Legacy

Order this book online at www.trafford.com
or email orders@trafford.com

Most Trafford titles are also available at major online book retailers.

Photographs courtesy of The d'zert Club, The Library of Congress Prints and Photographs Division, Lynn Johnson, and The Atlanta Journal-Constitution.

Edited by Bianca Morris Rhym and Krishnan Anand
Typeset by Jeffrey Henon for Henon Design
Layout by Denise Nicole Cheeves for kohl, inc.
Graphic Design by Jeffrey Henon for Henon Design
Cover Design by Denise Nicole Cheeves for kohl, inc.

Print information available on the last page.

ISBN: 978-1-4120-4359-5 (sc)

Trafford rev. 03/30/2023

www.trafford.com

North America & international
toll-free: 844-688-6899 (USA & Canada)
fax: 812 355 4082

Legacy

Horace Cheeves
Denise Nicole Cheeves

NAKLo. Publishing

Dedicated to the memory and spirit of
Jeff Carter Sr. and Lillian Arthur Carter Cheeves

About the Authors

Horace Cheeves

As an organizer and advocate in the consumer movement for nearly a decade, Horace opposed the holder in due course doctrine, the discriminatory practice of redlining committed by realtors, and fraudulent car deals, as well as other acts of fraud.

Due to the rampant land and mineral loss throughout the Middle District of Georgia, Horace founded the National Association of Kaolin Landowners (NAKLo.), in 1993. NAKLo. advocates for those who have lost their land or kaolin rights through outright theft and/or fraudulent mineral leases. The organization not only supports those with kaolin, but all disgruntled landowners, including those with other natural resources (i.e. oil, coal, gas, etc.) and farmers.

Denise Nicole Cheeves

After studying Art and Art History at Spelman College in Atlanta, Georgia, School of Visual Arts in New York City, and Lorenzo De' Medici in Florence, Italy, Denise Nicole worked as an organizer of NAKLo. in Atlanta. While writing *LEGACY* and compiling her family's genealogy, she freelanced as a photographer, designer, and fashion stylist. Her work has appeared in publications such as Essence, Beatdown, and HealthQuest magazine. She also assisted in the *Cheeves v. Alston & Bird, et al* case filed in Federal District Court in April 1994, the appeal for the Eleventh Circuit in 1998, and the U.S. Supreme Court in 1999. Presently, she teaches yoga to athletes, beginners, and children in the Philadelphia area.

Foreword

As is usually true with any large undertaking, especially one requiring in-depth research, there are always several motivating factors. Initially, ours was to substantiate our family's rights to realty that had been in our family for years, but had been stolen from us decades ago. The brutal eviction was committed in Georgia in 1950 when Blacks had no "rights" under the law. Jim Crow etiquette did not require that Blacks be given receipts or other proofs of legal transactions. It has been our hope to expose the ramifications of these practices and eradicate the damage as much as possible.

We set out to reverse this status in light of modern legislation, and social awareness, and promptly learned that our only hope was to provide a detailed genealogy of our family, and to document all legal claims in or out of court.

Much of what follows in this book is complex, and sometimes the legalese becomes cumbersome, but all of it is necessary to grasp the full picture of what has transpired. Even in the 21st century, the "law" - regardless of how discriminatory, irresponsible or unethical - is the law, and remains largely unchallenged, especially with regard to inheritance and land claims made by people of color.

My great-grandfather, Jeff Carter, Sr., acquired at least 803 acres of mineral (kaolin) rich land in Georgia, despite the fact that he was born during slavery. Commencing around 1950, Black landowners in Washington County, Georgia, as well as surrounding areas, were often legally and violently, stripped of their land by the kaolin (mineral/chalk/clay) industry. Many of our relatives thrived in those communities, despite their second-class status amongst whites. Most of them, however, lost the minerals and realty that would have been extremely valuable to their heirs, had they been allowed to inherit it.

In these pages, you will read a great deal about the Tarbutton family. With the assistance of their representatives (i.e. agents 'strawmen', lawyers, and judges), they have proven to be one of our greatest adversaries in achieving the justice we seek. As a family, independently and collectively, we have taken our case to lawyers, and to court. We have yet to win, but we have not given up either. Through this book, it is my goal to make others conscious of the brutal holocaust and ongoing land swindle that has deprived so many Black families, including the Carter heirs, of their inheritance.

Horace Cheeves

Foreword

Table of Contents

INTRODUCTION

Maafa - African Holocaust

"The events which transpired five thousand years ago; Five years ago or five minutes ago, have determined what will happen five minutes from now; five years from now or five thousand years from now. All history is a current event."
—Dr. John Henrik Clarke

Maafa is a Kiswahili term for "disaster" or "terrible occurrence". It is used to describe more than five hundred years of exploitation of Africa through "slavery", "colonialism", and "imperialism". A "colony" is a settlement in one land supported by another land, and "imperialism" is the practice of building empires to support trade.

Slavery or the concept of forced labor has always existed in world history. When Muslims invaded Africa they contributed greatly to the development of the institution of slavery. They seized women for their harems and men for military and menial service. By purchase and conquest, they shipped African people to Arabia, Persia, and other lands of Islam. Because the demand for Blacks depended mostly on the wealth of "masters"; many "slaves" were essentially servants. The institution showed little of the harshness and severity it possessed when it was itself the foundation on which wealth was built.

The European Renaissance (1400 - early 1500s) was a time of transition that bridged the end of the middle ages and the on-set of the modern era. This period of transition into "modernity" was centered on Italy, but was carried into Northern Europe through commerce and by scholars. The fundamental principles of white supremacy were flagrantly exerted during the Renaissance when a relatively small group of wealthy, powerful Europeans played a significant role in shaping the events of their day. Unfortunately, their power gave them the freedom to destroy and exploit the rights of others.

The Commercial Revolution was a result of the breakdown of feudalism (a system of indentured servitude), the rise of towns, heightened interest in commercial activities, new recognition of strength, and power of capital. Under the new national monarchies, most notably those of Portugal, Spain, the Netherlands, and England, markets grew wider and more secure. Commercial expansion was supported by technical improvements in seafaring, and from about 1450 explorations were made, first to Africa, then to Asia and the "New World". Modern credit facilities also appeared. New institutions included charter banks, the state bank (Bank of Amsterdam - 1609, Bank of London - 1694); the stock exchange (Bourse of Antwerp); the futures market; the promissory note; insurance companies (Lloyd's of London); and other new media of exchange were created. All of these factors revitalized Europe's economy. Some of the effects of the Commercial Revolution were inflation, an increase in the population and the emergence of a middle class, an increase in world trade, and most notoriously, the African "slave trade" (Triangle Trade), which, beginning in the 13th century, created the modern institution of "slavery", fostering competition and ruthless exploitation of any commodities – inanimate or human - that could be viewed as economic. Sadly, the importation and exportation of African men, women and children as human chattel was such a successful enterprise, that it continued well into the 19th century.

The Holocaust Gets The Church's Blessing

Some of the African people sold during Muslim domination certainly ended up in markets of Western Europe. By the end of the 14th century, Africans were regularly being enslaved and brought to Europe. Spanish and Portuguese sailors went to the Canary Islands and many other ports mainland, as far as the Gulf of Guinea. African men, women, and children were being physically and mentally tortured. Europeans believed subjugation of the African would give them "the opportunity to cast off their heathenism and embrace the Christian religion".

> *Dey talks a heap 'bout de niggers stealin'. Well, you know what was de fust stealin' done? Hit was in Afriky, when de white folks stole de niggers jes' like you'd go get a drove o' hosses and sell 'em. Dey's bring a steamer down dere wid a red flag, 'cause dey knowed dem folks liked red, and when dey see it dey'd follow it till dey got on de steamer. Den when it was all full o' niggers dey'd bring 'em over here and sell 'em*
> —**Shang Harris,** *Augusta Georgia*

It was the Portuguese who first took enslaved Africans to Europe. Around 1460, they exported approximately 800 Africans to Portugal to work on the sugar plantation, Spain and the islands of Fernando Po, Sao Tome and Principe. In fact, toward the 15th century, sailors and merchants from Portugal recognized the economic advantages afforded by the "slave trade". This realization was largely due to Portugal's Prince Henry, also known as Henry the Navigator (1394-1460). In the early - mid 1400s, he sent numerous sailors to explore the African coast. His navigators were thorough in their conquest of West Africa. Henry became noted for establishing "slave" and gold trades. He ordered Christopher Columbus to capture and export twelve Africans from West Africa to Lisbon, the capital of Portugal. The captives were given to Pope Eugene IV (1388 - 1431), who completely forgave the sins of anyone that engaged in further raids and conquest. By the end of the 15th century, Europeans were scrambling for monopoly of the "slave trade". The Spaniards and Portuguese erected forts and trading posts for relations with Africans, rationalizing slavery within Christianity as a "holy cause". They led the Europeans with the missionary zeal of Christianity and carried with them the blessing of their king and church.

In 1517, despite his reputation as a defender of the oppressed (because he condemned Indian servitude), Bishop Bartolomeo de Las Casas (1474 - 1566) formally began the "slave trade". He encouraged immigration to the Americas and the Caribbean by permitting Spaniards to export African people. The vast natural resources and undeveloped regions in the "New World" made the exploitative nature of "slavery" and the "slave trade" irresistible to Europeans. English and Spanish invaders had become frustrated with both Native Americans and poor whites from Europe. They found them insufficient, ineffective at clearing forests and cultivating fields. Many sued their "masters" and ship captains for illegal detention; others ran away making it difficult and expensive to apprehend them.

So it was concluded Blacks would be easier to apprehend and could be purchased outright. This would end the fluctuation of the captor's supply. Many Europeans believed skin color dictated superiority and that Africans were "heathens" who had not been exposed to the ethical ideals of Christianity. Christian doctrines or religion was believed to allow for the practice of slavery as a way to convert people to the faith. This gave them a sense of superiority in civilization and values. Therefore, Africans should be handled rigidly and be morally and spiritually degraded for the sake of stability on the plantation. The value and "cost" of Black life was also considered less. This made Black labor the solution to the Europeans' most difficult problem - accountable, cheap labor.

4
Big Business

Around 1501, a number of Africans were exported to the Americas from Lisbon, Portugal. Forty years later, Africans were being transported directly from the Guinea Coast. By 1630, the demand for Blacks increased tremendously because of new farms opened up by the English, Dutch, the French in the Caribbean, and Brazil.

In 1618, Sir William St. John and thirty others were incorporated as "a Company of Adventurers of London trading into the ports of Africa" to engage in the profitable trade in African people. Known as the Guinea Company, they could not raise fresh capital, so they granted licences to private traders, referred to as interlopers. One prominent interloper was Sir Nicholas Crispe (1599 - 1666), who is said to have built the first permanent English settlement at Kormantin (a few miles east of Cape Coast Castle). In 1631, Crispe and his partners were issued with a patent giving them a monopoly for 31 years of trade on the entire west coast of Africa, and prohibiting all others from importing African goods into England. On November 22, 1632 Charles gave Crispe and five others an exclusive right to trade to the Guinea coast. Crispe got redwood from Guinea and had a sole importation right. By the late 1630s, the London customs farmer established an English "slave depot" and refreshment base for East India shipping on the African coast of Kormantin, whose faction sought a royalty-backed monopoly on Moroccan trade. The wealth Crispe accumulated from "slaving" and other businesses in 1640, enabled him to contract for two large customs farms, and on that security he and his backers gave the king use of £253,000.

With the Restoration, West India merchants in London persuaded Charles II to retain Jamaica as a "royal colony". During this period, the East India Company directors gave gifts of their loyalty, and the king gave them a favorable charter and accepted loans over 16 years of £170,000. By about 1660, more than half of the beneficiaries of the capital in the Royal Adventurers to Africa were peers or members of the Royal Family including the Duke of York, and Princesses Maria and Henrietta. More common investors included some of the greatest mercantile figures of Restoration London including Sir John Robinson, deputy-governor of the Hudson's Bay Company and director of the East India Company.

In 1661, Robert Holmes of the Royal Adventurers into Africa, expelled the Courlanders (Latvians) from the mouth of the Gambia River; James Island was occupied by the English. There was trading to Sherbro and Sierra Leone, but the Dutch placed obstacles, so in 1664, Holmes captured Dutch settlements at Cape

Verde. By 1661, the East India Company had a revised charter, which allowed it to maintain forts and raise troops for their defense. This began a new era with paid-up capital of £370,000 and permanent joint-stock. The sole objective of the Royal Adventurers Trading into Africa in 1662, was to oust the Dutch in the "slave trade". The East India Company, now the third English-Africa Company, leased Kormantin which was a few miles east of the Dutch Cape Coast Castle. They took over the East India Company factory, Cape Coast Castle, and Elmina Castle. The Duke of York contributed £3600 to the Africa Company, which surrendered its charter in 1663 and had a new one issued, to the Company of Royal Adventurers of England Trading into Africa. This charter mentioned "slaving", specifically the idea of being able to supply Blacks to the West Indies on credit. The new company took over Kormantin and Cape Coast Castle, but was soon troubled by the Dutch which led to a series of wars between Britain and Holland. In 1665 they began a purely commercial war, Anglo-Dutch, which stemmed from conflict on the African west coast. Captain Robert Holmes took Goree north of the Gambia River and Cape Coast Castle on the Gulf of Guinea.

Thomas Crispe became the chief agent on the Gold Coast for Rowland Wilson, Maurice Thompson, John Wood and Thomas Walter, whom he called The Guinea Company. Crispe had been active in the Africa trade since 1625. The original site of Cape Coast Castle in Africa had been given to the English, taken by the Swedes, then re-taken by the English, all in Crispe's time on the coast. Crispe claimed to have established what became the prime English "slaving depot", which he had bought for £64 worth of goods (in the small coastal kingdom of Fetu).

By 1645, Barbadians imported 1000 enslaved Blacks. Between 1710 and 1810, 250,000 Blacks were brought to Barbados alone of Britain's "sugar islands". In 1647, evidently unsatisfied with other supply lines, the Barbados settlers Thomas Modyford and Richard Ligon had gone out themselves looking for Blacks, horses, and cattle. Their ship went to Africa, where they bartered for their own Blacks. By 1654, Barbados had developed its own unique way of life, including its own "slave code" which was later exported to Jamaica and then Virginia.

By the end of the 18th century, Dutch influence in Africa, the Americas and the Caribbean had begun to decline, but it was long after they had already reaped a bountiful harvest from the trade of Africans.

The business of trading Africans was a source of great wealth, and the last major development of the Commercial Revolution. Charles II (1660 - 85) issued licenses to several Flemish traders to transport Africans into the Spanish colonies. Based on their bid, the Dutch, Portuguese, French, and English each held the monopoly on the trade in Black people at various times. The "slave trade" and "slavery" became the biggest, most lucrative businesses in the history of the world. As West Indian plantations grew in size and importance, the "slave trade" became a huge, profitable undertaking, employing thousands with a capital outlay of millions of dollars. The investment was staggering.

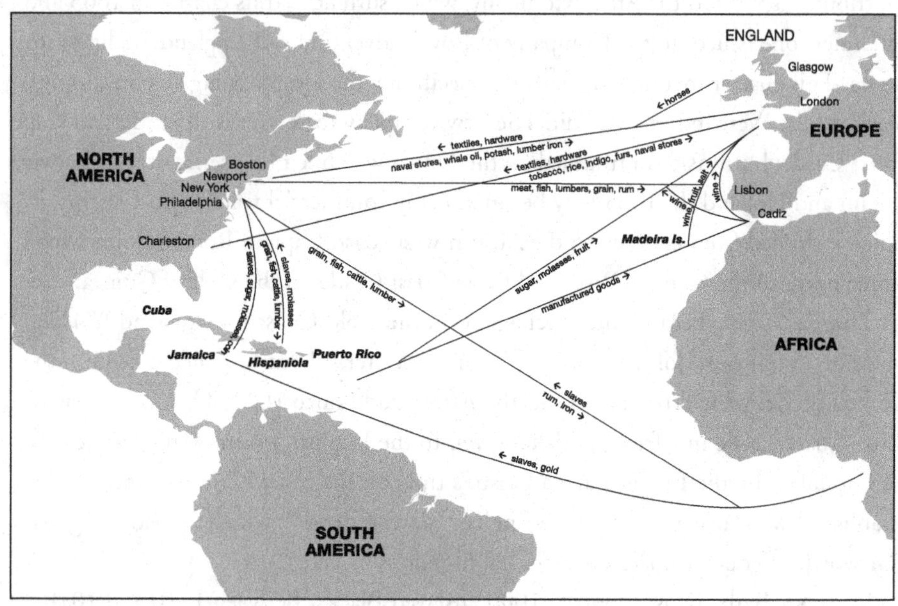

Atlantic Slave and Trade Routes (Allen Weinstein and Frank Otto Gatell, *Freedom and Crisis: An American History,* Vol. I, New York, 1981, pg. 33.)

Ships leaving Europe first stopped in Africa where they traded weapons, ammunition, metal, liquor, and cloth for captives taken in wars or raids. The ships then traveled to America and the Caribbean, where Africans were exchanged for sugar, rum, salt, and other island products. The ships completed the triangle loaded with products popular with Europeans.

Eventually Europeans explored the interior of Africa to expand the trade. By the 1800's, a "scramble for Africa" occurred. Five European powers - England, France, Germany, Belgium, and Italy "colonized" almost the entire continent by 1900. They exploited the great mineral wealth of Africa and sought to expand their borders by moving into the continent.

"Colonial" rulers were often cruel and had little regard for Africans. King Leopold II of Belgium obtained "personal title" to the Congo in central Africa. He forced the native people to work under cruel conditions in his rubber plants. Every village was required to donate four people a year to work for Leopold. Villagers who failed to complete their duties were flogged; others had their hands or head cut off.

Dungeons And Castles

Elmina Castle was built by the Portuguese in 1471 and became the largest "slave-trading post" in the world. Africans were kept there until they were transported to their unknown destination. European officers raped African women in Elmina's female dungeons. Officers would choose their victims from a balcony as the female captives were routinely paraded through a courtyard below. This was the only time women were allowed out. Once selected, a woman was then sent off to be cleaned and later brought through a trap door into an adjoining room where she would be raped. The awful twist was that if by chance she became pregnant, she was set free and allowed to remain in Africa.

There is a cell for prisoners who tried to rebel against their captors in the courtyard. These men were condemned to death and left to starve. Across the way is the church where the European officers worshiped. Elmina is the oldest European structure in sub-Saharan Africa.

Cape Coast Castle is located on the coast of Ghana. In 1637 the lodge at Cape Coast was occupied by the Dutch. Then, in 1652 it was taken over by the Swedes, who in 1757 built Fort Carolusborg. The Castle was occupied by the Dutch in 1659, and then again by the Swedes, who altered and enlarged it until it became a fort in 1657. By 1663 the Dutch occupied it again. Finally, in 1664, after a four day battle, the fort was captured by the British and re-named Cape Coast Castle. The Castle served as the seat of the British Administration in the Gold Coast (Ghana) until the administration was moved to Christianborg Castle in Osu near Accra in 1877. Cape Coast Castle played a significant role in the gold and African "slave trade".

All 42 European castles and fortifications were used as dungeons for the millions who lost their lives and whose descendants compose the African diaspora today. In these hot, dark, tiny rooms, hundreds of Africans were crowded and chained for months in utterly inhumane conditions, before being shipped across the ocean. The dungeons were completely dark except for a bit of light that came from a tiny window. Food was dropped through a small hole and water was thrown, so Africans had to cup their hands to try to get a sip. This forced them to fight over the scarce food and water in a small space where they ate, drank, vomited, urinated, defecated, and slept. The only sanitation came in the form of a small drain that ran across the stone floor. Europeans lived comfortably in quarters above the sweltering prisons, which had only tiny openings for air.

Elmina Castle

Elmina Castle

Elmina Castle

Elmina Castle

Elmina Castle

Elmina Castle

Elmina Castle

Elmina Castle

Elmina Castle

Elmina Castle – The Door of No Return

The Door Of No Return

The "door of no return" is where many enslaved Africans passed through before leaving the shores of Africa. With the exception of Elmina Castle, Cape Coast Castle was the largest "slave-trading post" in the world. The coast of Ghana is littered with the highest concentration of forts and castles, more than any other coastline in Africa. They were built and occupied at different times by European traders and "adventurers" from Portugal, Spain, Denmark, Sweden, Holland, Germany, and Britain to safeguard trading posts.

Africans were packed like sardines in ships from the Guinea Coast. They were stripped naked and treated like animals. Europeans exchanged cotton, brass, rum, inferior guns and gun powder for captured Africans. Meanwhile Africa lost its most valuable resource, its people, who built the economies and prosperity of Europe, the Americas and the Caribbean.

The price for Blacks depended upon age and physical condition, period of trading, and location of post. As a means to conquer, European traders mastered the science of turning Blacks against one another. The use of gifts and other methods of persuasion on chiefs and locals enabled captors to scour villages to secure enough Blacks to meet the traders' demands. Naturally, Africans rigidly resisted being captured, sold, and kidnaped.

Bloody wars erupted between tribes when members of one tried to capture members of another to sell to Europeans. Because their desire to escape was so fierce, Africans were always brought to posts in chains. Europeans shackled the healthiest, largest, youngest, ablest, and most culturally advanced men, women and children. The onslaught of this massive kidnaping deprived the continent of one of its most valuable resources – its people, most of whom were from West Africa. On a modern atlas, this would include the areas known as the west Sudan, from Mali, Niger, and Chad, down to Cameroon. This area is also known as the Songhai region, where civilization was at its highest in the world outside of Kemet (land of the Blacks). Kemet is an African country further north renamed Egypt by the Greeks. Scholastically and culturally, no country outside of Africa could compete. This was particularly true of the sciences such as astronomy and mathematics.

The last post for traders to make transactions was Goree, on the coast of Senegal. They obtained supplies and principle foodstuffs from the natives, (such as Indian corn, kidney beans, yams, fruits, coconuts, and plantains) for the voyage to North and South America and the Caribbean. It was standard procedure to overcrowd ships, since more Blacks meant greater profits. The psychological and physical trauma of being captured, shackled, and crowded onto a ship for 40-50 days, destined for an unknown place and future, never to see family, friends, or home again, was immeasurably devastating. Whenever the opportunity presented itself, many captives ended their torment by doing the unimaginable - to escape from bondage; they leaped to the mouths of hungry sharks.

The Middle Passage

> *"The outrage to mortality which the Middle Passage must always be should not obscure the fact that it was also an outrage to sound economics".*
> —**K.G. Davies,** *The Royal Africa Company*

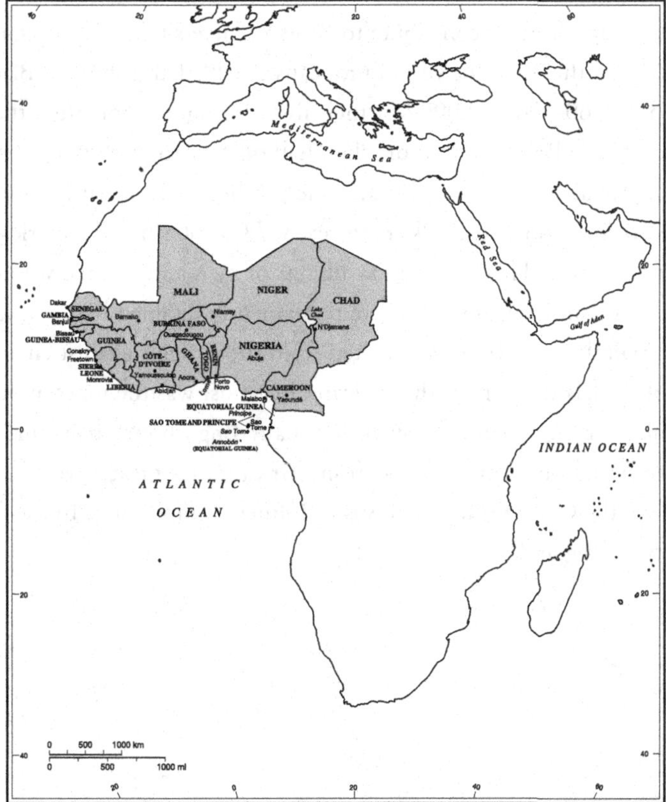

Map of the Songhai Region

Compounding their abrupt turn of misfortune, the incidence of disease for shackled Africans increased due to overcrowding. They spent 6 to 8 weeks chained and constricted during the Middle Passage (the trip across the Atlantic ocean). Most experienced epidemics such as smallpox, gonorrhea, syphilis, tuberculosis, and even more deadly, flux, which whites were somehow immune to. Hunger strikes, filth, stench, and waste, along with disease, added to physical and psychological illness, as well as mortality. Those who did not die of starvation were tortured to eat. Captors often put hot coals on shovels and placed them near the captives' lips. Another technique implemented was the speculum oris, a device used to forcefully open one's mouth (knocking out teeth if necessary), in an effort to shove food in.

Torture devices were manufactured in New England and Britain, employing hundreds of thousands of whites for more than a century and a half. In fact, the speculum oris was manufactured in a factory owned by Brown and Savitts in Boston, Massachusetts. The tremendous profits from the production of torture devices enabled them to significantly contribute to Brown University, an Ivy League institution. During the 400 plus years Europeans shackled and shipped Black people, it is estimated that 60-100,000,000 lost their lives during, or soon after, the journey known as the Middle Passage. No more than half of the people shipped were effective workers in the Americas or the Caribbean. The psychological, spiritual, and physical abuse suffered before captured Blacks even reached Caribbean and American shores is beyond comprehension. There were also millions of men and women who did not die of disease or commit suicide, but were permanently disabled by the ravages of disease or by maiming, which often resulted from the struggle against chains.

In the 17th and 18th century, the African Holocaust was the most important source of wealth for Europeans, so much that many English merchants made 100% profits. The importation of more Blacks from Africa meant greater wealth, particularly into the Caribbean, which was of immense importance to the grandeur and prosperity of England.

Slave Castle on Goree Island, Senegal, Africa

Slave Castle on Goree Island, Senegal, Africa

Slave Castle on Goree Island, Senegal, Africa

Slave Castle on Goree Island, Senegal, Africa

Slave Castle on Goree Island, Senegal, Africa

Slave Castle on Goree Island, Senegal, Africa

Royal African Company - RAC

The very being of the plantations depended on the supply of enslaved Blacks. Europe was seldom so unanimous as in its view of the value of Black labor. The African Adventurers Company was ruined by its losses. On January 10, 1663, King Charles II affirmed the charter of the Royal African Company, which dominated England's "slave trade" for almost a century. The ambitious company set up six forts on the Gold Coast (Ghana) and one on the "slave coast", while the French built up north of the Gambia in Senegal. According to K.G. Davies, author of The Royal Africa Company, the RAC was "the strongest and most effective of all European companies formed exclusively for the African trade".

In February of that year, the English seized Dutch possessions on the west coast of Africa. On March 24, 1663, the king awarded lands known as Carolina in America to eight members of nobility who assisted in his restoration; and on July 8th, he granted a charter to Rhode Island guaranteeing freedom of worship. On March 12, 1664, Charles II granted land in New Jersey to his brother James, the Duke of York, and ten days later gave him large tracks of land from west of the Connecticut River to the east of Delaware Bay in North America. James had invested in both the East India Company and the RAC. On September 5, 1664, after days of negotiation, the Dutch settlement of New Amsterdam surrendered to the British, who would rename it New York. The citizens of New Amsterdam petitioned Peter Stuyvesant to surrender to the English, which the Dutch did formally, four days later. That same year Jamaica adopted Barbados' "slave code".

The initials of the Royal African Company were branded on the chests of millions of men, women, and children. It became the single most important "slave-trading" group in the world. They jealously guarded the monopoly granted by the king, and tried to drive the French and Dutch out of West Africa. On September 27, 1672, the RAC charter passed the Great Seal, gaining legal recognition. A charter was the only legal way to become a limited liability joint-stock company. At the time the RAC received its charter, it was the second largest of the joint-stock companies after the East India Company. It could seize the goods and ships of any who infringed its monopoly. It sought gold, silver, and Blacks, and could make war and peace with "heathen nations", raise troops, and execute martial law. In 1671, West India planters owed the RAC £70,000 for Blacks in Jamaica alone. Through a "secret" treaty of Dover of 1671, Charles received cash from France for an attack on the United

Provinces. The Dutch had a tremendous impact on the African coast and the second Dutch war had been largely a result of rivalry. Many who knew of the "secret" Dover treaty subscribed to the RAC. By 1672, the primary problem of any African company was a shortage of liquid capital, and the RAC had raised too little. Turnover was slower due to long credit being extended to "slave-buying" planters. There was the infrastructure cost of fixing capital in forts, so the company had to borrow heavily. It traded in gold, ivory, dyewood, hides and waxes for the English market, and in buying Blacks for the West Indies. In 1672 the RAC and the Third Guinea Company merged. The new RAC had a sub-contract with the Asiento and an oblique entry was made possible to Spanish colonial markets; gold and ivory would supplement the trade in Blacks, and of course, sugar. The RAC was also granted a charter to expand the slave trade. Its shareholders included Prince Rupert and philosopher John Locke, who sold his £400 stock in 1675.

The Asiento Treaty

Religion played a pivotal role in sedating African "heathens", leading to laws that required they be baptized within at least 1 year after their arrival in the Americas and the Caribbean. A strict "slave code" was introduced in Latin America - earlier than in British America - where the Catholic Church played a significant role. Priests often accompanied European traders and insisted African people be instructed in Roman Catholic religion and baptized in the church. Missionaries suggested captives be given time to study Scripture and learn to read and write. This religious sanction of the enslavement of Black people made planters feel even more secure in the righteousness of the African Holocaust. The Catholic Church received $25 per Black, granted by the Asiento, which was the silver and financial exchange backing the supply of Africans from Africa to the Caribbean and South America.

On May 29, 1677, Charles II and twelve Virginia Indian chiefs signed a treaty that established a 3-mile non-encroachment zone around Indian land. (In 1997, the Mattaponi Indians invoked this treaty to protect against encroachment.) On July 10, 1679, the British crown claimed New Hampshire. On March 4, 1681, the king granted a charter to English Quaker William Penn for 48,000 square miles that later became Pennsylvania. Penn's father had bequeathed him a claim of £15,000 against the king.

The trade in African people played a pivotal role during the Commercial Revolution. Its significant impact on the economy, which established, of many things, insurance companies, such as the London coffee shop where shipping insurance was bought and sold. Lloyd's of London was opened by Edward Lloyd in 1688. On July 27, 1694, The Bank of England received a royal charter as a commercial institution.

Between 1695 - 1709, more than 11,000 Africans were sold in Virginia alone. England's settlement of St. Christopher Barbados, Nevis, Montserrat, Antigua, and Jamaica in the first half of the 17th century opened up a new realm of commercial possibilities. "Slave codes" were standard by the early 18th century. The bountiful productivity in their Caribbean and American territories paid handsome dividends. England's commerce came to dominate the world. They were able to supply the insatiable demand for African men and women with their strengthened navy and almost unlimited capital resources for investment. By the 18th century, the cornerstone of England's economy was the enslavement and trade of Black people.

In 1698, while free traders were also again assailing the East India Company in London and about India, the Parliament abrogated the Africa Company's monopoly and threw 'slaving" open to free trade. There was only a "10% " duty to a custom house for all goods exported to Africa for the purchase of "slaves". Goods included woolens (also part of the triangular trade), iron bars, guns and brass goods including pans and kettles. This increased the number of private ships allowed to enter the African trade. This 10% policy continued until 1712, when the African trade was made free. During the next decade, private traders flocked to the open market. By 1707 they outnumbered company ships 3 to 1. After the abolishment of the RAC's monopoly, English merchant's prices for Blacks rose along with the increased demand. Whereas in the 1670s and 1680s the RAC paid for Africans with about £3 in trade goods; by 1710 this price had quadrupled to £12. The planters' price for Blacks reflected increase. By 1700, "new Africans" cost between £25 and £30. The opening of the "slave trade" to a free market caused an explosion of activity both in the high seas and in Europe. Based on statistics provided by seventeenth century English economist Charles Davenant, England's total profit from trade amounted to £2 million. The triangular (Atlantic) trade pattern represented 36% of England's commercial profits. Davenant added that every individual in the West Indies was seven times more profitable than an individual in England. In 1700, British settlers began arriving to the Cayman Islands. Also that year, the English ship Henrietta Marie sank 35 miles off Key West, Florida on its way back to Europe. It had delivered 188 captured Africans to a "slave broker" in Jamaica in exchange for sugar and other goods bound for England. The wreck was found in 1972.

Thirteen "Original Colonies"

A rough estimate is that 40% of those sold in the "slave ports" such as Charleston, South Carolina, Savannah, Georgia, and New Orleans were of Bantu origin.

Originating in the Nok region of Nigeria, possibly 2,500 years ago, Bantu languages and culture spread over a large section of Central, South and East Africa. The "Congo-Angola" region became increasingly more important because the many channels and small islands at the Congo River's broad mouth made it easier for Africans to duck patrolling English and American ships. After 1700, Georgia, the Carolinas, Tennessee, and Mississippi maintained a Black majority for over two centuries. Well into the 20th century, African born, Bantu speaking ex-"slaves" still lived in America.

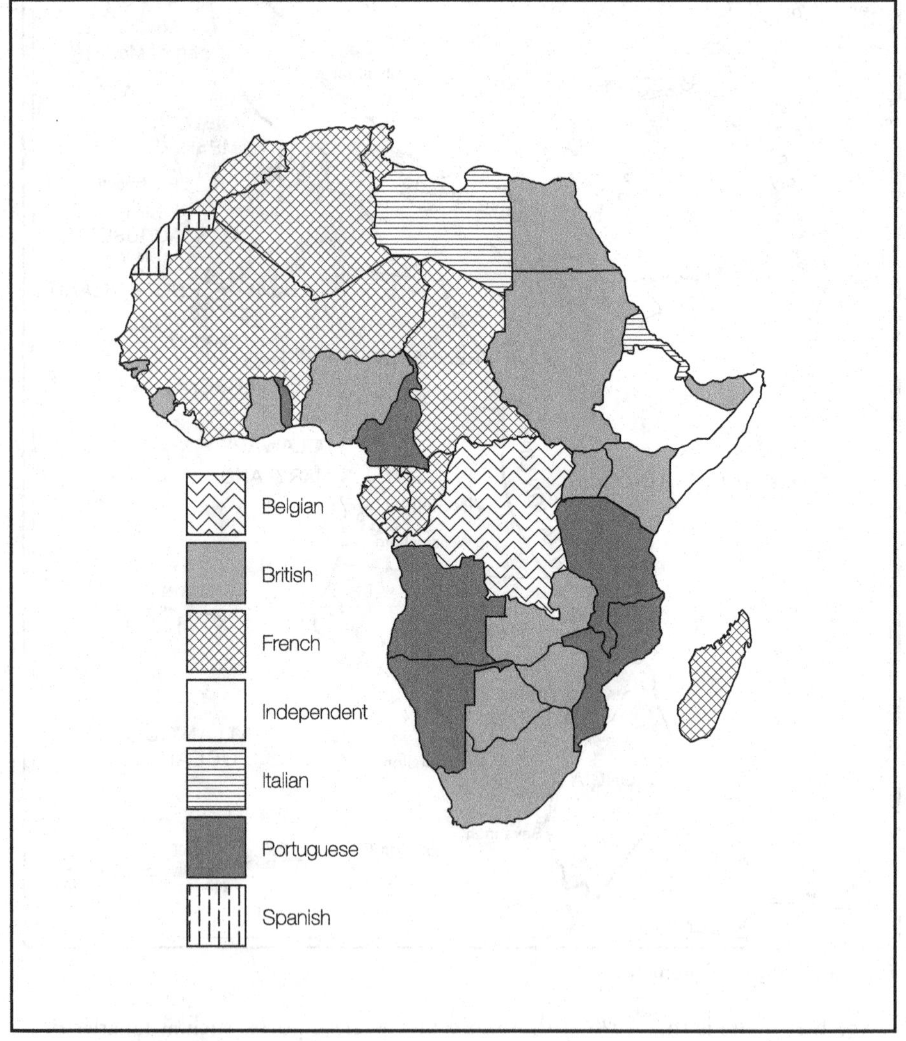

'Colonial' Africa, 1914

By the 18th century, as demand for Blacks increased in North America, re-exportation from the overpopulated Caribbean became a lucrative business for the many Europeans involved. Prices for Blacks went up as the demand increased. In another desperate attempt to increase the number of whites, planters were required to import a proportionate number of whites for all Blacks brought, but most preferred to pay the fines instead.

In 1702 in Maryland, the Anglican Church was established as the official church, financially supported by taxation imposed on all free men, male servants, and enslaved Blacks. Three years later, in Virginia, Blacks were assigned the status of real estate by the Virginia Black Code of 1705. In New York, a law against runaway slaves assigned the death penalty for those caught over 40 miles north of Albany. Massachusetts declared marriage between Blacks and whites illegal. In May of 1712, the "Carolina colony" was officially divided into North Carolina and South Carolina. In June, the Pennsylvania assembly banned the import of enslaved Blacks. In 1713, England was able to secure the asiento - the exclusive right to transport African people to Spanish "colonies" for 30 years. In 1716, the first group of Blacks were brought to the Louisiana territory. In June of 1732, Georgia, the 13th "English colony", was founded.

> *De place am so well managed by de Marster dat whuppin's am not necessary. Ise don't ever 'membahs of one whuppin's even. Marster had a method of keepin' de cullud fo'ks in line. If one of dem do somethin' not right to dem he say: "Don't go to wo'k tomorrow Ise 'spect de nigger drive am a-comin' pass an' Ise gwine to sell youse." Weuns all skeert 'bout gettin sold to de nigger driver. Youse see de nigger driver am a nigger trader. Deys go through de country buyin an' sellin' slaves. W'en a slave gets in de hands of a driver 'twas a big chance of him gettin' sold to a cruel Marster an' de cullud fo'ks am powerful skeert 'bout sich. Den 'twas a plant'tion next to weuns, Ledbetter am de name, who use de whup an' hard. Weuns could hear de cullud fo'ks pleadin', "Marster, oh Marster please have de mercy" and sich. W'ens weuns heah de pleadin' de Marster say to weuns, "Boys youse heah dat misery, weuns don't want any sich on dis place an' tis up to youse." Weuns know how it may be wid some tudder Marster. W'en de Marster call a slave an' say, "Don't go to wo'k 'cause Ise have to sell youse to de nigger driver." Youse den heah de nigger pleadin', "Forgive me Marster, dis time Ise sho wont does it 'gain."*
>
> —**Sam Kilgore,** *enslaved in Texas*

Sam Kilgore

Well, I come on out an' got in the wagon an' ole Marser drove me down to the 7th Street Wharf, to ole Joe Bruin's omnibus where they had them. Uncle Moses was standing there chained up with 40 or 50 other slaves what had been sold along with him. They all was runaways, there was a gang of them what had tried to get to Canada. All but ten had been caught, including Uncle Moses. He was de only one what belonged to Marser John, though. And all these runaways what had been sold was chained round they legs in rows of 12 each, an' each one had handcuffs round they wrist
—**Frank Bell**

Aw chile, woods stayed full of niggers an' sometimes dey would ketch 'em by dogs (sometimes) called bloodhounds. Lord, Lord, dem ole dogs scent ya up to de crick. Ef ya ar' runnin' 'way, jump in de crick. Dogs loose de scent of ya an' too, ef ya take a raw onion (and) rub feet bottom ya make de dogs loose ya.

Dese slaves stay in woods 'til dey git tired. Come back to marster, git a beatin' - "nine and thirty," dey use to call hit

—**Ishrael Massie,** *enslaved in Virginia*

England declared war on Spain in 1739. As a result, in America, hostilities broke out between Florida Spaniards, Georgia and South Carolina "colonists". Also three separate violent uprisings by enslaved Blacks occurred in South Carolina. One year later, fifty Blacks were hung in Charleston, South Carolina after plans for another revolt were revealed.

Despite government backing and participation by numerous prominent Englishmen, the Royal African Company could not outmaneuver the smaller, family-owned "slaving enterprises" such as the Browns of Rhode Island and the Hobhouses of Bristol. One of the Browns' more fruitful enterprises was a torture device-making factory in Massachusetts. They later contributed significantly to Brown University. The eventual demise of the RAC came in 1750.

From One Slave Plantation Owner To Another

The following are excerpts from a speech made by Willie Lynch in 1712:

Gentlemen:

I greet you here on the bank of the James River in the year of our Lord, 1712. First, I shall thank you, the gentlemen of the colony of Virginia, for bringing me here.

I am here to help you solve some of your problems with slaves. Your invitation reached me on my modest plantation in the West Indies where I have experimented with some of the newest and still the oldest methods for control of slaves.

Ancient Rome would envy us if my program is implemented. As our boat sailed south of the James River, named for our illustrious King James, whose Bible we cherish, I saw enough to know that your problem is not unique. While Rome used cords of woods and crosses for standing human bodies along the old highways in great numbers, you are here using the tree and the rope on occasion.

I caught the whiff of a dead slave hanging from a tree a couple of miles back. You are not only losing valuable stock by hangings, you are having uprisings, slaves are running away, your crops are sometimes left in the fields too long for maximum profit, you suffer occasional fires, your animals are killed, gentlemen...you know what your problems are; I do not need to elaborate. I am not here to enumerate your problems; I am here to introduce you to a method of solving them.

In my bag here, I have a foolproof method for controlling your Black slaves. I guarantee every one of you that if installed correctly it will control the slaves for at least 300 years. My method is simple, any member of your family or any overseer can use it.

I have outlined a number of differences among the slaves, and I take these differences and make them bigger. I use fear, distrust and envy for control purposes. These methods have worked on my modest plantation in the West Indies, and it will work throughout the South.

Take this simple little list of differences and think about them. On the top of my list is "age," but it is there because it only starts with an "A." The second is "color" or shade. There is intelligence, size, sex, size of plantations, attitude of owners, whether the slave lives in the valley, on a hill, east, west, north, south, have fine or coarse hair, or is tall or short.

Now that you have a list of differences, I shall give you an outline of action - but before that, I shall assure you that distrust is stronger than trust, and envy is stronger than adulation, respect or admiration.

The Black slave, after receiving this indoctrination, shall carry on and will become self-refueling and self-generating for hundreds of years, maybe thousands.

Don't forget you must pitch the old Black vs. the young Black male, and the young Black against the old black male. You must use the dark skin slaves vs. the light skin slaves and the light skin slaves vs. the dark skin slaves.

You must use the female vs. the male and the male vs. the female. You must also have your servants and overseers distrust all Blacks, but it is necessary that your slaves trust and depend on us. They must love, respect and trust only us.

Gentlemen, these kits are your keys to control and use them. Have your wives and children use them. Never miss an opportunity. My plan is guaranteed, and the good thing about this plan is that if used intensely for one year, the slaves themselves will remain perpetually distrustful.

The Destruction Of Families

Unsurprisingly, the mortality rate for those who survived the Middle Passage was high. The aggressive, oppressive assault waged on the minds, bodies and souls of Black people, made mere survival an act of tremendous will and fortitude. With so many forces working against them, it was extremely difficult for Black families to sustain themselves. Throughout captivity, there were many miscarriages, infant deaths, suicides, murders by the whip, and illnesses compounded by acclimation.

Mammy's name was Leonora and she was cook for Marse Tim Walton what had de plantation at Tuscaloosa. Dat am in Alabamy. Papa's name was Joe Tatum and he lived on de place 'jinin' ourn. Course, papa and mamy wasn't married like folks now, 'cause dem times de white folks jes' put slave men and women together like hosses or cattle.

Dey allus done tell us it am wrong to lie and steal, but why did de white folks steal my mammy and her mammy? Dey lives clost to some water, somewheres over in Africy, and de man come in a little boat to de sho' and tell dem he got presents on de big boat. Most de men am out huntin' and my mammy and her mammy gits took out to dat big boat and dey locks dem in a black hole what mammy say so black you can't see nothin'. Dat de sinfulles' stealin' dey is.

De captain keep dem locked in dat black hole till dat boat gits to Mobile and dey is put on de block and sold. Mammy is 'bout twelve year old and dey am sold to Marse Tim, but Grandma dies in a month and dey puts her in de slave graveyard.

Mammy am nuss gal till she git older and den cook, and den old Marse Tim puts her and papa together and she has eight chillen. I reckon Marse Tim warn't no worser dan other white folks. De nigger driver sho' whip us, with de reason and without de reason. You never knowed. If dey done took de notion dey jes' lays it on you and you can't do nothin'.

One mornin' we is all herded up and mammy am cryin' and say dey gwine to Texas, but can't take papa. He don't 'lon to dem. Dat de lastes' time we ever seed papa. Us and de women am put in wagons but de men slaves am chained together and has to walk.

Marse Tim done git a big farm up by Marshall but only live a year dere and his boys run de place. Dey jes' like day papa, work us and work us. Lawd have mercy, I hear dat call in de mornin' like it jes' jesterday. "All right, everybody out, and you better git out iffen you don't' want to feel dat bullwhip 'cross you back."

My gal I lives with don't like me to talk 'bout dem times. She say it ain't no more and it ain't good to think 'bout it. But when you has live in slave times you ain't gwine forgit dem, no, suh!

—**Josephine Howard,** *born on Tim Walton's plantation near Tuscaloosa, Alabama.*

For the most part, Black men and women were treated the same. Pregnant women were forced to work until childbirth, and were lashed severely if they didn't keep up with others. After women gave birth, they were allowed 1 month maximum for recovery. If they paused in the fields to care for their babies, whom they carried on their backs, they were lashed with cart whips for idling away their time. Notwithstanding the epidemic of miscarriages, many babies survived despite the abuse inflicted on their mother's while still in utero. Unfortunately, they too would eventually witness and experience the same or similar abuses first-hand.

I ploughed, hoed, split rails. I done the hardest work ever a man ever did. I was so strong, iffen he needed me I'd pull the men down so the marster could handcuff 'em. They'd whop us with a bullwhip. We got up at 3 o'clock, at 4 we done et and hitched up the mules and went to the fiel's. We worked all day pullin' fodder and choppin' cotton. Marster'd say, "I wan' you to lead dat fiel' today, and if you don' do it I'll put you in de stocks." Then he'd whop me iffen I didn' know he was talkin' to me.

My poppa was strong. He never had a lick in his life. He helped the marster, but one day the marster says, "Si, you got to have a whoppin'," and my poppa says, "I never had a whoppin' and you cain't whop me." An the marster says, "But I kin kill you," an' he shot my poppa down. My mama tuk him in the cabin and put him on a pallet. He died.

My mama did the washin' for the big house. She tuk a big tub on her head and a bucket of water in her hand. My mama had two white chillen by marster and they were sold as slaves. I had two chillen, too. I never married. They allus said we'd steal, but I didn' take a thing. Why, they'd put me on a hoss with money to take into town and I'd take it to the store in town, and when I'd git back, marster'd say, "Anne, you didn' take a thing."

When women was with child they'd dig a hole in the groun' and put their stomach in the hole, and then beat 'em. They'd allus whop us."
—**Anne Clark,** *enslaved in Misssissippi*

Husbands allays went to de woods when dey know de wives was due fo' a whippin', but in de fiel' dey dare not leave. Had to stay dere, not darin' even look like dey didn't like it. Charlie Jones was one slave dat had his wife workin' in de same fiel' wid him. Was plantin' tobacco - he was settin' out an' she was hillin'. Annie was big wid chile an' gittin' near her time, so one day she made a slip an' chopped a young shoot down. Ole man Diggs, de overseer, come runnin' up screamin' at her an' it made her mo' nervous, an' she chopped off 'nother one. Ole overseer lif' up dat rawhide an' beat Annie 'cross de back an shoulders 'till she fell to de groun'. An Charlie he jus' stood dere hearin' his wife scream an' astarin' at de sky, not darin' to look at her or even say a word
—**Jordan Johnson,** *enslaved in Virgina*

I wus born...on Mr. Bill McDowell's place, an' dat wus er big farm. Marse Bill wus mi'ty tough on his slaves. I wes jes' a boy, but I will niver fergit how he whup'ed his slaves. I ken name ebry one uf his slaves: dar was Viney - she done de cookin'; Zias wus er fiel' han' an' he driv de carriage: My uncle Irwin, he fed de hosses, an' he wus a bad nigger an' got whup'd fur stealin all de time; Jim was de rice beater, an' he beat de rice ebery Friday; Sara wus er fiel' han' - Relia wurk in de fiel' an milked, an' had ter go to de cow pen bar'footed an' her feet got frost bit, an' dat made her cripple; Hager wus er fiel' han' an' Peggy wus er fiel' han' an' afte' Relia got crippled Peggy he'p milk; Monday wus er fiel hand' but he wus bad 'bout runnin way from home an' de patroller wud git him; Patience, dat was my mammy, she milked an' wurk in de fiel'...

My pappy wus a carpenter, an wurk in de fiel' an dun de buildin' dat wus dun on de place, an' he driv de ox team to Osyka to git sugar an' flour, an' he allus hed ter grease de wagon wid tar: Dat wud make it run easy.

Marse Bill had no overseer dat I remember: he an' young Marse Russ toted de whup, an' wud ride ober de fiel an' make de slaves wurk an' day wud shore whup iffen dat wurk wusnt dun. Den Marse Bill had er old poll parrot dat he put on a limb in de fiel' sum times, an' dat parrot wud tell who it wus dat didnt wurk. Marse Bill wud tie dem slaves an' whup hard, and all de slaves wud say "O, pray, marster; O, pray, Marster!"
—**Ebenezer Brown** *worked on a Mississippi plantation*

Women worked in de field same as de men. Some of dem plowed jes' like de men and boys. Couldn't tell 'em apart in de field, as dey wore pantelets or breeches. Dey tied strings 'round de bottom of de legs so de loose dirt wouldn't git in deir shoes. De horn blow'd to start work and to quit. In de morning when de signal blow'd, dey all tried to see who could git to de field first... Us didn't pay much mind to de clock. We worked from sun to sun
—**George Fleming,** *enslaved in South Carolina*

...No one ain't see papa, but dere it is. One time he brung us dresses, and Uncle Big Jake heered 'bout it and he sho' mad 'cause he can't cotch papa, and he say to mama he gwine to whip her 'less she tell him where papa is. Mama say, "Fore God, Uncle Jake, I don't know, 'cause I ain't seed him since he run 'way," and jus' den papa come 'round de corner of de house. He save mama from de whippin' but papa got de hot grease drapped on him like I told you Uncle Big Jake did, and got put in de stockhouse with shackles on him, and kep' dere three days, and while he in dere mama has de goin' down pains and my sister, Rachel, is born
—**Sarah Ford,** *enslaved in Texas*

Sarah Ford

Courtship and the normal relationship preliminary to marriage seldom existed. There were instances where whites insisted on religious ceremonies to unite Black couples, but were generally distressed when Blacks wanted to marry persons on other plantations. They feared this would reduce their efficiency because they would be away from their "own plantation" at various times. Blacks were encouraged to marry on the plantation, or the "slaveholder" would sell them, or buy their spouse.

> *We slaves knowed that them words wasn't bindin' Don't mean nothin' lessen you say "What God done jined, cain't no man pull asunder. But dey never would say dat. Jus' say, "Now you married."*
>
> **—Mathew Jarrett**

Lack of adequate medical care had a particularly negative impact on the health of Black women during pregnancy, childbirth, and the period thereafter. The high death rate of many Black infants, in many ways, was a reflection of this. One Englishman noted that "one of the most serious evils of slavery is its tendency to blight domestic happiness; and the anxiety of parents for their sons, and constant fear of licentious intercourse with slaves is painfully great". Black women were sometimes granted freedom after "giving her master" 10 children.

Black women were frequently forced into cohabitation and eventually impregnated, by their white "master". Miscegenation was largely the result of Black women being raped by white men; only a small percentage of the race mixing was a result of Black men and white women. If Black women resisted the physical compulsion of white men, they were frequently beaten in the most vicious manner. Many Black women were permanently scarred when they resisted their "owner's" advances. Other Black women did not resist, either because of futility, or because of the material advantages that might accrue from it. The Black children from these unions were "slaves" too. White fathers had various reactions: some had no feeling at all and sold their Black children when the opportunity presented itself. Resenting the presence of children fathered by their husbands, white women often encouraged their sale. Some old repentant men "atoned" by freeing the Black children they fathered (years later), and in some cases giving them land and/or money.

> *Sukie was her name. She was a big strappin' nigger gal dat never had nothin' to say much. She used to cook for Miss Sarah Ann, but ole Marsa was always tryin' to make Sukie his gal. One day Sukie was in the kitchen makin' soap. Had three gra' big pots o' lye jus comin to a bile in de fireplace when ole Marsa come in for to get arter her 'bout somep'n*
>
> *He lay into her, but she ain't answer him a word. Den he tell Sukie to take off her dress. She tole him no. Den he grabbed her an' pull it down off'n her shoulders. When he done dat, he fo'got 'bout whuppin' her, I guess, 'cause he grab hold of her an' try to pull her down on de flo'. Den dat black gal got mad. She took an' punch ole Marsa an' made him break loose an' den she gave him a shove an' push his hindparts down in de hot pot o' soap. Soap was near to bilin', an' it burnt him near to death. He got up holdin' his hindparts an' ran from de kitchen, not darin' to yell, 'cause he didn't want Miss Sarah Ann to know 'bout it.*

Well, few days later he took Sukie off an' sol' her to de nigger trader. An' dey put Sukie on de block, an' de nigger traders 'zamined her an' pinched her an' den dey open her mouf, and stuck dey fingers in to see how her teeth was —story related by **Fannie Berry,** *enslaved in Virginia*

My father took me away from my mother when at age of six weeks old and gave me to my grandmother, who was real old at the time. Jus' befo' she died she gave me back to my father, who was my mammy's master. He was a old batchelor and run saloon and he was white, but my mammy was a Negro. He was mean to me.

Finally my father let his sister take me and raise me with her chillen. She was good to me, but befo' he let her have me he willed I must wear a bell till I was 21 years old, strapped 'round my shoulders with the bell 'bout three feet from my head in steel frame. That was for punishment for bein' born into the world a son of a white man and my mammy, a Negro slave. I wears this frame with the bell where I couldn't reach the clapper, day and night. I never knowed what it was to lay down in bed and get a good night's sleep till I was 'bout 17 year old, when my father died and my missy took the bell offen me.

Befo' my father gave me to his sister, I was tied and strapped to a tree and whipped like a beast by my father, till I was unconscious, and then left strapped to a tree all night in cold and rainy weather. My father was very mean. He and he sister brung me to Texas, to North Zulch, when I 'bout 12 year old. He brung my mammy, too, and made her come and be his mistress one night very week. He would have kilt every one of his slaves rather than see us go free, 'specially me and my mammy.

My missy was purty good to me, when my father wasn't right 'round. But he wouldn't let her give me anything to et but cornbread and water and little sweet 'taters, and jus' 'nough of that to keep me alive. I was allus hongry. My mammy had a boy called Frank Adds and a girl called Marie Adds, what she give birth to by her cullud husban', but I never got to play with them. Missy worked me on the farm and there was 'bout 100 acres and fifteen slaves to work 'em. The overseer waked us 'bout three in the mornin' and then he worked us jus' long as we could see. If we didn't get 'round fast 'nough, he chain us to a tree at night with nothin' to eat, and nex' day, if we didn't go on the run he hit us 39 licks with a belt what was 'bout three feet long an' four inches wide.

I wore the bell night and day, and my father would chain me to a tree till I nearly died from the cold and bein' so hongry. My father didn't 'lieve in church and my missy 'lieved there a Lord, but I wouldn't have 'lieved her if she try larn me 'bout 'ligion, 'cause my father tell me I wasn't any more than a damn mule. I slep' on a chair and tried to res' till my father died, and then I sang all day, 'cause I knowed I wouldn't be treated so mean. When missy took that bell offen me I thinks I in Heaven 'cause I could lie down and go to sleep. When I did I couldn't wake up for a long time and when I did wake up I'd be scairt to death I'd see my father with his whip and that old bell. I'd jump out of bed and run till I give out for fear he'd come back and git me
—**J.W. Terrill,** *the son of his owner, enslaved in DeSoto, Louisiana*

About three hundred negro families living in box-type cabins made it seem like a small town. Built in rows, the cabins were kept whitewashed, neat and orderly, for the Master was strict about such things. Several large barns and storage buildings were scattered around the plantation. Also, two cotton gins and two old fashioned presses, operated by horses and mules, made Miller's plantation one of the best equipped in Mississippi.

Master John was quite a character. The big plantation didn't occupy all his time. He owned a bank in Vicksburg and another in New Orleans, and only came to the plantation two or three times a year for a week or two visit.

Things happened around there mighty quick when the Master showed up. If the slaves were not being treated right - out go the white overseer. Fired! The Master was a good man and tried to hire good boss men. Master John was bad after the slave women. A yellow child show up every once in a while. Those kind always got special privileges because the Master said he didn't want his children whipped like the rest of them slaves.

My own Mammy, Mary, was the Master's own daughter! She married Salomon Oliver (who took the name of Oliver after the War), and the Master told all the slave drivers to leave her alone and not whip her. This made the overseers jealous of her and caused trouble. John Santhers was one of the white overseers who treated her bad, and after I was born and got strong enough (I was a weakling for three-four years after birth), to do light chores he would whip me just for the fun of it. It was fun for him but not for me. I hoped to whip him when I grew up. That is the one thing I won't ever forget...

My mother was high-tempered and she knew about the Master's orders not to whip her. I guess sometimes she took advantage and tried to do things that maybe wasn't right. But it did her no good and one of the white men flogged her to death. She died with scars on her back!

—**Salomon Oliver,** *enslaved in Mississippi*

Breeding

In 1796, a South Carolina man declared that the fifty Blacks he was offering for sale were purchased for "stock and breeding". By 1832, Virginia was declared a "Negro raising state" and was to export 6,000 per year because of breeding. One citizen of Fredericksburg, Virginia asserted: "The chief pecuniary resource in the border states is the breeding of slaves; and I grieve to say that there is too much ground for the charges that general licentiousness among the slaves for the purpose of a large increase, is compelled by some masters and encouraged by many".

Even experiments on "slave rearing" were carried on. One "respectable" Virginia planter boasted his women were "uncommonly good breeders" and that he never heard of babies coming so fast as they did on his plantation. The "gratifying" thing about it was that "every one of them...was worth $200 the moment it drew breath".

I was de oldest...Ma was almost fifteen when I was born. Having me was what kilt her, I was so big and fat. She had sebenteen mo' chilluns but it finally got her. She died wid a pain in her stomach when she was ninety year ole

—**"Grammaw"**

Papa's name was Mike and he's a tanner and he come from Tennessee and sold to Massa Kit by a nigger trader. He wasn't all black, he was part Indian. I heard him say what tribe, but I can't 'lect now. When I's growed mama tells me lots of things. She say de white folks don't let de slaves what works in de field marry non, dey, jus' puts a man and breedin' woman together like mules. Iffen the woman don't like the man it don't make no diff'rence, she better go or dey gives her a hidin'

—**Sarah Ford,** *enslaved in Texas*

The systematic breeding of Black people maintained a plentiful "supply" while demand was high. It became one of the most approved methods of increasing agricultural capital. "Slave-breeding owners" were far more common and much more highly esteemed in their community. "Breeding" was so profitable that many Black girls became mothers at thirteen and fourteen years of age. By the time they were twenty, some young women had given birth to five children.

> *Dere am one thing Massa Hawkins does to me what I can't shunt from my mind. I knows he don't do it for meanness, but I allus holds it 'gainst him. What he done am force me to live with dat nigger, Rufus, 'gainst my wants.*
>
> *After I been at he place 'bout a year, de massa come to me and say, "You gwine live with Rufus in dat cabin over yonder. Go fix it for livin'." I's 'bout sixteen year old and has no larnin', and I's jus' igno'mus chile. I's thought dat him mean for me to tend de cabin for Rufus and some other niggers. Well, dat am start de pestigation for me.*
>
> *I's took charge of de cabin after work am done and fixes supper. Naw, I don't like dat Rufus, 'cause he a bully. He am big and cause he so, he think everybody do what him say. We'uns has supper, den I goes here and dare talkin', till I's ready for sleep and den I gits in de bunk. After I's in, dat nigger come and crawl in de bunk with me 'fore I knows it. I says, "What you means, you fool nigger?" He say for me to hush de mouth. "Dis am my bunk, too," he say.*
>
> *"You's teched in de head. Git out," I's told him, and I puts de feet 'gainst him and give him a shove and out he go on de floor 'fore he knew what I's doin'. Dat nigger jump up and he mad. He look like de wild bear. He starts for de bunk and I jumps quick fer de poker. It am 'bout three feet long and when he comes at me I lets him have it over de head. Did dat nigger stop in his tracks I's say he did. He looks at me steady for a minute and you's could tell he thinkin' hard. Den he go and set on de bench and say, "Jus' wait. You thinks it am smart, but you's am foolish in de head. Dey's gwine larn you somethin'."*
>
> *"Hush yous big mouth and stay 'way from dis nigger, dat all I wants," I say, and jus' sets and hold dat poker in de hand. He jus' sets, lookin' like de bull. Dere we'uns sets and sets for 'bout an hour and den he go out and I bars de door.*
>
> *De nex' day I goes to de missy and tells her what Rufus wants and missy*

say dat am de massa's wishes. She say, "Yous am de portly gal and Rufus am de portly man. De massa wants you-uns for to bring forth portly chillen."

I's thinkin' 'bout what de missy say, but say to mysef, "I's not gwine live with dat Rufus." Dat night when him come in de cabin, I grabs de poker and sits on de bench and says, "Git 'way from me, nigger, 'fore I busts yous brains out and stomp on dem." He say nothin' and git out.

De nex' day de massa call me and tell me, "Woman, I's pay big money for you and I's done dat for de cause I wants yous to raise me chillens. I's put yous to live with Rufus for dat purpose. Now, if you doesn't want whippin' at de stake, yous do what I wants.

I thinks 'bout massa buyin' me offen de block and savin' me from bein' sep'rated from my folks and 'bout bein' whipped at de stake. Dere it am. What am I's to do? So I 'cides to do as de massa wish and so I yields...

I never marries, 'cause one 'sperience am 'nough for dis nigger. After what I does for de massa, I's never wants no truck with any man. De Lawd forgive dis cullud woman, but he have to 'scuse me and look for some others for to 'plenish de earth

—Rose Williams

The "trading and breeding" of Black men and women perpetuated the practice of dividing families, who were frequently advertised as being for sale together. However, it was not considered good business since Black men, women and children brought higher prices when sold separately. The large number of single Blacks on the market bears testimony to the ruthless separation of families.

...Babies was snatched from dere mother's breas' an' sold to speculators. Chilluns was separated from sisters an' brothers an' never saw each other ag'in.

Course dey cry; you think dey not cry when dey was sold lak cattle? I could tell you 'bout it all day, but even den you couldn't guess de awfulness of it.

It's bad to belong to folks dat own you soul an' body; dat can tie you up to a tree, wid yo' face to de tree an' yo' arms fastened tight aroun' it; who take a long curlin' whip an' cut de blood ever' lick.

Folks a mile away could hear dem awful whippings. Dey was a turrible part of livin'...

I never seed non of my brothers an' sisters' 'cept brother William...Him an' my mother an' me was brought in a speculator's drove to Richmon' an' put in a warehouse wid a drove of other niggers. Den we was all put on a block an' sol' to de highes' bidder.

I never seed brother William ag'in. Mammy an' me was sold to a man by de name of Carter, who was de sheriff of de county.

No'm dey warn't no good times at his house. He was a widower an' his daughter kept house for him. I nursed for her, an' one day I was playin' wid de baby. It hurt its li'l han' an' commenced to cry, an' she whirl on me, pick up a hot iron an' run it all down my arm an' han'. It took off de flesh when she done it.

Atter awhile, marster married ag'in; but things warn't no better. I seed his wife blackin' her eyebrows wid smut one day, so I thought I'd black mine jes' for fun. I rubbed some smut on my eyebrows an' forgot to rub it off, an' she kotched me. She was powerful mad an' yelled: "You black devil, I'll show you how to mock your betters."

Den she pick up a stick of stovewood an' flails it ag'in' my head. I didn't know nothin' more 'till I come to, lyin' on de floor. I heard de mistus say to one of de girls: "I thought her thick skull and cap of wool could take it better than that."

I kept on stayin' dere, an' one night de marster come in drunk an' set at de table wid his head lollin' aroun'. I was waitin' on de table, an' he look up an see me. I was skeered, an' dat made him awful mad. He called an overseer an' tol' him: "Take her out an' beat some sense in her."

I begin to cry an' run an' run in de night; but finally I run back by de quarters an' heard mammy callin' me. I went in, an' raght away dey come for me. A horse was standin' in front of de house, an' I was took dat very night to Richmon' an' sold to a speculator ag'in. I never seed my mammy any more.

I has thought many times through all dese years how mammy looked dat night. She pressed my han' in bofe of hers an' said: "Be good an' trus' in de Lawd."

Trustin' was de only hope of de pore black critters in dem days. Us jest prayed for strength to endure it to de end

—**Delia Garlic,** *enslaved in Virginia, Georgia, and Louisiana*

Delia Garlic

...Pray we stay together an' have lots of chillun an' none of 'em git sol' way from de parents. Den she lay a broomstick 'cross de sill of de house we gonna live in an' jine our hands together. Fo' we step over it she ast us once mo' if we was sho' we wanted to git married. "Course we say yes. Den she say, "In de eyes of Jesus step into Holy land of mat-de-money." When we step 'cross de broomstick, we was married. Was bad luck to tech de broomstick
—**Caroline Johnson Harris**

Exter done made me a weddin' ring. He made it out of a big red button wid his pocket knife
—**Tempie Herndon Durham,** *enslaved in North Carolina*

The sale of single young children privately and publicly was frequent and notorious. It was normal to see advertisements in which traders sought children from eight to twelve years of age. Some traders even specialized in buying and selling young children. To justify separating families, they argued that Blacks were indifferent. Consequently, Black "fugitives" frequently escaped to wherever they may have had a wife, husband, or child.

> *I was born in Chester, South Carolina, but I was mos'ly raised in Alabama... When I was 'bout fo' or five years old, I was loaded in a wagon wid a lot mo' people in 'hit. Whar I was boun' I don't know. Whatever become of my mammy an' pappy I don' know for a long time...*
>
> *I was tol' there was a lot of slave speculators in Chester to buy some slaves for some folks in Alabama. I 'members dat I was took up on a stan' an' a lot of people come 'roun' an' felt my arms an' legs an' chist, an' ast me a lot of questions. Befo' we slaves was took to de tradin' post Ol' Marsa Crawford tol' us to tell eve'ybody what ast us if we'd ever been sick to tell 'em dat us'd never been sick in our life. Us had to tell 'em all sorts of lies for our Marsa or else take a beatin'.*
>
> *I was jes' a li'l thang; tooked away from my mammy an' pappy, jes' when I needed 'em mos'. The only caren' that I had or ever knowed anything 'bout was give to me by a frein' of my pappy. His name was John White. My pappy tol' him to take care of me for him. John was a fiddler an' many a night I woke up to find myse'f 'sleep 'twix' his legs whilst he was playin' for a dance for de white folks. My pappy an' mammy was sold from each yuther too, de same time as I was sold. I use' to wonder if I had any brothers or sisters, as I had always wanted some. A few years later I foun' out I didn't have none...*
>
> *De nex' time dat I saw my mammy I was a great big boy. Dere was a 'oman on de place what ever'body called mammy, Selina White. One day mammy called me an' said, "Mingo, your mammy is comin'." I said, "I thought dat you was my mammy."... One day I was settin' down at de barn when a wagon come up de lane. I stood 'roun' lack a chile will. When de wagon got to de house, my mammy got out an' broke and run to me an' th'owed her arms 'roun' my neck an' hug an' kiss me. I never even put my arms 'roun' her or nothin' of de sort. I jes' stood dar lookin' at her. She said, "Son ain't you glad to see your mammy?" I looked at her an' walked off.*

Mammy Selina call me an' tol' me dat I had hurt my mammy's feelin's, and dat dis 'oman was my mammy. I went off an' studied and I begins to 'member thangs. I went to Selina an' ast her how long it been sence I seen my mammy. She tol' me dat I had been 'way from her since I was jes' a li'l chile. I went to my mammy an' tol' her dat I was sorry I done what I did an' dat I would lack for her to fergit an' forgive me for de way I act when I fust saw her. After I had talked wid my real mammy, she told me of how de family had been broke up an' dat she hadn't seed my pappy sence he was sold. My mammy never would of seen me no mo' if de Lawd hadn't a been in de plan

—Mingo White

Bimeby Miss Betsy died an' az I sed, she had her own property an' Master Reuben had to sell her property to settle wid de chilluns; dey tuk us an' put us in what dey called "de traders yard" whar de visitors an' de speculators c'ud see us, an' den dey set a day fer to sell us; I wuz on de back po'ch when dey tol' me to cum to de block; de man puts me up on de block an' ses: "Here's a little girl 12 years old she's got de scofula (scrofula) but she's young an' will out gro' hit." Dey put my sister on de block the same day dey did me, an' dey sol' her in anudder direction, up de country, an' I ain't never seen her to dis day. Didn't no body buy me; I 'spose dey wuz skeered uv de scofula; dem dat dey c'dn't sell in Kentucky, the trader decided to tak' to Mississippi to see ef he c'ud sell, dey put us in a big 6 horse stage coach, an' bro't us to Grenada

—Mattie Dillworth

Before "Jim Crow"

Wherever captive Africans were brought (Jamaica, Nevis, Montserrat, St. John, St. Christopher, St. Thomas, St. Vincent, St. Lucia, Haiti, Cuba, Antigua, Barbados, Dominican Republic, Puerto Rico, Mexico, Panama, Colombia, Peru, Argentina, Venezuela, Ecuador, Cartagena, Chile, Uruguay, Brazil, or America), their numbers generally equaled, when they didn't completely outnumber, whites. This alarmed "slave-holders" and made them apprehensive, particularly about mixing and rumors of conspiracies and rebellion.

There were clear signs of dissatisfaction and plots, and where it was not evident, general disrespect for the law prevailed. This preponderance of Blacks over whites promoted the enactment of "Slave Codes" of excessive severity. Black people were forbidden from learning how to read or write, leaving the plantation without a pass, or carrying a weapon. If a "slave" struck a Christian, he was severely whipped, and branded on the face with a hot iron. If the "owner" whipped a Black person to death, he was not subject to fine or imprisonment; after all, Africans were being brought in at an increasing rate well into the 19th century.

> *Oh, them patrollers! They had a chief and he git'em together and iffen they caught you without a pass and sometimes with a pass, they'd beat you*
> —**Daniel Dowdy,** *enslaved in Georgia*

> *...The patrolers would break up their prayer meetings and whip all caught in attendance - unless, of course, a Nigger saved himself in flight.*
>
> *My father was once attending a prayer meeting in a house which had only one door. The slaves had turned a large pot down in the center of the floor to hold the sounds of their voices within. (No sounds can escape from a closed room, if a big pot be turned down in the middle of it.) But, despite their precaution, the patrolers found them and broke in. Of course, every Nigger present was "in" for a severe whipping, but the Lord must have spoken to my father. Thinking fast and acting quickly (as if he were inspired), my father stuck a big shovel in the fireplace, drew out a peck or more of hot ashes and cinders and flung them broadcast into the faces of them patrolers. The room was soon filled with smoke and the smell of burning clothes and white flesh and, in the confusion and general hubbub that followed, every Negro escaped.*
>
> *Teasing, and playing pranks on, the patrolers were favorite pastimes of some of the slaves. One of their choicest stunts was to tie a grapevine across some narrow, dark stretch of road where they knew the patrolers would pass. And, as the patrolers usually rode in a gallop, these vines would be sure to catch the foremost rider or riders somewhere between their saddle horns and necks and unhorse at least one or more of them*
> —**W. B. Allen,** *enslaved in Alabama*

> *On Sundays they would let us go to church up at Sassafras Stage, near Bethel. Was the fust church for niggers in these parts. Wasn't no white*

church, niggers built it an' they had a nigger preacher. 'Couse they wouldn't let us have no ser'vices lessen a white man was present. Most times the white preacher would preach, then he would set dere listenin' while the colored preacher preached. That was the law at that time. Couldn' no nigger preacher preach lessen a white man was present, an' they paid the white man what attended the colored services. Niggers had to set an' listen to the white man's sermon, but they didn' want to 'cause they knowed it by heart. Always took his text from Ephesians, the white preacher did, the part what said, "Obey your masters, be good servant."

Can' tell you how many times I done heard that text preached on. They always tell the slaves dat ef he be good, an' worked hard fo' his master, dat he would go to heaven, an' dere he gonna live a life of ease. They ain' never tell him he gonna be free in Heaven. You see, they didn't want slaves to start thinkin' 'bout freedom, even in Heaven

—**Beverly Jones,** *enslaved in Virginia*

Virginia's "Slave Code" reflected many of the aforementioned abuses and restrictions, along with hanging Blacks found guilty of murder or rape, and for "major offenses" such as robbing a house or store, Blacks received sixty lashes and were placed in the pillory where their ears were then cut off. For "petty offenses", such as insolence and associating with whites or free Blacks, enslaved Blacks were whipped, branded, and/or maimed. In 1667, Europeans enacted the "Act to Regulate the Negroes on the British Plantation", which referred to Blacks in the Caribbean as "of wild, barbarous, and savage nature to be controlled only with strict severity". By 1694, Blacks in Virginia were so "ungovernable", Governor Edmund Andros complained enforcement of their "slave code" was insufficient, although it regulated most of a person's actions.

When the white preacher come to the plantation to preach to us niggers, he pick up his Bible and claim he gitting the text right out fom the good book, and he preach: "The good Lord say: 'Don't you niggers steal chickens fom your missus. Don't you niggers steal your marster's hogs.'" And that would be all he preach

—**Richard Carruthers**

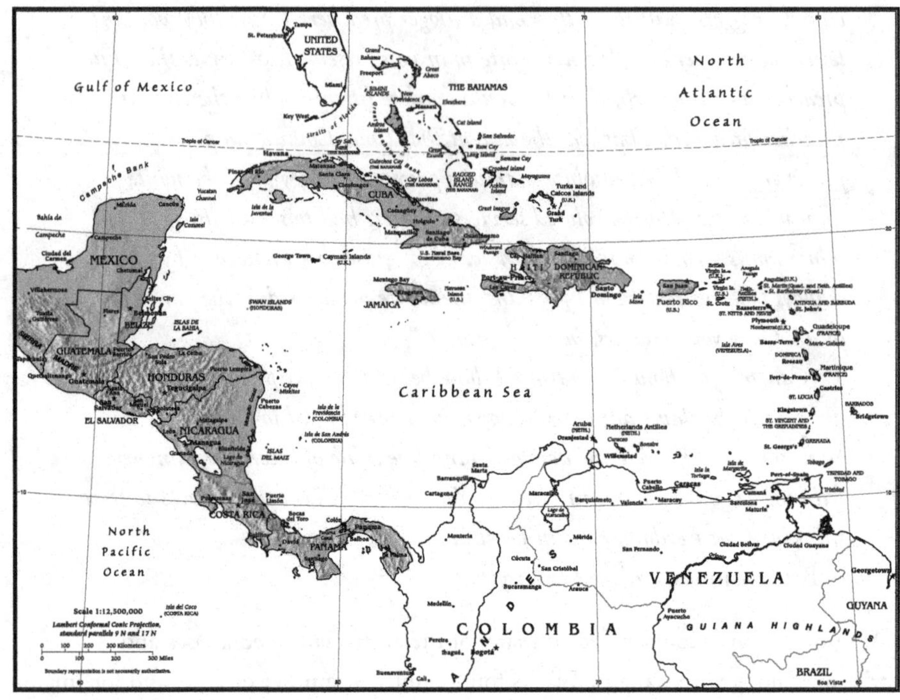

Central America and the Caribbean Islands

An important ingredient in the "seasoning process" was the overseer's lash, typically made of plaited cowhide. The omnipotent whip could draw blood through pants; in fact, some wounds were so large a man's finger could fit inside. Blacks were often hung from trees by ropes with iron weights tied around their neck and waist. In Brazil, they used various torture devices including the tronco, which was constructed of wood or iron, by which Blacks' ankles were fastened in one place for several days; the libambo, did the same thing to the arms. Black people were tied face down to instruments known as novenas and trezenas and beaten for 9 or 13 consecutive nights.

South America

...In dem days, preachers wuz just as bad and mean as anybody else. Dere wuz a man who folks called a good preacher, but he wuz one of de meanest mens I ever seed. When I wuz in slavery under him he done so many bad things 'til God soon kilt him. His wife or chillun could get mad wid you, and if dey told him anything he always beat you. Most times he beat his slaves when dey hadn't done nothin' a t'all. One Sunday mornin' his wife told him deir cook wouldn't never fix nothin' she told her to fix. Time she said it he jumped up from de table, went in de kitchen, and made de cook

go under de porch whar he always whupped his slaves. She begged and prayed but he didn't pay no 'tention to dat. He put her up in what us called de swing, and beat her 'til she couldn't holler. De pore thing already had heart trouble; dat's why he put her in de kitchen, but he left her swingin' dar and went to chuch, preached, and called hisself servin' God. When he got back home she wuz dead. Whenever your marster had you swingin' up, nobody wouldn't take you down. Sometimes a man would help his wife, but most times he wuz beat afterwards.

Another marster I had kept a hogshead to whup you on. Dis hogshead had two or three hoops 'round it. He buckled you face down on de hogshead and whupped you 'til you bled. Everybody always stripped you in dem days to whup you, 'cause dey didn't keer who seed you naked. Some folks' chillun took sticks and jobbed (jabbed) you all while you wuz bein' beat. Sometimes dese chillun would beat you all 'cross your head, and dey Mas and Pas didn't know what stop wuz.

Another way marster had to whup us wuz in a stock dat he had in de stables. Dis wuz whar he whupped you when he wuz real mad. He had logs fixed together wid holes for your feet, hands, and head. He had a way to open dese logs and fasten you in. Den he had his coachmen give you so many lashes, and he would let you stay in de stock for so many days and nights. Dat's why he had it in de stable so it wouldn't rain on you. Everyday you got dat same number of lashes. You never come out able to sit down.

I had a cousin wid two chillun. De oldest one had to nuss one of marster's grandchildren. De front steps wuz real high, and one day dis pore chile fall down dese steps wid de baby. His wife and daughter hollered and went on turrible, and when our marster come home dey wuz still hollerin' just lak de baby wuz dead or dyin'. When dey told him 'bout it, he picked up a board and hit dis pore little chile 'cross de head and kilt her right dar. Den he told his slaves to take her and throw her in de river. Her ma begged and prayed, but he didn't pay her no 'tention; he made 'em throw de chile in

—Leah Garrett

Marse Easterlin wuz sho' a stern master. He believed in whippin' his slaves. I'se seed him put my ma 'cross a barrel an' whip her. She wuz a fiel' hand an' wuked powerfully hard. One ob de cruelest things I ever seen done to a slave wuz done by my Master. He wanted to punish one ob de slaves what had done some 'em dat he didn't lak, a kinda subborn one. He took dat darkie an' hitched him to a plow an' plowed him jes' lak a hors. He beat him an' jerked him 'bout 'till he got all bloody an' sore, but ole Marse he kept right on day after day. Finally de buzzards went to flyin' over 'em...dem buzzards kept a flyin' an' old Marse kept on a plowin him 'till one day he died. After dat Ole Marse got to being haunted by dat slave an' buzzards. He could alwas' see 'em an' hear de groans ob dat darkie an' he was hainted dat way de res' ob his life.

My pa an' ma wasn't owned by de same masters. My pa wuz owned by Marse Bill Brown who owned a plantation near Marse Easterlin. An' Marse being curious lak he wouldn't let pa come to see ma an' us. At night he would slip over to see us an' ole Marse wuz mos' alwa's on de look out fer everything. When he would ketch him he would beat him so hard 'till we could tell which way he went back by de blood. But pa, he would keep a comin' to see us an' a takin' de beatins

—**Vinnie Busby,** *enslaved on a Mississippi plantation*

Well, here's how it happened. She put a piece of candy on her washstan' one day. I was 'bout eight or nine years ole, an' it was my task to empty de slop ev'y mornin'. I seed dat candy layin' dere, an' I was hungry. Ain't had a father workin' in de fiel' like some of de chillun to bring me eats - had jes' little pieces of scrapback each mornin' throwed at me from de kitchen. I seed dat peppermint stick layin' dere, an' I ain't dared go near it 'cause I knew ole Missus jus' waitin' for me to take it. Den one mornin' I so hungry dat I cain't resist. I went straight in dere an' grab dat stick of candy an' stuffed it in my mouf an' chew it down quick so ole Missus never fin' me wid it.

Nex' mornin' ole Missus say: "Henrietta, you take dat piece o' candy out my room?" "No mam, ain't seed no candy." "Chile, you lyin' to me. You took dat candy." "Deed Missus, I tel de truf. Ain't seed no candy." "You lyin' an' I'm gonna whup you. Come here." "Please, Missus, please don't whup me. I ain't seed no candy. I ain't took it." Well, she got her rawhide down from de nail by de fire place, an' she grabbed me by de arm an' she try to turn me 'cross her knees whilst she set in de rocker so's she could hol' me. I twisted an' turned till finally she called her daughter. De gal come an' took dat strap like her mother tole her and commence to lay it on real hard whilst Missus holt me. I twisted 'way so dere warn't no chance o' her gittin' in no solid lick. Den ole Missus lif' me up by de legs, an she stuck my haid under de bottom of her rocker, an' she rock forward so's to hol' my haid an' whup me some mo'. I guess dey must of whupped me near a hour wid dat rocker leg a-pressin' down on my haid.

Nex' thing I knew de ole Doctor was dere, an' I was lyin' on my pallet in de hall, an' he was a-pushin' an' diggin' at my face, but he couldn't do nothin' at all wid it. Seem like dat rocker pressin' on my young bones had crushed 'em all into soft pulp. De nex' day I couldn' open my mouf and' I feel it an dey warn't no bone in de lef' side at all. An' my mouf kep' a-slippin' over to de right side an' I couldn't chaw nothin' - only drink milk. Well, ole Missus musta got kinda sorry 'cause she gits de doctor to come regular an' pry at my mouf. He git it arterwhile so's it open an' I could move my lips, but it kep' movin' over to de right, an he couldn't stop dat. Arter a while it was over jes' whar it is now. An' I ain't never growed no mo' teef on dat side. Ain't never been able to chaw nothin' good since. Don't even 'member what it is to chaw. Been eatin' liquid, stews, an' soup ever since dat dey, an' dat was eighty-six years ago.

Here, put yo' han' on my face - right here on dis lef' cheek - dat's what slave days was like

—Henrietta King

Some white folks might want to put me back in slavery if I tells how we was used in slavery time, but you asks me for the truth. The overseer was 'straddle his big horse at three o'clock in the mornin', roustin' the hands off to the field. He got them all lined up and then come back to the house for breakfas'. The rows was a mile long and no matter how much grass was in them, if you leaves one sprig on your row they beats you nearly to death. Lots of times they weighed cotton by candlelight. All the hands took dinner to the field in buckets and the overseer give them fifteen minutes to git dinner. He'd start cuffin' some of them over the head when it was time to stop eatin' and go back to work. He'd go to the house and eat his dinner and then he'd come back and look in all the buckets and if a piece of anything that was there when he left was et, he'd say you was losin' time and had to be whipped. He'd drive four stakes in the ground and tie a nigger down and beat him till he's raw. Then he'd take a brick and grind it up in a powder and mix it with lard and put it all over him and roll him in a sheet. It'd be two days or more 'fore that nigger could work 'gain. I seed one nigger done that way for stealin' a meat bone from the meathouse. That nigger got fifteen hundred lashes. The li'l chaps would pick up eggs shells and play with them and if the overseer seed them he'd say you was stealin' eggs and give you a beatin'. I seed long lines of slaves chained together driv by a white man on a hoss down the Jefferson road

—**Wes Brady,** *enslaved in Texas*

Wes Brady

Compass at Elmina Castle

Many "masters" boasted of their "slaves" docility, which was achieved through the enactment of a comprehensive "slave code". These "codes" contained provisions for punishment designed to break even the most irascible Blacks, with the sheriffs, courts, and even "slaveless" whites on their side. In 1722, justices in Georgia were authorized to search Blacks for guns, swords, "and other offensive weapons" and to take them unless the "suspect" could produce a permit less than 1 month old authorizing him to carry such a weapon. Patrols were given authority to search Blacks and whip those deemed dangerous to peace and good order.

> *Mammy an' daddy wa'nt never lawful' wedded. Dey don't do dat in dem days...My daddy, he was a fine man an' treated us chullun jus' dandy. He stay wid Marster Gill, an' mammy stay wid Missus Rosa...Missus Rosa was a doctor woman, an' she run dat plantation all by herself. Us colored folks would step right lively when she speak up an' say, "Do dis an' do dat." She was kin' an' good, but she sho' don't stan' no foolishness.*
>
> *Mammy an' de res' of de colored folks, dey lived out in de Quarters in separate cabins of dey own. Dey job was to he'p Missus Rosa in de fields, an'*

h. White motorists had the right-of-way at all intersections.

Jim Crow etiquette operated in conjunction with Jim Crow laws (Black codes). When most people think of Jim Crow they think of laws (not the Jim Crow etiquette) which excluded Blacks from public transport and facilities, juries, jobs, and neighborhoods. The passage of the 13th, 14th, and 15th Amendments to the Constitution had granted Blacks the same "legal" protections as whites. However, after 1877, and the election of Republican Rutherford B. Hayes, southern and border states began restricting the liberties of Blacks. The Supreme Court helped undermine the Constitutional "protections" of Blacks with the Plessy v. Ferguson (1896) case, which legitimized Jim Crow laws and the Jim Crow way of life.

In 1890, Louisiana passed the "Separate Car Law," which purported to aid passenger comfort by creating "equal but separate" cars for Blacks and whites. This was a ruse. No public accommodations, including railway travel, provided Blacks with equal facilities. The Louisiana law made it illegal for Blacks to sit in coach seats reserved for whites, and whites could not sit in seats reserved for Blacks. In 1891, a group of Blacks decided to test the Jim Crow law. They had Homer A. Plessy, who was seven-eighths white and one-eighth Black (therefore Black), sit in the white-only railroad coach. He was arrested. Plessy's lawyer argued that Louisiana did not have the right to label one citizen as white and another Black for the purposes of restricting their rights and privileges. In Plessy, the Supreme Court stated that so long as state governments provided legal process and legal freedoms for Blacks, equal to those of whites, they could maintain separate institutions to facilitate these rights. The Court, by a 7-2 vote, upheld the Louisiana law, declaring that racial separation did not necessarily mean an abrogation of equality. In practice, Plessy represented the legitimization of two societies: one white and advantaged; the other, Black, disadvantaged and despised.

Blacks were denied the right to vote by grandfather clauses (laws that restricted the right to vote to people whose ancestors had voted before the Civil War), poll taxes (fees charged to poor Blacks), white primaries (only Democrats could vote, only whites could be Democrats), and literacy tests ("Name all the Vice Presidents and Supreme Court Justices throughout America's history"). Plessy sent this message to southern and border states: Discrimination against Blacks is acceptable.

Jim Crow states passed statutes severely regulating social interactions between the races. Jim Crow signs were placed above water fountains, door entrances and exits, and in front of public facilities. There were separate hospitals for Blacks and whites, separate prisons, separate public restrooms, and separate public accommodations. In most instances, the Black facilities were grossly inferior - generally older, less well-kept. In other cases, there were no Black facilities - no Colored public restroom, no public beach, no place to sit or eat. Plessy gave Jim Crow states a legal way to ignore their constitutional obligations to their Black citizens.

In October 2001, American RadioWorks conducted a special report called *Remembering Jim Crow*. In the early 1990s, dozens of graduate students at Duke University in North Carolina, as well as other schools, traveled throughout the south with tape recorders and microphones to capture and preserve stories of 20th century oppression and segregation. Correspondent Stephen Smith sifted through hundreds of recorded interviews of Black women and men who experienced and remember Jim Crow.

> *I can remember my mother would have the occasion to send me to this grocery store... that was approximately a mile away, she would give me instructions before I'd leave home and tell me, say, "Son, if you pass any white people on your way, you get off the sidewalk. Give them the sidewalk. You know, you move over. Don't challenge white people*
> **—Grafton**

> *You couldn't go to eat in a restaurant. If they served you at all you went around to a window at the back of the place, right at the kitchen. You see?*
> **—Welch**

> *My grandfather, he was just afraid of a white man as he was a rattlesnake. Because he'd been beaten and knocked about so much, no matter what you say or do let them have their way, don't you say nothing back to them. No matter what they did*
> **—Pointer**

> *Well my grandmother always told me, "you have a certain place, and stay in it." That was automatic, you didn't have to think about it. You knew it and you were taught it*
> **—Randolph**

According to Glenda Elizabeth Gilmore, professor of history at Yale University, "Jim Crow was a word that white and black southerners used for an elaborate system of white supremacy, a system that was established both through legislation and the courts, and through custom. It could mean anything from being unable to vote, to being segregated, to being lynched. It was part and parcel of a system of white supremacy. Sort of like we use the word apartheid as a codeword to describe a certain kind of white supremacy...Jim Crow was a political movement that began with state constitutions. For example in Mississippi, writing in laws that took the right to vote effectively took the right to vote away from black people. Basically it's about power: who has it, who keeps it, who vies for it."

They'd ask college professors with PhDs to write certain parts of the Constitution, to prove that they could read and write. Long passages. And they would say, didn't put a period, didn't write straight on the line. Anything like that. And of course our registrars could hardly read or write themselves
—**Sulling**

There wasn't any opportunity unless you taught school or was a preacher. That was it. Only the domestic folks that had decent jobs with the white folks where took care of the washing and ironing for the white folks were the only ones who had a decent place to stay unless you owned your own land or something. That was it. The only people you saw with shirt and tie on through the week was a school teacher or a preacher. And if them white folks caught you with a shirt and tie on they wanted to know what the hell you was doing
—**Maurice Lucas,** *Mayor of the town of Renova, Mississippi, located about 90 miles south of Memphis*

For instance here's a man with 10 children. In December he's told, and this goes for all of the plantations, he's told to come to the big house and have a settlement. Okay the settlement would go like this. "Well, John, you made 25 bales of cotton. And now you know that the old mule died, had to have another mule, got to pay for that. Now John, your daughter took sick and

you called me and told me you had to take her to the doctor and I had to call the doctor up. You know it costs some money for that so I'll take that out. Now John, you're almost out of debt, but you're not out of debt yet
—Robinson

When my granddaddy was sharecropping, it was a system designed to keep you owing them. You never got free
—Lucas

My name is Thomas Christopher Columbus Chatman, Sr. I was born in Coffee County, Georgia. When we had gathered our crops, sold all the money crops like tobacco, peanuts, and cotton, my father told me that Saturday, "Well boy, let's go and settle up." So we went up to Mr. Thomas' house to the back yard as usual and he came out on the back porch. I had kept a record myself of everything we had got from that man that year and I know we didn't owe him any money. So he came out on the porch and he started thumbing through his book, and finally he looked up at my father and said: "John, you don't have any money coming but you cleared your corn." Well when he said that I reached for my book, my daddy stepped on my foot because he knowed them crackers would kill you if you'd dispute their word, you know. The first thing went through my mind was, how could this man take all our money and my father had six other children down there, raggedy, no money, winter was coming and he's going to take it all.

"There were a lot of rules to follow. Blacks visiting a white home were expected to use the back door. If a white employer was driving his black maid home, she had to sit in the back seat. Blacks were never supposed to contradict white people. And perhaps the most serious rule of all: under no circumstances could a black man show interest in a white woman", correspondent Stephen Smith

Some white man might feel that I don't like the way that Negro looks at my wife or that white woman. And string him up to a tree. And when they would get ready to lynch him, they'd have a picnic. They'd have told the people, we're gonna have a lynching. And hundreds of people would come.

The wives would bring a picnic basket and bring her little children, and they would have the lynching
—Robinson

And you had this big belly sheriff going to sit on that square, the little square. And if you came through there and you were black, you were going to be stopped. And once you got stopped you were going to have to pay out that 15 dollars, which was a lot of money. You going to pay something. We would watch three or four carloads of blacks go through. We'd give them about five minutes or ten minutes to get into Pageland. And we know that sheriff has them. And that was what we called running the gauntlet. We would go through driving ten miles an hour, fifteen miles an hour. But the minute you got out of his sight you'd better hit it down, because as soon as he would take care of those three blacks, you were going to be next
—Davis

If he had a big house, he had a small house. And this house for his black mistress. And one man he had another young girl wasn't but 13 years old. And she came there to wash dishes for his wife. When his wife knew anything she's pregnant, and she's having babies one after the other. And she stayed there and took it. Now, I wouldn't taken that
—Pointer

I guess that's the one thing my father did say, he always used to say, "you have to be very careful where you go, what you do, because anytime something goes wrong, and if you're there whether you're guilty or not, your guilty by association
—Cemore Morton Newsome

My mother told me nobody ever knows what goes through your head. She used to say, that lady I work for is foolish enough to believe that I really like her. She said I'm not thinking about her one way or the other. Just pay me what she owes me. And I learned, too, that I could smile on the outside
—Sutton

A 37-year-old black woman named Gladys Stephenson stopped at an appliance store in Columbia, Tennessee to pick up her radio, which was being fixed. Her 19-year old son James was with her. He was just back from serving in World War II. Gladys and the appliance store clerk got into an argument about the cost of the repairs. James intervened.

> *The clerk said, "What you stop back here for boy, to get your teeth knocked out?" I said, "Yeah, if that's what it takes," so I kept walking and when I got to the door he hit me in the back of the head and I turned around and grabbed him, smacked outside the door and hit him three times: bam! bam! bam! Turn him loose, he fell through the window*
> **—James**

Although James Stephenson was a Navy boxing champ, the clerk was the brother of a local cop. Whites started gathering in the square at the news that a black man had beaten a white man.

> *At that time, you did something that you shouldn't do if you were black they'd hang you. We got wind that the whites were going to come and get him. So the bird got around, if you got guns come down, we'll just have to have a showdown. Got tired of being kicked around*
> **—Edward Kimes**

More than a hundred men gathered in the black part of town, which whites like Bernard Stofel called Mink Slide." I was a policeman back in '46. They got to shooting down at the slide, on east 8th Street. And they shot out all the streetlights, it done got dark then. And we said well we better go down there and talk to them boys. They were shooting right up that sidewalk. And they got all four of us."The police officers were shot but they all recovered. James Stephenson slipped away to a northbound train. Tennessee state patrolmen stormed the black neighborhood the next morning, arresting people and destroying black businesses. The news made national headlines.

Some Key Moments Of The Jim Crow Era:

1863 "The Emancipation Proclamation"
1865-72 Freedmen's Bureau
1866-71 Ku Klux Klan
1865-77 Reconstruction
1868 Fourteenth Amendment
1870-71 Enforcement Acts
1875 Civil Rights Act Passed
1876 Election of 1876
1881 Founding of Tuskegee
1883 Civil Rights Act Overturned
1892 Ida B. Wells Flees Memphis
1895 Atlanta Compromise Speech
1896 Plessy v. Ferguson
1898 Spanish American War
Williams v. Mississippi
Wilmington Riot
1900-10 The Birth of the Blues
1900-70 The Great Migration
1903 The Souls of Black Folk
1905 Niagara Movement
1906 Atlanta Riot
Brownsville Affair
1909 NAACP
1910 The Crisis
1913 Government Segregation
1915 The Birth of a Nation
1917 World War I
1919 The Red Summer
1917-35 The Harlem Renaissance
1921 Tulsa Riot
1922 Moore v. Dempsey
1925-27 Fisk Protest
1929-39 The Great Depression

1931 Scottsboro Case
1938 Gaines v. Canada
1941 March on Washington
1941-45 World War II
1944 Smith v. Allright
1946 Morgan v. Virginia
1947 Jackie Robinson
1947-48 Truman Supports Civil Rights
1954 Brown v. Board of Education

Legacy

In what follows, is an attempt to provide a full description of the events and people who led us to present-day litigation. It is provided so there can be no question regarding the research and documentation utilized in the discovery of our ancestry.

The controversy surrounding the estate of Jeff Carter compelled us to examine his genealogy. It was then discovered Jeff was one of Burrell Carter's sons. Burrell was born in Sandersville, Georgia in May 1833. Around 1860 he married Mary Ann "Molly" Lane. Their union produced 9 children, 8 of whose names are known: Milly, Jeff D. Sr., Gracie, John, Burrell, Sallie, Virgil, Susie, and Mary. Burrell also adopted Alonzo Dixon who was born in May of 1887.

1870 CENSUS – U..ITED STATES

State Georgia County Washington Town/Township Bucks Dist. 98th P.O. Hebron Call No. M593 roll 18[illegible]

enumerated 1 July 1870 by Henry A. Cat[illegible]

Page	Dwelling No.	Family No.	Names	Age	Sex	Color	Occupation, etc.	Value - Real Estate	Value - Personal property	Birthplace	Father Foreign born	Mother Foreign born	Month born in year	Month married in year	School in Year	Can't Read or Write	Eligible to vote	Date of Enumeration
340	210	207	Carter, Burrell	41	M	B	Farm Black Smith			Georgia						//		
			— Mary	32	F	B	Keeping House			"						//		
			— Milly	10	F	B	Work at Home			"						/		
			— Jeff D.	8	M	B				"								
			— Gracie	6	F	B				"								
			— Burrell	2	M	B				"								

Burell Carter, 1870 Census

The 1880 Agriculture Census shows Burrell rented a farm in Washington County where he had at least 35 acres of improved land. He planted 15 acres of Indian corn, 20 acres of cotton yielding 4 bales, 1 acre of sugar cane, and an acre of sweet potatoes. He owned 1 horse, 1 working oxen, 1 milk cow, 1 calf, 16 swine, and 12 barn-yard fowl. Thirty cords of wood were cut on the farm during 1879. Burrell did not hire extra hands to assist in the farming of this land. It is estimated that Burrell died between 1900 and 1910.

E.D. 128 — 1880 CEN. — UNITED STATES

STATE: Georgia — COUNTY: Washington — TOWN/TOWNSHIP: The 98th Dist — CALL NUMBER: T9, Roll 171

PAGE	DWELLING NUMBER	FAMILY NUMBER	NAMES	COLOR	SEX	AGE PRIOR TO JUNE 1st	MONTH OF BIRTH IF BORN IN CENSUS YEAR	RELATIONSHIP TO HEAD OF HOUSE	SINGLE	MARRIED	WIDOWED	DIVORCED	MARRIED IN CENSUS YEAR	OCCUPATION	MISCELLANEOUS INFORMATION	CANNOT READ OR WRITE	PLACE OF BIRTH	PLACE OF BIRTH OF FATHER	PLACE OF BIRTH OF MOTHER	ENUMERATION
7	60	60	Carter, Burrell	Mu	M	50		Head		✓				Farmer		✓	Ga	Ga	Ga	
			Mary	B	F	40		wife		✓				Keeping House		✓				
			Milly	B	F	19		dau	✓					Laborer		✓				
			Jeff	B	M	18		son	✓					Laborer		✓				
			Gracy	B	F	16		dau	✓					Laborer		✓				
			John	B	M	14		son	✓					Laborer						
			Sallie	B	F	9		dau	✓					at home						
			Virge	B	M	7		son	✓					at home						
			Susie	B	F	4		d	✓					at home						
			unnamed	B	F	2/12		d	✓					at home						
			James	Mu	M	4		G. Son	✓											
			Joseph	Mu	M	2		G. Son	✓											

Burell Carter, 1880 Census

The Jeff Carter Estate

On January 19, 1887, Jeff Carter, Sr. married Ella Hooks, when he was about 24 years old and she was about 21. Ella was the daughter of Mary and James Hooks. The following year they gave birth to their first child, Mary Ethel. Bertha soon followed, and by March 1890, their third daughter Annie was born. Lora Ella, Jeff Jr., Lillie Ruth, and Virgil 'Virge', Sr. added to Jeff and Ella's growing family. In August 1899 Boysie was born, and about 5 years later, Ella gave birth to Crawford 'Crawf'. Their youngest daughter Minnie was born around 1907. Unfortunately, Ella died from complications during the birth of this child.

On February 8, 1908, Jeff married again. His second wife, Easter, was the daughter of Berry Gordy, Sr. And Lucy Hellum, also of Sandersville. Easter gave birth to two children, Rodell 'Coot' and Esther, who was born May 7, 1914. Easter died during childbirth, so Esther was raised by her maternal grandmother, Lucy Gordy. When Esther turned five, the family moved to Detroit, Michigan.

On December 12, 1916, Jeff wed Delia Howard of Sandersville, and adopted her daughter Lizzie Dixon.

As Jeff's family grew, his estate flourished. His first wife Ella acquired 103 acres in a deed from her father, James Hooks, on July 10, 1900. On October 23, 1902, Jeff purchased 100 acres of land from A.E. and R.H. Gilmore by warranty deed. He purchased 200 acres on October 27, 1913, from T.D Davis, and 200 more acres from him on November 15, 1916. On the same day he bought another 200 acre tract of land from Ben 'B.J.' Tarbutton, Sr. In all, he purchased 4 tracts of land, which, in addition to the 103 acres Ella inherited from her father, totaled 803 acres, or 1.380 square miles.

Comparable in acreage, Central Park in New York City was developed on 843 acres of land. In 1853 the area above 38th Street was largely undeveloped. Sixteen hundred people were displaced, including New York's first significant community of property owning Blacks, called Seneca Valley. It has become one of the most significant public parks in the country.

Jeff also accumulated 2 buggies, 2 large farm wagons, plows, harnesses, and other agricultural implements. The livestock consisted of 3 mules, approximately 15 to 20 hogs, turkeys, chickens, and at least 1 horse.

Page 181

No.

MARRIAGE LICENSE.

State of Georgia, Washington County.

By the ORDINARY of said County.

To any JUDGE, JUSTICE OF THE PEACE or MINISTER OF THE GOSPEL,

You are Hereby Authorized to Join

Jeff Carter col and Ella Hooks col

In the Holy Estate of Matrimony, according to the Constitution and Laws of this State; and for so doing, this shall be your sufficient License.

And you are hereby required to return this License to me, with your Certificate hereon of the fact and date of the Marriage.

Given under my hand and seal of office, this 15 *day of* January *188*7

M Newman (L.S.)

Ordinary.

GEORGIA, Washington County.

I CERTIFY, that Jeff Carter col *and* Ella Hooks col *were joined in Matrimony by me, this* 19 *day of* January *Eighteen Hundred and Eighty* Seven

Wm Aug. Smith J. P.

Recorded: .... *Ordinary.*

J. W. BURKE & CO., PRINTERS, MACON, GA.

Jeff Carter and Ella Hooks, Marriage License, January 19, 1887

Jeff averaged 18 bales of cotton per season; 9 or 10 bales of his own, and 8 or 9 from his tenants. After the cotton was baled, he stored it until there was a scarcity. Later he would sell it at a better price. Of course there were difficult times, but sales from cotton, timber, and agricultural crops, enabled Jeff to earn $3,000 annually, by conservative estimates. Jeff amassed more land and wealth than most Blacks in Sandersville.

According to his grandchildren, Jeff's house was an impressive, wooden structure, with a circling porch. Several trees surrounded the homeplace, and a large elm tree stood in front of the house. Rail fences kept wildlife off, and amongst his many crops grew a variety of melons, while landscaped orchards grew peaches, apples, plums, pears, berries, and grapes. There were also 6 tenant houses and 2 barns. Jeff's grandchildren participated in daily chores by working in the kitchen and on the farm, milking cows before school. Inside were four large rooms, decorated with photographs and paintings, reflecting his love of art. The house was fully furnished, including a piano and organ in the front sitting room, which was reserved for entertainment.

MICROFILM NUMBER .623 — 1900 CENSUS – UNITED STATES

STATE: Georgia | TOWN/TOWNSHIP: Hebron | SUPV. DIST. NO.: | SHEET NUMBER: 8

COUNTY: Washington | CALL NUMBER: | DATE: | ENUM. DIST. NO.: 94 | PAGE NUMBER: 72

LOCATION				NAME		PERSONAL DESCRIPTION									NATIVITY			CITIZENSHIP			OCCUPATION		EDUCATION					
Street	House Number	Dwelling Number	Family Number	of each person whose place of abode on June 1, 1900, was in this family	Relation to head of family	Color	Sex	Month of birth	Year of birth	Age	Single, married, widowed, divorced	Number of years married	Mother of how many children	Number of these children living	Place of birth	Place of birth of father	Place of birth of mother	Year of immigration to United States	No. of years in U.S.	Naturalization	Type	Number of months not employed	Attended school (months)	Can read	Can write	Can speak English	Home owned or rented	Home owned free
		158	159	Carter, Jeff	H	B	M	Aug	1864	35	M	13			Ga	Ga.	Ga.				Farmer			n	n	y	O	F
				—, Ella	W	B	F	Sep	1866	33	M	13	6	6	Ga.	Ga.	Ga.							y	y	y		
				— Ethel	D	B	F	Jan	1887	12	S				Ga.	Ga.	Ga.				at sch.		3	y	y	y		
				— Annie B	D	B	F	Mar	1890	10	S				Ga.	Ga.	Ga.				at sch.		4	y	y	y		
				— Lorie E.	D	B	F	May	1892	8	S				Ga.	Ga.	Ga.									y		
				— Jeff. Jr.	S	B	M	Sep	1894	5	S				Ga.	Ga.	Ga									y		
				— Lilly L.	D	B	F	Feb	1897	3	S				Ga.	Ga.	Ga.						–			y		
				— Boysie	S	B	M	Jun	1899	9/12	S				Ga.	Ga.	Ga.											

Jeff Carter, 1900 Census

Crawf recalls his father telling him that Ben Tarbutton wanted to buy back the land he sold him. A sharp entrepreneur, Jeff was not interested. He was always punctual with his payments, and saved whatever money remained. Jeff did not believe in borrowing.

Jeff suffered three strokes during his life, the last being the most probable cause of his death. On January 24, 1930, he died without a will (intestate), leading to one of the most brutal and unjust battles over an estate in Washington County. The assault on the Carter heirs for Jeff's highly valued estate has led to emotional breakdown, poverty, and death.

From the time of Jeff Carter's death in 1930 until his daughter Lora Ella's eviction from the estate in 1950, the law never recognized the Carter heirs' rights. When he died, Jeff owned at least 803 acres, free and clear of any note, security deed, or debt instrument. Analysis of the probate record shows there has never been an official appraisal of the estate.

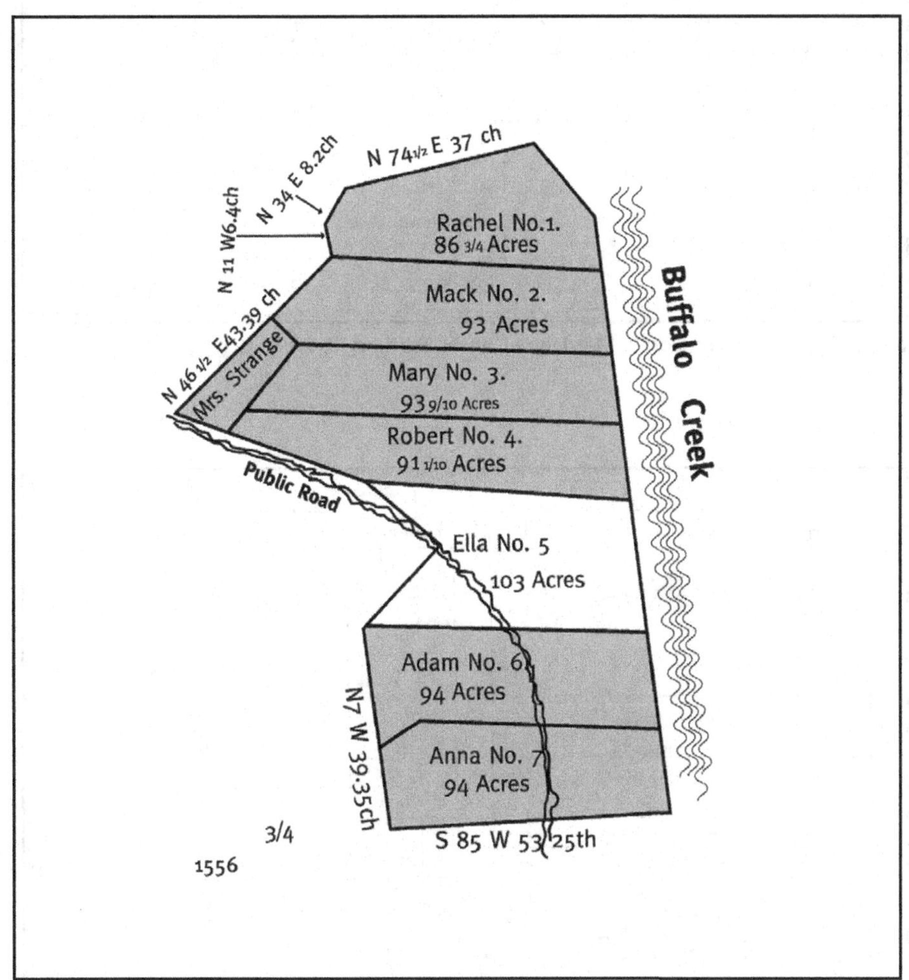

Plat of James Hooks' Estate, Washington County, Georgia. Filed and recorded July 10,1900

MARRIAGE LICENSE. NO.

STATE OF GEORGIA, WASHINGTON COUNTY.

TO ANY JUDGE, JUSTICE OF THE PEACE, OR MINISTER OF THE GOSPEL:

You are hereby authorized to join Jeff Carter, col and Easter Gordon col in the Holy State of Matrimony, according to the Constitution and laws of this State, and for so doing this shall be your license; and you are hereby required to return this license to me, with your certificate hereon of the fact and date of the marriage.

Given under my hand and seal, this 8" day of February, 1908

C. D. Thigpen, (L. S.)
ORDINARY.

GEORGIA, WASHINGTON COUNTY. CERTIFICATE.

I certify that Jeff Carter col and Easter Gordon, col were joined in matrimony by me, this 8" day of February, Nineteen Hundred and eight

G. H. Holmes, M. G.

Recorded Mar 19", 1908 C. D. Thigpen, Ordinary.

Jeff Carter and Easter Gordy, Marriage License, February 8, 1908.

1910 CENSUS - UNITED STATES

STATE: Georgia | COUNTY: Washington | TOWN/TOWNSHIP: Hebron | ENUM. DIST. NO. 107 | PAGE 5

Street Name	House Number	Visitation Number	Family Number	Name of each person whose place of abode on April 15, 1910, was in this family	Relation to Head of House	Sex	Race	Age	Single/Married/Widowed/Divorced	Number of Years Present Marriage	No. of Children Born This Mother	Number of These Children Living	Place of Birth of This Person	Place of Birth of Father	Place of Birth of Mother
		87	87	Carter, Jeff	H	M	B	46	M	2			Ga.	Ga.	Ga.
				— Easter	W	F	B	27	M	2	1	1	Ga.	Ga.	Ga.
				— Louella	dau	F	B	15	S				Ga.	Ga.	Ga.
				— Jeff	son	M	B	14	S				Ga.	Ga.	Ga.
				— Lucy	dau	F	B	11	S				Ga.	Ga.	Ga.
				— Virgie	son	M	B	7	S				Ga.	Ga.	Ga.
				— Crawford	son	M	B	5	S				Ga.	Ga.	Ga.
				— Minnie	dau	F	B	3	S				Ga.	Ga.	Ga.
				Lundy? Eugene	Lo	M	B	18	S				Ga.	Ga.	Ga.

Jeff Carter, 1910 Census

MARRIAGE LICENSE. No.______

STATE OF GEORGIA. WASHINGTON COUNTY.

TO ANY JUDGE JUSTICE OF THE PEACE OR MINISTER OF THE GOSPEL:

You are hereby authorized to join Carter Jeff (col) and Delia Howard in the Holy State of Matrimony, according to the Constitution and laws of this State, and for so doing this shall be your license; and you are hereby required to return this license to me, with your certificate hereon of the fact and date of the marriage.

Given under my hand and seal, this 18 day of Feb, 1916

C D Thiggpen, (L. S.)
ORDINARY.

GEORGIA, WASHINGTON COUNTY. CERTIFICATE.

I certify that Jeff Carter and Delia Howard were joined in matrimony by me, this 12 day of Dec, Nineteen Hundred and fifteen

R. H. D. Strange

Recorded Jan 12, 1917 C D Thiggpen, Ordinary.

Jeff Carter and Delia Howard, Marriage License, December 12, 1916

STATE Georgia
COUNTY Washington
TOWNSHIP OR OTHER COUNTY DIVISION
NAME OF INSTITUTION

1920 CENSUS — UNITED STATES

NAME OF INCORPORATED PLACE 98th Militia
ENUMERATED BY ME ON THE 12 DAY OF January, 1920

SUPERVISOR'S DISTRICT # 14
ENUMERATION DISTRICT # 143
SHEET NO. 5-6-
WARD OF CITY —
ENUMERATOR Wm H. Barksdale

PLACE OF ABODE				NAME	RELATION	TENURE		PERSONAL DESCRIPTION				CITIZENSHIP			EDUCATIO	
STREET, AVENUE, ETC.	HOUSE NUMBER OR FARM	NUMBER OF DWELLING HOUSE (VISITATION ORDER)	NUMBER OF FAMILY (VISITATION ORDER)	OF EACH PERSON WHOSE PLACE OF ABODE ON JANUARY 1, 1920, WAS IN THIS FAMILY	RELATIONSHIP TO HEAD OF HOUSEHOLD	HOME OWNED OR RENTED	IF OWNED, FREE OR MORTGAGED	SEX	COLOR OR RACE	AGE AT LAST BIRTHDAY	SINGLE, MARRIED WIDOWED, OR DIVORCED	YEAR OF IMMIGRATION TO U.S.	NATURALIZED OR ALIEN	IF NATURALIZED, YEAR OF NATURALIZATION	ATTENDED SCHOOL ANYTIME SINCE SEPT. 1, 1919	ABLE TO READ
1	2	3	4	5	6	7	8	9	10	11	12	13	14	15	16	17
	Fm	88	90	Carter, Jeff	Head	O	F	M	Mu	54	M					No
				— Delia	wife			F	Mu	36	M					Yes
				— Crawford	son			M	Mu	16	S					Yes
				— Minnie	dau			F	Mu	13	S				Yes	Yes
				— Roy Del	son.			M	Mu	9	S				Yes	Yes
				Howard Lizzie	S dau.			F	B	17	S				Yes	Yes
	Fm	89	91	Carter Jeff Jr.	Head			M	Mu	22	M					Yes
				— Generaia	wife			F	Mu	19	M					Yes
				— May Julie	dau			F	Mu	3	S					
				— Lily Arthur	dau			F	Mu	1	S					

Jeff Carter, 1920 Census

Administrator/Bond

When one has died intestate, an administrator is appointed to handle their affairs. S/he manages the estate of a deceased person who leaves no executor. In other words, s/he acts as an instrument established by law "for performing the acts necessary for the transfer of the effects left by the deceased to those who succeed to their ownership." If a decedent dies with a will, an executor then carries out those responsibilities.

APPLICATION FOR ADMINISTRATION

GEORGIA—Washington County:
Virge Carter having in proper form applied to me for permanent letters of administration on the estate of Jeff Carter late of said county, this is to cite all and singular the creditors and next of kin of Jeff Carter to be and appear at my office within the time allowed by law, and show cause, if any they can, why permanent administration should not be granted to Virge Carter on Jeff Carter's estate.
THOS. J. SWINT, Ordinary.
(pd)

Sandersville Progress, April 10, 1932

For an appointment to be made, the majority of the heirs must first agree on who should apply to become administrator. In Georgia, the chosen heir must petition the court to become administrator. Then, s/he must publish the application so that any creditors and next of kin are given time to show cause, if any, why permanent administration should not be granted. If no objection is made, the court permits the petitioner to become administrator after posting bond.

The purpose of the bond and good security is to protect the heirs from any mismanagement or wrongdoing to the estate, in addition to any debts incurred on behalf of the estate without the acknowledgment of the probate court. The sum of the bond should equal double the value of the estate, payable to the judge of the probate court in that county.

The Carter heirs agreed that Virge would handle family affairs, since his older brother, Jeff Jr., was too ill to fulfill the obligation. However, there is no record in the probate log of Virge applying or being granted permission to legally act as administrator of the estate.

The "Ennis Deed"

E. N. Ennis owned a general store in Washington County where, like most farmers, the Carters made purchases. On January 27, 1933, Ennis "acquired" a deed to secure debt, supposedly signed by Jeff Carter's heirs at law, securing a promissory note in the sum of $1,471.19. The heirs, however, were unaware the deed existed. Although her name appears on the document, Jeff's daughter, Esther Scott Hinton did not sign the Ennis note and deed to secure debt.

On March 2, 1936, without the approval of the probate court or Esther Scott Hinton's signature, E.N. Ennis transferred and assigned the deed to secure debt (promissory note) to Fannie Belle Hatch for $1,471.19. The note had allegedly been in default for over two years, with a $949.13 balance. The Carters had been making regular payments to E.N. Ennis, so it is highly unlikely they accumulated a $950 debt, let alone a $1400 one.

On September 6, 1984, attorney Roger Moister and kaolin (a mineral) industry agent Robert Lee Watkins deposed Adam Renfroe Sr. in Moister's Atlanta office. Adam stated that in 1933, he brought the signature page of the Ennis deed to secure debt to Philadelphia. The pretense was the heirs were in danger of losing their land because of a debt, and their signatures would prevent the loss. Some of the heirs refused to sign because they did not believe there was a significant debt on the self-sufficient estate. The timber alone was worth at least $2,000. Lillie Ruth was the only heir to sign, as witnessed by her daughter, Blanche Holley.

Adam says he returned the deed to Robert Hooks, Jr. in Sandersville. In his deposition, however, Robert claimed he had no knowledge of the deed or the collection of the signatures in Philadelphia. Adam later testified under oath to forging the signatures of Bertha and Crawford Carter, and "... Johnny Renfroe's signature as a witness".

In 1933, Esther Scott was still living in Detroit, Michigan. The Ennis note and deed to secure debt contained a blank line for the signature of "I.V. Scott". In 1932 Esther married I.V. Scott in Detroit. However, Esther never signed the Ennis deed, so on December 7, 1937 when Mrs. Hatch foreclosed upon the deed to secure debt, it was done without Esther's knowledge. Lizzie Dixon Carter's signature was also absent from the deed. Since none of the Carter heirs ever saw the note and deed, than the purported encumbrance of the Jeff Carter estate constitutes at best, a fraudulent scheme to divert the principal assets of the estate from the Carter heirs to the Tarbuttons.

James H. Kelley, a member of The American Society of Questioned Document

Examiners and Chief Document Examiner of The Georgia State Crime Laboratory, challenged the authenticity of the Ennis note and deed to secure debt. Mr. Kelley pointed out numerous other irregularities in the documents, such as the typed names versus the signatures of those names. He further stated that some of the signatures on both the Ennis deed and note might appear so similar they could have been traced from a common pattern or possibly from one another. He also stated the following:

1| The name of Mrs. Mary Young was signed using abbreviations and initials *"M.E."* for the given name of that person rather than spelling out her name. The other given names used on the deed were spelled out by the persons who signed their names.

2| The signature line for the person named I.V. Scott was not signed on the deed. The signature line is blank on the deed. This indicates that a necessary party to the deed never participated in the transaction.

3| Several discrepancies exist between the typed names and the signed names as follows:

a| The typed named Virgil Carter was signed *"Virge Carter Admr."*

b| The typed named Rodel Carter was signed using a different spelling *"Rodell Carter"*.

c| The typed name Mrs. Homer Dawson was signed on the deed as *"Lora E. Dawson"*.

d| The typed name Mrs. Jeff Carter Sr. was signed *"Delia Carter"* on the deed.

e| The typed name Bertha Renfroe was misspelled when signed *"Bertha Renfrow"*.

f| The typed name Mrs. Sam Turner was signed *"Lillian Turner"*; the handwritten name *"Mrs. Sam Turner"* appears to have been written above the handwritten signature *"Lillian Turner"*.

Additionally, Mr Kelley noted, "Further, from inspecting the Ennis Deed to Secure Debt and the Note, I conclude that the person referred to as Esther Scott may have been related to I.V. Scott (her husband), for whom there was a signature line on the Ennis Deed. The last name 'Scott' connects the two persons. The interest of I.V. Scott in the land which was subject to the Ennis Deed to Secure Debt, must have had some value because he was an apparent necessary party to the transaction. If his interest had value and if someone named Esther Scott was signing in his place to convey it, it was probably a taxable transaction. An interest of value was being conveyed for presumably a fair amount of valuable consideration".

Mr. Kelley also stated in his affidavit that he "finds it unusual that Virgil Carter signed his name *'Virge Carter, Admr.'* without reference in the Deed to any pending estate administration. Such reference would usually appear by a specific recital in the Deed identifying the estate which was being administered. Another typical reference in a Deed to estate administration would be the use of an administrator's deed itself, which the administrator would sign. Neither of these typical references were used by *'Virge Carter, Admr.'* which causes me to speculate why not".

Johnnie Dark Renfroe states in his affidavit that the signature "appearing as 'Johni Renfrow' is not my signature. I never signed the Deed to Secure Debt and have never seen the document. I was ten years old in January 1933 and living in Sandersville, Georgia. I did not go to and was not in Philadelphia, Pennsylvania on or about January 27, 1933. I did not see Crawford Carter, Mrs. Bertha Renfroe or Mrs. Sam Turner in the city of Philadelphia sign this document in my presence. The alleged signature of my name...is a forgery. I did not authorize anyone to sign my name to the Deed to Secure Debt".

In The Face Of Jim Crow

In an effort to reclaim his father's estate, Crawf, who was living in Philadelphia, made a trip to Sandersville in 1936. He went to B.J. Tarbutton Sr.'s office and asked to speak with him. A young man asked Crawf who he was and what the nature of his business was. Crawf told him (who he later learned was one of Tarbutton's sons) he was Jeff Carter's son, and had come from Philadelphia to arrange payments on the debt against his father's place. The young Tarbutton asked, "Can't Virgie take care of it here?"

Crawf answered, "I'm Jeff Carter's son, too, and I have a good job in Philadelphia and could borrow the money as soon as I make arrangements with Mr. Tarbutton".

"Mr. Tarbutton isn't in", his son replied.

Crawf left Tarbutton's office, but returned a few days later. He sensed Mr. Tarbutton did not wish to speak with him from the actions of those in the office.

Crawf left but made a third visit. That time he knew Mr. Tarbutton was in the office, but again he refused to speak with Crawf. The next day was Sunday and Crawf returned to Philadelphia, dismayed by his unsuccessful attempt.

Virge Carter

As on every Sunday, the Carter family attended Fullers Church. But on this first day of June, Jeff's daughter Lora Ella, stayed at the homeplace due to her pregnancy with Wilhemina 'Candy'. Meanwhile, the rest of the family was attending service when they received word that Virge was critically ill, and to return home immediately. They frantically rushed to the homeplace where they were stunned to discover Virge had passed.

When Crawf arrived in Philadelphia, he was horrified to learn of his brother's untimely death. Considering his confrontation with the Tarbuttons only a few days earlier, during which they inquired about Virge's ability to manage the Carter estate, his death was particularly ironic.

The Probate Record

The first entry concerning the Jeff Carter Sr. estate in the probate log is during the July 1936 Term, on page 211. Ella's brother, Robert Hooks Sr., was appointed administrator de bonis non of the estate, meaning he wasn't the first administrator. Because there was no mention of an administrator on the probate record prior to this, Robert Hooks Sr. should have been the first administrator, not de bonis non. According to Crawf, his father and Uncle Robert were "never on friendly terms". Jeff and Robert's poor relationship, coupled with Lora Ella's vehement opposition to her Uncle Robert for malicious attacks he made on her, the Carter land, and its crops, makes Robert's appointment to administrate Jeff's estate tenuous.

According to the record, on June 9, 1936, the same day that Robert Hooks Sr. allegedly posted a $10,000 bond, he was appointed administrator de bonis non of the estate. It would have been procedurally correct to allow next of kin and creditors to make objections or claims to Robert Hooks Sr.'s appointment, if they could show just cause. The record also states that notices had been issued, published, and posted in the court, and no valid objection had been made. This would have been the time for Fannie Belle Hatch to assert her alleged deed with the $950 balance against the estate. The bond Robert Hooks Sr. was said to have posted certainly would have covered the alleged "debt". That day, in chambers with the Ordinary of the Court, Thomas Swint, the following was recorded:

> *Citation having been duly issued and published, requiring all and singular the creditors and heirs of Jeff Carter, late of said County, deceased, to show cause at the present term of this Court why Letters of Administration de bonis non on Jeff Carter's Estate on said estate should not be granted to*

> *Robert Hooks, Sr.; and no valid objection being made in the premises, it is considered that such Letters be granted to said Robert Hooks, Sr. on his giving bond in the sum of Ten Thousand & no/100 Dollars, with The heirs at law of Jeff Carter surety, and taking the oath of office.*

This entry is also the first time there was any mention that on May 5, 1930, Virge applied for and was granted permission to become administrator, after allegedly posting an $8,000 bond. These documents are dated February 14, 1930. They were hidden in other records, and intentionally not filed in the probate log.

Ordinary Swint signed his name on these false documents that were strategically misfiled. This made it appear as if Virge applied for and was granted a permanent letter of administration to the estate of Jeff Carter Sr., after posting an $8,000 bond. There is no evidence of Virge ever paying the bond required to qualify as administrator. If the bond had been paid, then any debts tacked onto the estate should have been covered by it as well. No debt has ever legally existed against the estate, because neither the estate nor the note have been probated. Virge was the only heir who could have argued the validity of the Ennis deed, again giving credence to the suspicion surrounding his death. The facade that Virge was the administrator may have been created to gain access to the names of the heirs and their signatures. Since Virge was not the administrator, there was no debt he could have acquired to encumber the land. No other heir had the legal right to do so either.

At the bottom of page 211 is the typed name Jeff Carter Jr. On page 212 the names Lova (sic) Ella Dawson, Lillie Turner, Bertha Renfroe, and Mamie Carter are typed. One could assume that the Carter estate was valued at $5,000 because the bond is supposed to be twice the value of the estate. However, there had still been no official appraisal of the estate by the probate court. There are few recordings in the probate record during the time Robert Sr. was administrator, and the "Ennis debt" still had not appeared.

The next entry in reference to the Jeff Carter Sr. Estate is dated April 10, 1937 on page 349, April term. Robert Hooks Sr. described 262 acres of land rented to tenants. He requested to waive the tenants rent in exchange for a crop loan from the Government of the Farm Crediting Administration. On that same day, he was granted an order authorizing the waiver. Robert Sr. never divulged to the Carter heirs what was done with the loan.

The next and final entry is dated December 6, 1937 on page 421, December term. Robert Hooks Sr., was granted leave to sell 300 acres of the Carter estate. He claimed the purpose was to pay debts and make distributions to heirs.

It must be noted here that the heirs were unaware that these entries into the record existed at all. As a result, there was no way to challenge their existence, or alleged dates of recordation. It was not until 1993, nearly 60 years later, after contacting Judge Lord in the Washington County probate court, did we become aware of the existence of these entries.

The Hatch to Hooks "Jr." Warranty Deed

Meanwhile, Mrs. Fannie Belle Hatch, holder of the alleged Ennis deed, advertised the subject property for foreclosure sale in the Sandersville, Georgia paper. The next day, Tuesday, December 7, 1937, the Carter estate was "sold" at foreclosure sale by Mrs. Fannie Belle Hatch, to Mrs. Fannie Belle Hatch, the "highest bidder for cash."

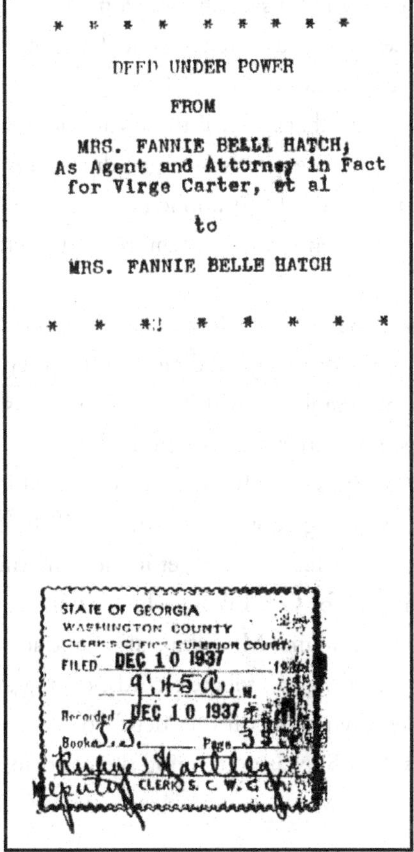

* * * * * * * * *

DEED UNDER POWER

FROM

MRS. FANNIE BELLE HATCH,
As Agent and Attorney in Fact
for Virge Carter, et al

to

MRS. FANNIE BELLE HATCH

* * * * * * * *

STATE OF GEORGIA
WASHINGTON COUNTY
CLERK'S OFFICE SUPERIOR COURT
FILED DEC 10 1937
9:45 A. M.
Recorded DEC 10 1937
Book 33 Page 35
Rufus Hartley
Deputy CLERK S. C. W. C. GA.

Two days later, on December 9th Mrs. Hatch passed the "Ennis deed" to Robert Hooks Jr. According to one of his depositions, he paid her $400 cash and signed two promissory notes: $418.79 due November 1, 1938, the other for $418.80 due November 1, 1939 totaling $1,237.59. Fulfillment of the deed is indicated by Mrs. Hatch's signature on the back, dated April 12, 1940. The two promissory notes "signed" by Robert Hooks Jr., have inscribed thereon in long hand: "Paid by B.J. Tarbutton, Apr. 13, 1940, Mrs. Fannie Belle Hatch by G.J. Elkins" (Mrs. Hatch's brother).

Mr. James H. Kelley points out that the Hatch to Hooks Warranty Deed dated December 9, 1937, is suspicious. He explains, "The deed shows 4 alterations on its face where the word 'Sr.' was changed to 'Jr.' by handwriting. None of these changes were initialed by the signer of the deed, Robert Hooks Jr. It is standard practice for typed changes on a legal document, such as a deed or mortgage, to be approved by the signer of the document, who would initial the changes in the margin of the document. The absence of any initials on this instrument raises suspicion in my mind about the genuineness of the document on its face, and the intent of the parties themselves in the transaction."

It is to be emphasized again that none of the Carter heirs knew of these transactions or actions. This was in 1930s Georgia, during Jim Crow, and there was no legal protection in place for Blacks. If public notices, for example, were required for the sale of a white person's land, no such requirement existed for the sale of a Black person's property.

Consequently, the Carter heirs were unaware that these transactions, beginning with the botched Ennis deed, were not legally binding, and that they had no responsibility to honor them. These events, combined with Virge's mysterious death, created a great deal of confusion amongst the Carter heirs regarding the status of their estate.

In his August 14, 1985 deposition, Robert Hooks Jr. said it was decided by the Jeff Carter heirs that he " would go down there and see if [he] could buy the place back and, then they [the Carter heirs] could get it back any time they got ready ". He had worked half of his life for G.J. Elkins, who was in charge of his sister's (Fannie Belle Hatch) business affairs. Mr. Elkins also conducted business regularly with B.J. Tarbutton Sr. According to probate records, during the same time that Robert Hooks Jr. was allegedly paying off the "debt" to get the estate back for the Carter heirs, his father Robert Sr. was petitioning the court for permission to sell 300 acres to pay the "debt".

There was obviously collusion between the probate court and Tarbutton; Robert Sr. and Tarbutton; Robert Jr. and Tarbutton; and Elkins/Hatch and Tarbutton.

The "Scott Deed"

A warranty deed from Esther Carter Scott [Hinton] to B.J. Tarbutton, dated January 31, 1938, allegedly conveyed her interest in the Jeff Carter Sr. Estate. Esther Scott's signature on this document was clearly forged. The record of the deed was typed and shows only a notary public, Charles E. Williams, as a witness. However, the original deed had two witnesses: Charles E. Williams, Notary Public, and his wife, Maude Williams. The original was re-recorded June 21, 1984 in the Washington County Superior Court.

In her August 19, 1985 deposition, Esther contends she never saw the original deed, did not authorize anyone to sign her name to a deed in January 1938, and does not know the Notary Public who claims to have witnessed her signing the deed. Although she allegedly signed the deed in Detroit, Michigan, she had been living in Los Angeles, California since early 1937. Like other deeds recorded in reference to the Jeff Carter Sr. Estate, the Scott deed was manufactured, forged, filed, and re-filed. These transactions laid the foundation for the deception that followed in future courts. Mr. Kelley again noted differences between Esther Scott's signature on the deed and her actual signature. They indicate to him that Esther Scott's signature was most likely forged. "I am also suspicious about the genuineness of the Esther Scott

Warranty Deed from its face based on my inspection of the document. The deed does not show a revenue stamp on it which would have been placed there by the County Clerk when recording the deed. Such stamps indicate the amount and payment of a transfer tax on the deed. If no transfer tax was due or payable, usually there is a notation to that effect by the Clerk. The absence of either a revenue stamp on the deed or a notation by the Clerk that no tax was due is unusual to me.

The absence of the revenue stamp therefore makes me suspicious of the Scott Deed on its face. Either the recited consideration of $1.00 was grossly inadequate for the payment of the interest conveyed, or the tax should have been paid on the deed when it was recorded if the conveyance was bona fide. I note that other original deeds which I have inspected in the chain of title to the Carter property have revenue stamps on them. They are the Deed Under Power by Mrs. Fannie Belle Hatch, as agent dated December 7, 1937, which shows a fifty cent revenue stamp; the Deed from Mrs. Fannie Belle Hatch to Robert Hooks Jr., dated December 9, 1937, shows $1.50 in revenue stamps; the Deed from Robert Hooks Jr. to B.J. Tarbutton, dated February 19, 1938, showing $1.00 in revenue stamps."

The "Hooks Jr. to Tarbutton Deed"

There were rumors that Robert Hooks Jr. was interested in the Carter estate as well. He, along with Mary Ethel's (Carter) husband Charlie Young, and her brother Rodell 'Coot', were led to B.J. Tarbutton, Sr., by E.N. Ennis' nephew, Luther Ennis, to negotiate a deal. It was their understanding Mr. Tarbutton would hold the "debt" on the estate until the heirs paid it off.

A meeting was held with Mr. Tarbutton's attorney, Jack Harris, at D.E. 'Stick' McMaster's office in Sandersville. Mr. Harris' partner, Mr. McMaster, is related to the Tarbutton family. Their signatures appear on a notarized copy of the deed to the Carter estate which was "sold" by Robert Hooks Jr. to B.J. Tarbutton Sr. for $640. This deed, dated February 19, 1938, is fraudulent. Robert, neither the trustee nor the administrator, was nonetheless permitted to "transfer" the Carter estate to Mr. Tarbutton.

Later, Robert claimed he did not understand what he had signed and that when he requested a second option, Mr. Tarbutton said, "If they don't pay it, I will let you have it back."

Robert said he didn't insist the second option be put in writing because he "didn't have no power to do nothing else," and he "would have been afraid to protest anything he [Mr. Tarbutton] said." He added, "This was in 1938. You look around here and see all of these white people and me Black. Who am I protesting?"

This "sale" took place 19 days after Tarbutton produced the forged Esther Scott deed. To make their chain of title appear legitimate, the Scott deed was not recorded until March 30, 1938 for $1.00.

Peonage

The 13th Amendment to the Constitution was passed in 1863 during the Civil War. It not only prohibits slavery, but also forbids "peonage" which is a condition of involuntary servitude based on indebtedness. The 14th Amendment was ratified in 1868 shortly after the civil war ended. It guarantees that all persons born in any state of the United States is a citizen of that state and of the United States, and is guaranteed the privileges and immunities due to citizens of the United States, and to due process and equal protection of the laws. It was originally passed to provide federal protection for the rights of individuals freed from slavery by the Thirteenth Amendment.

The name Jim Crow is often used to describe the segregation laws, rules, and customs which arose after Reconstruction ended in 1877 and continued until the mid-1960s. By 1838, the term "Jim Crow" was being used as a collective racial epithet for Blacks, not as offensive as nigger, but as offensive as coon or darkie. The popularity of minstrel shows aided the spread of Jim Crow as a racial slur. By the end of the 19th Century, the words Jim Crow were less likely to be used to derisively describe Blacks; instead, the phrase Jim Crow was being used to describe laws and customs which oppressed Blacks.

Stetson Kennedy, the author of *Jim Crow Guide,* offered these simple rules that Blacks were supposed to observe in conversing with whites:

1| Never assert or even intimate that a White person is lying.

2| Never impute dishonorable intentions to a White person.

3| Never suggest that a White person is from an inferior class.

4| Never lay claim to, or overly demonstrate, superior knowledge or intelligence.

5| Never curse a White person.

6| Never laugh derisively at a White person.

7| Never comment upon the appearance of a White female.

The Jim Crow laws and system of etiquette were undergirded by violence, real and threatened. Blacks who violated Jim Crow norms, for example, drinking from the white water fountain or trying to vote, risked their homes, their jobs, even their lives. Whites could physically beat Blacks with impunity. Blacks had little legal recourse against these assaults because the Jim Crow criminal justice system was all-White: police, prosecutors, judges, juries, and prison officials. Violence was instrumental for Jim Crow. It was a method of social control. The most extreme forms of Jim Crow violence were lynchings.

Most of the victims of Lynch-Law were hanged or shot, but some were burned at the stake, castrated, beaten with clubs, or dismembered. The great majority of lynchings occurred in southern and border states. Many whites claimed that although lynchings were distasteful, they were necessary supplements to the criminal justice system because Blacks were prone to violent crimes, especially the rapes of white women. Most Blacks were lynched for demanding civil rights, violating Jim Crow etiquette or laws, or in the aftermath of race riots.

Lynchings were most common in small and middle-sized towns where Blacks often were economic competitors to the local whites. These whites resented any economic and political gains made by Blacks. Lynchers were seldom arrested, and if arrested, rarely convicted. Lynching served many purposes: it was cheap entertainment; it served as a rallying, uniting point for whites; it functioned as an ego-massage for low-income, low-status whites; it was a method of defending white domination, and helped stop or retard the fledgling social equality movement.

Lynch mobs directed their hatred against one (sometimes several) victims. The victim was an example of what happened to a Black man who tried to vote, or who looked at a white woman, or who tried to get a white man's job. Sometimes the white mob was not satisfied to murder a single or several victims. Instead, in the spirit of pogroms, the mobs went into Black communities and destroyed additional lives and property. Their immediate goal was to drive out - through death or expulsion - all Blacks; the larger goal was to maintain, at all costs, White supremacy.

The mass media, especially newspapers often published inflammatory articles about "Black criminals" immediately before the riots; Blacks were not only killed, but their homes and businesses were looted, and many who did not flee were left homeless. The goal of the white rioters, as was true of white lynchers of single victims, was to instill fear and terror into Blacks, thereby buttressing white domination. The Jim Crow hierarchy could not work without violence being used against those on the bottom rung.

Jim Crow

It was therefore not unusual for whites to refuse to give Blacks receipts. Without receipts, it was impossible for one to show proof of past payments on claims of debts. This made it difficult to prove the validity, or lack thereof, of debts such as the Carter's.

After the "sale", Robert Hooks, Jr. told the Carters they would have two years to pay Mr. Tarbutton off by making regular deliveries of cotton to his cotton warehouse in Sandersville, Georgia.

Lora Ella, her family, and the tenants delivered bales of cotton toward payment on the "debt" from 1938 until 1950. Mr. Tarbutton never wrote any receipts for these deliveries. Lora Ella even made special day-long trips to Sandersville in hopes of getting receipts - although the bus stop was an 8 or 9 mile walk from her home.

Tarbutton's receptionist would say that either he was not in or he was out of town. Lora Ella was told other times to come back the following Saturday and the receipts would be ready for her then.

Despite the run-around she was given, Lora Ella persevered. She was determined to clear her family's "debt". She often brought her daughter Eloise 'Honey' into town with her. During one trip, they were walking down the street and saw Mr. Tarbutton. Lora Ella told him she brought some cotton and wanted to speak with him about the property. He continued walking and said, "Lora Ella, come around to my office". Upon entering, she anxiously announced her business to the receptionist, who promptly exited but returned shortly with the response, "Mr. Tarbutton is tied up...[so], come back next week".

Eloise witnessed Tarbutton berating her mother. She experienced first hand the intimidation one felt as a Black person facing white power during Jim Crow. "There were no demands, and it just seemed like it was an understood thing...I don't know whether it was just so far above us as minorities, you just had that feeling. You just couldn't say anything to him. You asked and he didn't give you anything and you just couldn't demand nothing it seemed like. We just couldn't challenge him... There was something about him and I guess his powerfulness...it looked like you couldn't talk to him."

It became painfully clear to Lora Ella that Mr. Tarbutton was shrewdly maneuvering to keep their land. She made several attempts to attain a lawyer who would help. In Eloise's deposition she states that one of the attorneys was "D.D. Veal of Eatonton, Georgia. He looked into the case but did not do anything. Another was a lawyer in Atlanta by the name of Holloway, I believe. He also said that he was unable to do anything in the case. Finally, my mother paid Benton Evans, a lawyer in Sandersville, to try to get the land back. These attorneys were willing to look into the case, but they were unable or unwilling to pursue it when they realized that it would mean opposing Mr. Tarbutton, who was wealthy and powerful in the Sandersville community. The message was clear to my mother and me that none of them wanted to take on a fight with Mr. Tarbutton."

Lora Ella convinced her sister Lillie Ruth, who was living in Philadelphia, to come to Georgia. When they went to Mr. Tarbutton's office, he gave them more excuses. Sometimes, he wouldn't even speak with them; he would lie and say his secretary wasn't in, or have his secretary say he wasn't in. During one of their trips, they told Mr. Tarbutton all they wanted was their land. Mr. Tarbutton's outlandish response was, "If you can pay the $3,000, than you can have your land back".

The sisters then negotiated with Mac Smith, a local mortician, and borrowed the money from the George D. Warthen Bank, in Sandersville. Accompanied by Robert Hooks Jr., they went to attorney Ed Avery's office, where Mr. Tarbutton was supposed to meet them. The lawyer called Mr. Tarbutton and told him they were there and had the money. Mr. Tarbutton had not anticipated the Carters would raise the money, so he changed his demand. He then claimed the debt must be paid through farm resources. After paying attorney fees and working feverishly to raise the money, Lora Ella and Lillie Ruth were devastated. They returned home in tears.

One Saturday afternoon a few weeks later, a fire started at the homeplace. In no time at all, the wooden structure was destroyed; little could be saved. This was during the late 1940s when house burning, like lynching, was a fearful reality for southern Blacks; a threat for them to abandon their land.

Abuse of Power

From 1947 until 1951, B.J. Tarbutton Sr. served as Mayor of Sandersville. He was also a State Senator from 1947 until 1948 and a State Legislator from 1949 until 1954.

In 1949, having returned home to Philadelphia after yet another failed effort in Sandersville, Lillie Ruth collected $650 from her brother Crawf and her daughter Blanche. Again, she traveled to Georgia in an effort to recover her father's estate from Mayor Tarbutton. During the meeting, Tarbutton was particularly harsh and hostile with Lillie Ruth's sister Lora Ella. Throughout the meeting, he verbally assaulted the sisters.

Lillie Ruth told Blanche that Mr. Tarbutton "...Carried her around back to a filthy, dirty, fearsome room and frightened her to death, telling her that she had come down there to stir up trouble. He took the money and didn't give her a receipt...She was humiliated and cried tears like a baby. She did not protest Mr. Tarbutton because she was lucky to be out of Sandersville and back in Philadelphia alive. That is how she feared for her life."

Soon after in 1950, under the orders of Mayor Tarbutton, Sheriff A.W. Smith attacked Lora Ella with what has been described as a "blunt instrument". He tossed her belongings on each side of the road and in a water-filled ditch. He then pad locked her door.

Her daughter Candy was coming home from school with her cousin Eugene and saw "...something down the road...we walked faster as we got closer. A lot of our things were put on the road, everything, they didn't even put it in the yard, we called it a ditch. Clothes were torn up...when I got to the house, my mother had a big gash above her eye, and she said, 'That low down A.W. Smith hit me...', she was bleeding. My sister and Sarah [Robert Hooks Sr.'s wife], had come across the road. The tenants were not thrown out, only Carter heirs. My sister says A.W. Smith actually used Black men to kick the family off the land. It's my understanding that she was picking up some of her prize possessions, family pictures, when the Sheriff struck her. Unbelievable, but it really happened".

Lora Ella's son Cornelius and her five year old granddaughter, Grace also witnessed the attack. Later, when Robert Hooks Jr. was asked why he didn't assist his cousin Lora Ella, he said, "I wasn't going to have Mr. A.W. beating my head".

With the help of his agents, Mayor Tarbuttton created a mirage that the Carters owed a "debt" and refused to pay. This lent legitimacy to his claim to their land. Sheriff A.W. Smith and his thugs represented the crippling intimidation of white supremacy. The Carters couldn't even report it to the authorities because the authorities were the ones who committed the savage attack. The brute force and intimidation used to eject the heirs from their estate was also effective in frightening others who might dare to involve themselves. Fear paralyzed them from even attempting to protect a battered woman and her children, who had violently and abruptly been made homeless.

Due to these outstanding circumstances, a white woman named Mrs. Frannie Mae, who operated a grocery/dry goods store with her husband, let Lora Ella and her children stay in her cow pasture that cold evening. They removed some hay and placed what belongings they had salvaged inside the barn, where they lived for a year before moving to West Palm Beach, Florida.

In the 1950s, Eloise went to Savannah, Georgia with her Aunt Lillie Ruth to speak with a lawyer about trying to get their land back. They met the attorney to discuss the case, and when he realized he would have to oppose Mayor Tarbutton, he told them he would not be able to assist them. Again, the message was clear. Although the Carter family legitimately owned the land, no lawyer was willing to represent the family in their effort to settle this ongoing feud with the Tarbuttons.

Eloise also went to see MW Dukes, an attorney in Sandersville. She paid him $25 to look into the issues surrounding the Jeff Carter Sr. Estate. The attorney told her there was nothing he could do about the situation.

Around 1955, Virge's widow Mamie went with her son Virgil, Jr. from their home in Brooklyn, NY, to Mr. Tarbutton's office in Savannah, Georgia. Their purpose was "...to get the Jeff Carter property back from him". It was Virge, Jr.'s idea to see if they could redeem the land.

Upon entering his office, Virge, Jr. immediately asked how much was owed on the property. In a deep voice, Mr. Tarbutton replied, "$3,000". Virgil reached in his pocket and offered him the money. To Mr. Tarbutton's surprise, his bluff had been called. He then informed Virge, Jr. he "...was too busy and would not accept it...Come back in three years and talk to me then".

Virge, Jr. made another trip to Sandersville and spoke with one of Tarbutton's sons about getting the land back. This attempt was unsuccessful as well.

Lillie Ruth never stopped worrying about the land. In 1963, she asked her son O' Neal to speak with the Tarbuttons about the family's claim. O' Neal called and spoke with Mrs. Tarbutton. She referred O' Neal to her son, Ben, Jr.

O' Neal wrote a letter to the Tarbuttons on behalf of his mother. Lillie Ruth received a response, dated March 5, 1963, which read:

> *Dear Lilly:*
> *My brother and I own the old Carter Farm, and at the present time we are not interested in selling.*
> *However, if and when we ever decide to sell we will give you the opportunity to purchase the property.*

Lillie Ruth Carter Turner

Later, O'Neal contacted M.W. Dukes, the Sandersville attorney his cousin Eloise contacted several years before. He went to the courthouse, obtained a copy of a deed, and gave it to O' Neal. The deed had typed names on it, so it was of absolutely no help. The deed was not recorded from a photocopy of the original, so the signatures weren't clear. Apparently, the original deed was not available for inspection. Mr. Dukes indicated he would not be able to take the case and referred O' Neal to Baxter Jones, an attorney in Macon, Georgia.

O' Neal wrote to Baxter Jones on September 7, 1964. Mr. Jones replied by letter, dated September 12, 1964. O' Neal commented, "I was overwhelmed with how picky Mr. Jones was in reviewing my letter. Also, I was a little suspicious of his endeavor since he did not charge me a fee". It was clear he did not want to pursue the case.

Eloise then went to see Mrs. Tarbutton about the land and explained Mr. Tarbutton had taken it from her family many years ago. She stressed that it was not intended for him to keep the land forever. Mrs. Tarbutton said she was not living on the property and her sons were in charge of it.

Later, Eloise met with Tarbutton's sons about the land. First, she spoke with B.J. Tarbutton, Jr. Later, Hugh came into the room and she discussed the matter with him. At the end of the meeting, Hugh stated, "...If we ever decide to sell the land, we will notify you as one of the first to know".

It was apparent to Eloise that they were not interested in hearing anymore about the Carter family claim, or dealing with her about the matter, and that she should conclude her business and leave for the day.

Lora Ella, sometimes accompanied by her eldest daughter Elizabeth, continuously tried to settle the dispute over the land by seeking a competent attorney. Every summer, she returned to Georgia to walk across the Carter estate. Her efforts continued until the stress of the ordeal led to a nervous breakdown.

Lora Ella Breaks Down

Lora Ella's son Homer was 17 when the family was evicted from the homeplace. "My mother talked all my life about this place", he says. "She said Uncle Robert (Hooks, Sr.) was nothing but a crook...she sensed it, and it has proven over the years. Tarbutton also knew he was crooked and could use him to get information. He hated the ground my mother was going to walk on in the next state. Like westerns on Bonanza, somebody has a big place, then somebody has a place next door...jealousy. Her brothers and sisters didn't believe her, like she didn't know what she was talking about. Today I feel she's in her grave with a broken heart because of this land. We could never sit down with her and have a conversation and it not come up. I feel she died of a broken heart. It was too late when they [her brothers and sisters] realized what had happened".

One evening in 1964, about two years before Lora Ella's death (she had been ill), her daughter Candy remembers coming home from work, and her mother saying, "We gotta get out of this house because of those white people, and I don't want no problems". She began to talk this way regularly. "She went to her grave hurt," Candy says, "but if you had an inheritance, and somebody took it and left a scar on you, a scar in your heart, a scar on your body, anything could happen, you could have a heart attack, anything. This is hard on her children. I couldn't bring my mind together to tell this story seven years ago because it hurts. You have to wonder why God allows certain things to happen. A man that had everything [Tarbutton] with no compassion whatsoever for those struggling people, to take their possessions. As I grow older it affects me more; I feel the hurt now greater than ever. I hope every day of my life that justice could be done because, this is a brutal act, I feel the property was brutally taken".

"She never wanted to live anywhere else," Homer recalls. "The night she died, she was in the hospital. I was going to Miami the next day...I had to see her to tell her I was coming back on the weekend. I went in, she was talking about Candy's daughters, Kay and Ruthie, and my two youngest kids, Wendy and Nellie... She said, 'I want to go back to the homeplace one more time and walk across the field, and carry the little ones with me...,' she liked little ones around. That Monday morning at five something she died. The Carter land was taken...that hurt her every second until the last. Somebody take something from you like that...hurt me just to see her, and for such a long time her brothers and sisters act like they don't care. Later they tried, but at first Uncle Robert could do no wrong...I hurt today from it."

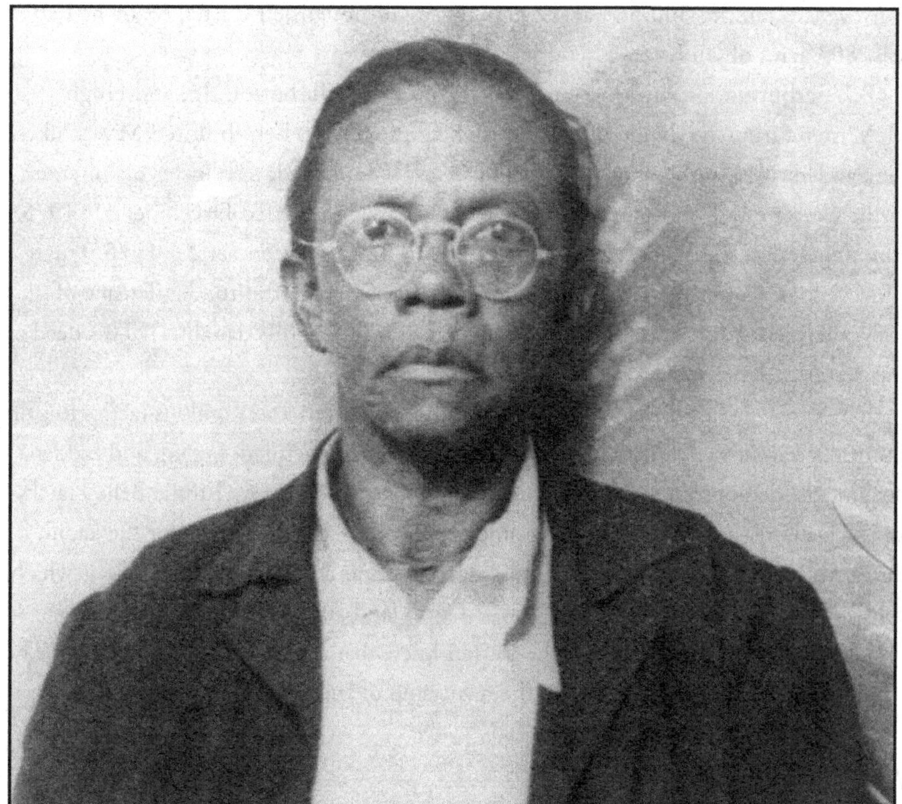

Lora Ella Carter Dawson

White Gold

> ***kaolin*** *\Ka"o*lin\ n. [Chinese, kaoling, high ridge, the name of a hill where it is found.] a fine white clay used in making porcelain, as a filler in textiles, paper, ceramics, paints, rubber, fiberglass, cosmetics, etc., and medicine.*

B.J. Tarbutton, Sr. executed a mineral lease on the Carter estate, dated December 7, 1950, to Stick McMaster. It was recorded 16 years later, on August 10, 1968. Thereafter, Mr. Tarbutton conveyed the property to his sons, Ben J. Tarbutton, Jr., and Hugh McMaster Tarbutton, by deed dated December 27, 1952. He recited as consideration his "natural love and affection for" his sons. Stick McMaster, lessee, transferred the lease to Georgia Kaolin on May 4, 1954. These and subsequent conveyances refer to 500-585 acres, more or less although Jeff Carter, Sr. owned at least 803 acres of land.

B.J. Tarbutton, Sr. died in September 1962. Ben J. Tarbutton, Jr., and Hugh McMaster Tarbutton divided their jointly held properties. Ben, Jr. hired MW Dukes, the Sandersville attorney both Eloise and O' Neal contacted, to transfer his interest in the Carter estate and other property to Hugh by deed, dated December 31, 1975. The transaction was recorded on January 23, 1976. On December 21, 1976, Hugh conveyed the Carter estate to Loulie Eugenia Kernaghan Tarbutton, as Trustee of Irrevocable Trust for Benefit of Loulie Eugenia Tarbutton (his daughter). This deed was recorded December 31, 1976.

For years B.J. Tarbutton and the kaolin cartel employed unscrupulous tactics to gain control of kaolin-rich land. Their consistent use of manufactured, forged, and hidden documents, demonstrates their turpitude. Luther and E.N. Ennis, Fannie Belle Hatch and G.J. Elkins, and Stick McMaster among others, all acted as agents for the kaolin cartel. Historically, agents created similar documents and performed transactions which consistently led to the theft of Black owned farm land and minerals.

Naturally, at the time, none of the Carters knew that the land was rich in kaolin. The family's pursuit was simply to regain the ownership of lands that were rightfully theirs.

The Struggle Continues

Virge, Jr., the grandson of Jeff, Sr., wrote a letter to the County Tax Commissioner of Washington County, Georgia with a copy to the Clerk of the Superior Court, dated January 11, 1978 . His intention was to give notice to Mr. Tarbutton of the Carter family claim to the Jeff Carter Sr. Estate. On February 17, 1978, he wrote to the Tarbuttons asserting his inherited right to the property, and asked for return of the land. The letter also asked whether the Tarbuttons intended to file any resistence or response to the request.

On April 1, 1979, Virge Jr.'s letter to the Judge of the Superior Court of Washington County renewed his request to reclaim the land. He indicated to the Judge that he had been unable to get competent counsel and that he was going to seek assistance through the Columbus Legal Aid Society.

Lillie Ruth was hospitalized for five months in 1979. She had been emotionally and mentally distraught for over 30 years. Day and night she cried out, "Uncle Robert, Uncle Robert!" The nurses and attendants asked, "Who is Uncle Robert?"

Uncle Robert and his son participated in the scam that allowed BJ Tarbutton to gain control of her father's estate. Lillie Ruth died in March 1980. Until she lost consciousness, she cried out, "Uncle Robert, Uncle Robert!".

In July 1980, Lillie Ruth's daughter Blanche contacted the National Association of Landowners in New Orleans, Louisiana. Alverez Ferroughelett was the legal counselor. She spoke to him by telephone and explained the problem concerning her family's land. She also wrote letters to him about the matter. He referred her to the Emergency Land Fund in Atlanta.

Blanche corresponded with the Emergency Land Fund and initially spoke with Kay Young, Director of Legal Services, about her concern. Blanche mailed her a set of deeds regarding the land and a copy of O' Neal's letter to Baxter Jones.

Kay Young and attorney Katrina Breeding, went to Sandersville in July 1980. Mrs. Young asked Blanche to obtain sworn statements about the land and facts surrounding the Carter claim. They went to Sandersville to examine records at the courthouse and investigate by speaking with people who had knowledge of the case. Blanche paid $125 for their travel expenses.

Communication with Kay Young and the Emergency Land Fund continued until approximately June 1981, when it suddenly stopped. "I never knew if or how Kay Young may have used the statements and the letter which I obtained for her. I never got a written report from Kay Young and Katrina Breeding about their trip to Sandersville. I called the Emergency Land Fund and asked to speak to Kay Young and Katrina Breeding repeatedly after June 1981, but was unable to speak to them".

On July 16, 1980, the Tarbuttons ordered Robert Hooks Jr. into Stick McMaster's office for interrogation in an effort to cover up the fraud alleged by the Carter heirs. Robert was sworn in and questioned by Mr. McMaster and Hugh McMaster Tarbutton. They asked what he remembered about the "sale" of the Carter land and whether all of the heirs signed the deeds transferring the land to B.J. Tarbutton Sr. They were particularly interested in whether or not Esther Scott signed the Ennis deed, which she had not.

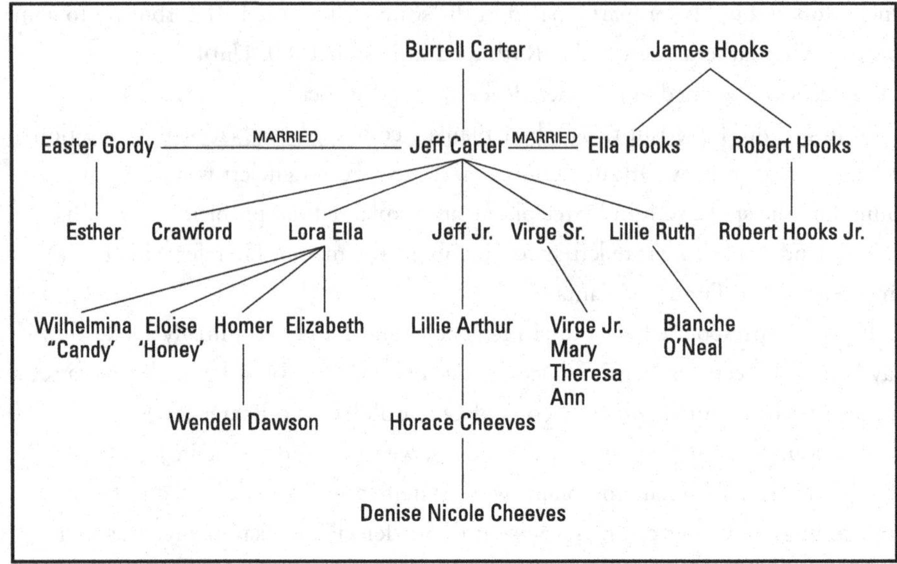

The Carter Family Tree

Dr. Harry Hollien, a professor of linguistics, Speech and Criminal Justice at the University of Florida, has been employed as an expert witness in numerous criminal and civil cases. After examining the two tape recordings of Robert Hooks Jr.'s interview, and the transcript of the interview, he found it physically unremarkable. In his affidavit, he stated that he made three (3) major findings that relate to questions of authenticity. Second, he found four (4) dozen (48) instances where modification or tampering could have occurred. He also stated other violations, such as hearing words on the tape that are not on the transcript, and noticed a break in the tape which indicates that the integrity of the recording has been compromised.

At this time, the Carter heirs had know way of knowing the fraud and forgery involved in the theft of their family estate. They were unaware of the value of kaolin, known to most as "chalk", and the treacherous industry it spawned in Georgia. The kaolin industry's power extended from the probate court, to many of the areas top attorneys (some of whom the heirs contacted), and city, state, and federal political figures.

Land Loss Equals Lost Legacy

Twenty-five years after the Civil War, the 1890 Census showed that 60 percent of all employed Blacks were farmers or farm laborers. In the South, the figure was 65 percent. In 1910, Black farmers owned over 16 million acres of farmland nationally, but that dropped to 3.1 million acres in 1982. In 1920, Blacks owned 1 out of every 7 farms in the U.S. By 1992, the number of Black farmers dropped from 925,710 to 18,816, some 98%.

There were 925,000 Black farmers in 1920. That is little more than 34,000 square miles, an area three times the size of Maryland. In 1970, that number had dwindled to 23 percent. In 1999, the number of Black farmers dwindled to less than 17,000, and less than 2.5 million acres. Black landowners are losing land at the rate of about 1000 acres per day.

In August 1997, Black farmers brought a lawsuit against the USDA charging it with discrimination in denying them access to loans and subsidies. The lawsuit was filed on behalf of 4,000 of the nation's 17,000 Black farmers and former farmers. A Consent Decree was signed in January 1999. The estimated cost of the settlement ranges from $400 million to more than $2 billion.

Gary Grant, a Tillery, North Carolina resident and a plaintiff in the Black farmers' lawsuit, is president of the Black Farmers and Agriculturalists Association (BFAA). His family was forced out of farming in 1991. Mr. Grant recognized the danger with a consent decree that fails to accurately compensate the farmers for all damages, previous and present.

> *This consent decree will ensure the demise of Black farmers in two to five years ... There is nothing in the document that will pay off debt that has been incurred because of racist actions of USDA officers. Many of the farmers no longer owe USDA but owe private lenders. If their property is freed up, then the private lender will be able to come after it with less reserve.*
>
> *... The government records are filled with examples where Black farmers were systematically treated different from White farmers. Black farmers were routinely given less money for the same land than White farmers. They were also denied access to programs that aided White farmers. These were common practices. Fifty thousand dollars is not a lot of money. We are talking about a small business stolen, people's jobs, credit rating, and livelihoods ruined, life savings and investments taken, and spirits broken. No amount of money can repay the pain and suffering inflicted on Black farmers.*
>
> *... To my knowledge, none of the USDA agents who perpetrated this*

injustice have been terminated. As a matter of fact, nobody was fired that I know of and some of them are getting promotions.

...My community, Tillery, is a New Deal Resettlement community established in the 1940s. The federal government bought 18,000 acres of former plantation land and divided it up into forty to eighty-acre tracts and made it possible for Black people to purchase that land. The Black landowners have been the thorn in the side of the political power in Halifax County, North Carolina ever since, because we have not been dependent on them for our survival. Through our struggle, we've managed to save most of the land. Now the population of Halifax is about 52% African American and the community of Tillery is 99% African American. We still probably own 90% of the land, however White farmers are farming 98% of it.

Tillery had over 300 Black farmers in the 1950s. Today it has none. My family has been in foreclosure for 23 years and we continue to raise that issue. I am part of the class action because the USDA denied me the opportunity to assume my father's debt and to continue to operate our farm. My nieces and nephews have grown up in that 23 year time with a very bitter taste in their mouths and hearts about farming because they have seen the toll taken on my father and mother and my brother and wife. We are not sure that any of them will enter farming. We are not even encouraging them that strongly, but it has brought us together much closer to the understanding of the power of the land.

Land ownership has to be a major theme that takes the African American community into the 21st century. As a people, we must understand the value and the power of land ownership. One generation removed from slavery, Black folks were able to acquire more than 16 million acres of farmland. We have nearly lost it all. This land has been in my family for 52 years and another tract that was in jeopardy has been in my family for about 100 years. The only power that there really is in this country is land ownership, which produces economics, which is green stuff... The constitution and the founding fathers believed that if you were not a land owner you could not run for office...you could not vote.

...Also, as we lose this land no one is asking what happens to it and that is where we can also bring in the issue of environmental racism and

environmental injustice. On much of this land is where the sitting of polluting industries are being set.

...Institutional racism is alive and well in this country. Black people still have to fight like hell to enjoy the rights that Whites take for granted...[The] real lesson lies in what we can do as a people if we really will come together. Our case proved that we do have some political power. We got the statute of limitations set aside. We learned quickly that the media is largely controlled and our images manipulated in the headlines to suit the stereotypes of White people. Finally, it became clear that the African American community does not understand the real value and power of Black landowners and Black farmers. This is true for many of our Black churches, civil rights organizations, political groups, colleges and universities, and professional associations. For the most part, we did not have a whole lot of mass support from...African Americans.

...When you say Black farmer and ask someone what image comes to mind, many will see a dirty, ignorant, barefoot, uneducated person. Many Blacks see the stereotype. They don't understand that the Black farmer has been a mathematician, a scientist, a meteorologist, a doctor, a veterinarian, and even a lawyer. Until we are able to destroy that stereotype, Black farmers will always be misunderstood and unappreciated by our professional people.

...I would like Black institutions and Black people to believe that the Black farmers know what is needed...I would also like them to contribute financially, morally, physically, and spiritually...We need to begin a massive education program with our children on the importance of owning land. The historically Black colleges and universities or HBCUs, and especially the Land Grant schools, need to get on board. The Black farmers' struggle was a wake up call, and some of our institutions are still asleep. Our struggle challenged the plantation system...Our land grant universities need to design outreach and research that encourage their students to work with Black farmers and the Black community.

This country has not had to listen to Black farmers because the Black community has not said we are worth saving. I don't believe any of us will survive and progress unless we can come together around the central issue of the survival of Black farmers. It is imperative that we maintain land ownership so we can make sure our food supply is not poisoned. Land ownership is economic power, political power, and is the only avenue that we really have to ensure our children a legacy.

Black Wall Street

At one time a thriving Black community existed in Tulsa, Oklahoma that accounted for one- tenth of the segregated city's population of one hundred thousand. In fact, they were so successful that their business district was called "The Black Wall Street". Unfortunately, this Black district fell prey to the first air bombing in a U.S. city.

On May 31, 1921, a white female elevator operator accused Dick Rowland, a nineteen year old Black male who worked at a shoeshine stand, of attacking her. Rowland denied the charge, but was nevertheless jailed where a white mob soon gathered. Armed Blacks came to support and protect Rowland. A gun was fired and the riot began.

Whites invaded the Black district burning, looting, and killing. Eventually, the National Guard was called in and martial law declared. The police arrested more than four thousand Blacks and interned them in three camps. All Blacks were forced to carry green identification cards.

When Tulsa was zoned for a new railroad station, the tracks were routed through the Black business district, forever destroying it.

Rosewood

On January 1, 1923, a white woman named Fannie Taylor falsely alleged that an unidentified Negro had sexually assaulted her. In response, an angry white mob lynched and murdered an undetermined number of Black men, women, and children, destroying the town of Rosewood, Florida. The homes, churches, and schools that had once been part of a close- knit community were ravaged and burned to ashes.

When the lynch mob found the man they believed committed the crime, they dragged him outside of his house with a rope around his neck, and tied him to a Model T automobile. They then dragged him 3 miles from Rosewood to Sumner, an all-white community down the railroad tracks from Rosewood.

The man, Aaron Carrier, was left to die while the posse returned to his house to harass his wife, M.G. As with her husband, the vigilantes put a rope around her neck and dragged her down the stairs, clad only in her nightgown, out into the cold where they put guns to her head.

They tried to coerce her into saying Aaron Carrier was not at home the night Taylor was allegedly attacked. M.G. refused to lie, and was raped repeatedly by the white mob.

It took seventy-three years for the nine living survivors of the Rosewood massacre to receive some form of amends. In 1995, the state legislature awarded $150,000.00 to each of them. Descendants of one hundred and forty-three residents were awarded sums ranging from $375.00 to $22,535.00. However, many have yet to receive anything.

The Jeff Carter case, Rosewood, and Black Wall Street illustrate the sociological, political and physical antagonism and oppression our ancestors and their heirs endure. Black families (people of color throughout the Diaspora in general), can access the value of their inheritance by researching their genealogy.

No 40 Acres And A Mule? Black Farmers Win Suit

FEATURED IN BOOK: Rosewood massacre survivor Minnie Lee Langley, who died in December, is shown listening to testimony about the event in the Florida Legislature in 1994.

New book chronicles Rosewood tragedy

Painful return to Rosewood
A racial tragedy in Florida, from past to present

This Land Was Their Land
Department of Agriculture Policies Hurt Black Farmers

Louisiana Legislature Votes To Return Land And $55 Million To Heirs Of Property Owners

STATE OF GEORGIA,
WASHINGTON COUNTY. } **LETTERS OF ADMINISTRATION.**

BY Thos. J. Swint *Ordinary for Said County:*

Whereas, Jeff Carter

late of this County, deceased, died intestate, having while he lived, and at the time of his death, divers estates, real and personal, within the County aforesaid, by means whereof the full disposition and power of granting the administration of the estate of the said deceased, and also auditing the accounts of said administration, and a final dismission from the same, to the Court aforesaid, does of right belong; he desiring that the same may be well and truly administered and legally disposed of, do hereby grant unto Virge Carter administrator, full power, by the tenor of these presents, to administer the entire estate, both real and personal, of said deceased, which to him in his lifetime, and at the time of his death did belong, and to ask, demand, sue for, recover, and receive the same, and to pay the debts in which the deceased stood bound, so far forth as his assets will extend, according to law, and then the balance jointly to pay over to the legal heirs and distributees of the said deceased. And the said Virge Carter having given bond and security, and taken the oath, and performed all other requisites by law, necessary to his just qualification as administrator is, by order of said Court, and by virtue of these presents, ordained, constituted, and appointed administrator of the whole estate, both real and personal, of said deceased.

WITNESS my hand and Seal of Office, in Sandersville, this the 5th *day of* May 1930

Thos. J. Swint Ordinary.

GEORGIA, Washington County.

I do solemnly swear that Jeff Carter, deceased, died without any will, so far as I know or believe, and I will well and truly administer on all and singular the goods and chattels, rights and credits of the said deceased, and pay all his just debts, as far as the same will extend and the law requires And that I will make a true and perfect inventory and appraisement of all and singular, the goods and chattels, rights and credits, and a just return thereof when thereunto required. SO HELP ME, GOD!

Sworn to before me, this 5th *day of* May*, in the year* 1930

Thos. J. Swint ORDINARY.

Virge Carter

Virge Carter, Forged Letters of Administration, May 5, 1930. Introduced into the Tarbutton Chain of Title in 1984.

PETITION FOR LETTERS OF ADMINISTRATION

GEORGIA—Washington County.

TO THE ORDINARY OF SAID COUNTY:

The petition of Virge Carter a citizen of the United States, residing in said State, shows that Jeff Carter departed this life on or about the 24th day of January 1930, a resident of said county, leaving an estate of real and personal property of the probable value of Five Thousand Dollars and under the law it is necessary that said estate should be administered; that Petitioner is a son of the deceased and has been selected by a majorty of the heirs

Wherefore, Petitioner prays an order directing that citation be issued herein and published as the law requires and if no good cause be shown to the contrary, your petitioner be appointed Administrator of the estate of said deceased.

Virge Carter
Petitioner.

Washington County Court of Ordinary, at Chambers, February 14, 1930.

Upon reading the foregoing petition, it is ordered that citation be issued therein and published as required by law.

Thos. J. Swint
Ordinary.

GEORGIA, Washington County.

Virge Carter having in proper form applied to me for permanent Letters of Administration on the estate of Jeff Carter late of said county, this is to cite all and singular the creditors and next of kin of Jeff Carter to be and appear at my office within the time allowed by law, and show cause, if any they can, why permanent administration should not be granted to Virge Carter on Jeff Carter's estate.

Thos. J. Swint
Ordinary

Washington County Court of Ordinary May *Term,* 1930

THE PETITION OF Virge Carter for Letters of Administration on the estate of Jeff Carter, deceased, having been duly filed, and it appearing that citation therein was issued and published according to law, requiring all concerned to appear at this term and show cause, if any they could, why said Letters should not be granted; and it also appearing that said deceased died a resident of said County, intestate, and that said applicant is a citizen of this State and lawfully qualified for said administration, and no objection being offered thereto: It is therefore ordered by the Court, that the said Virge Carter be, and he is hereby appointed Administrator on the estate of said deceased, and that Letters be issued to as such upon his giving bond, with approved security, in the sum of Eeegh Thos. J. Swint Dollars and taking the oath as provided by law.

Thos. J. Swint Ordinary

Virge Carter, Forged Letters of Administration, pg.1, May 5, 1930. Introduced into the Tarbutton Chain of Title in 1984.

Georgia, Washington County.

To the Ordinary of said County.

We, the undersigned heirs at law of Jeff Carter hereby select Virge Carter, his son as administrator of the estate of Jeff Carter and ask that you approve of our selection and appoint him.

This 14th day of February, 1930.

Jeff Carter
Rodell Carter
Mary E. Young
Lona E. Dawson
Delia Carter

Virge Carter, Forged Letters of Administration, pg. 2, May 5, 1930. Introduced into the Tarbutton Chain of Title in 1984.

STATE OF GEORGIA, WASHINGTON COUNTY.

KNOW ALL MEN BY THESE PRESENTS:

THAT WE, Virge Carter, principal and United States Fidelity and Guar. Co. of Baltimore Maryland

Securities, are held and firmly bound unto the Ordinary of said County, and his successors in office, and assigns, in the just and full sum of Eight Thousand .... for the payment of which sum to the said Ordinary, and his successors in office, we bind ourselves, our heirs, executors and administrators, in the whole and for the whole sum, jointly and severally, and firmly by these presents.

Sealed with our seals, and dated this 5th *day of* May 1930

THE CONDITION OF THE ABOVE OBLIGATION IS SUCH, That if the above bound Virge Carter

Administrator of the estate, real and personal, of Jeff Carter

late of said County, deceased, do make a true and perfect inventory of all the estate, both real and personal, of said deceased, which have or shall come into the hands, possession or knowledge of the said Virge Carter

or the hands or possession of any person or persons, for him and the same so made to exhibit unto the said Ordinary, when he shall be hereunto required; and such Goods, Chattels, Credits, Lands and Tenements, do well and truly administer, according to law, and do make a just and true account of his actings and doing therein, when he shall thereunto be required by the Court; and the balance shall deliver and pay to such person or persons, respectively as he may be entitled to the same by law: And if it shall hereafter appear that any last Will and Testament was made by the deceased, and the same be proven before the Court of Ordinary, and the Executor obtain a certificate of the probate thereof, and he .... in such case, if required, render and deliver up the said Letters of Administration, then this Obligation to be void, else to remain in full force.

Signed, sealed and acknowledged in open court.

Virge Carter L. S.

United States Fidelity + Guar Co L. S.

By E. P. Wood L. S.

Document Alleging Virge Carter posted a bond, May 5, 1930. Introduced into the Tarbutton Chain of Title in 1984.

the day and year first above written.

Signed, sealed and delivered
in the presence of

Evelyn Rose | Wm Schley Howard (L.S.)

G. B. Tidwell (SEAL)
Notary Public, Fulton County, Ga.
State at Large
Notary Public, State at Large, Atlanta, Ga.
My Commission Expires January 26, 1937

Recorded October 18th, 1934. Roy H. Duggan, Clerk.

Virge Carter, Admr., Jeff Carter, Jr.
Minnie Butts, E.E.Young, et al To E. N. Ennis

STATE OF GEORGIA, WASHINGTON COUNTY.

THIS INDENTURE, Made the 27th day of January in the year of our Lord, One Thousand Nine Hundred and Thirty-Three, between Jeff Carter, Jr. Virgil Carter, Rodel Carter, Mrs.Mary Young, Mrs. Homer Dawson, Mrs. Jeff Carter, Sr., Mrs. Minnie Butts, all of Washington County, Georgia, and Crawford Carter, Mrs. Bertha Renfroe and Mrs. Sam Turner of Philadelphia, Pennsylvania, and I.V. Scott of Detroit, Michegan, all parties of the first part, and E.N. Ennis of the County of Washington, of the second part.

WITNESSETH, That the said parties of the first part for and in consideration of the sum of One Thousand Four Hundred Seventy-One and 19/100 ($1471.19) Dollars, in hand paid, at and before the sealing and delivery of these presents, the receipt whereof is hereby acknowledged, has granted, bargained, sold, aliened, conveyed and confirmed, and by these presents, does grant, bargain, sell, alien, convey and confirm unto the said party of the second part, his heirs, successors and assigns, all of their undivided interest in the following described tracts of land:

Tract No. 1: That certain tract in Washington County, containing One Hundred (100) acres, more or less, and known as the Strange Place, lying in the 98th District, G. M., of Washington County, Georgia, being bounded on the north by Mrs. Dr. Graybill, east by Robert Hooks, south by W. J. Cochran, and west by Tom Hodges.

Tract No. 2.: That tract containing Two Hundred (200) acres, known as the Davis Place, being in the 98th District, G. M., Washington County, Ga., and bounded on the north by Tom Hodges, east by Tract No. 1 above described, south by E. N. Ennis, and west by E.N. Ennis.

Tract No. 3.: That tract containing One Hundred (100) acres, more or less, known as the Jim Hooks Place, being place formerly owned by Mrs. Jeff Carter, located in the 98th District, G. M., of Washington County, Georgia, and bounded on the north by Robert Hooks, east by Robert Hooks, south by Sam Gordy and west by W. J. Cochran.

TO HAVE AND TO HOLD, The said bargained premises, with all and singular the rights, members and appurtenances thereunto appertaining, to the only proper use, benefit and behoof of the said party of the second part, his heirs, executors, administrators and assigns, in Fee-Simple: and the said parties of the first part the said bargained premises unto the said party of the second part, his heirs, executors, and administrators and assigns, against the said parties of the first part, their heirs, executors and administrators, and against all and every other person or persons, shall and will warrant and forever defend by virtue of these presents.

THIS CONVEYANCE is intended to operate as provided in Section 3306, 6037 and 3310 of the Code of 1910, in regard to the sales of property to secure debts, and to pass the title of the property described into the said party of the second part, the debt hereby secured being one promissory note for said sum of One Thousand Four Hundred Seventy-One and 19/100 ($1471.19) Dollars, the consideration aforesaid, dated this day and due upon the 15th day of October, 1933, with ten per cent on the principal and interest for Attorney's fees, if incurred in the collection of said note. The said parties of the first part also agree to keep the

Fraudulent 'Ennis Deed', January 27, 1933, pg. 1

said property insured during the continuance of this loan and to pay the premiums for insurance when due; and also to pay all taxes on said property when the same shall fall due and before any levy or advertisement of any tax execution thereon; and the said parties of the first part hereby agree that if any of said interest or principal installments are not promptly paid when the same become due (time being hereby expressly made of the essence), of if the parties of the first part shall fail to pay the premiums of insurance or the taxes aforesaid, then the entire principal of said debt shall become due and payable at once, if the party of the second part shall so elect; and the said parties of the first part hereby agree that if the debt to secure which this deed is made, is not p romptly paid at maturity according to the tenor and effect of said note, or it any one of said interest or principal installments is not promptly paid when it matures, or if said parties of the first part shall fail to pay the premiums of insurance and taxes aforesaid, then the said party of the second part, his agent or legal representatives or assigns, may, and by these presents, is authorized to, sell at public outcry, before the Courthouse door, in the County of Washington to the highest bidder for cash, all of said property to pay said principal with the interest thereon to the date of sale, and expenses of the proceeding, including Attorney's fees, if incurred, of ten per cent. on the amount of the principal and interest due after advertising the time, place and terms of sale in any newspaper published in said County of Washington once a week for four weeks prior to said day of sale, and it is hereby stipulated that the foregoing power of sale, being coupled with an interest shall be irrevocable by the death of either party thereto; and the said party of the second part, his agent or legal representatives or assigns, may bid at said sale should they desire, and the said party of the second part, his agent or legal representatives or assigns may make to the purchaser or purchasers of said property good and sufficient titles in Fee-Simple to the same, thereby divesting out of the said parties of the first part all right and equity that they may have in and to said property, and vesting the same in the purchaser or purchasers aforesaid.

The proceeds of said sale are to be applied first to the payment of said debt and interest, also all taxes and premiums of insurance that may have been paid on said property by the party of the second part, his agent or legal representatives or assigns, and the expenses of this proceeding, the remainder, if any, paid to the said parties of the first part. The said party of the second part, his agent or legal representatives or assigns, shall be authorized to proceed summarily to put the purchaser or purchasers in possession, the said parties of the first part covenanting and agreeing to surrender the same without let or hindrance of any kind. The method of sale hereinbefore provided for shall be cumulative of the othr remedies allowed by law.

IN WITNESS WHEREOF, The said parties of the first part have hereunto set their hand, affixed their seals, and delivered these presents, the day and year first above written.

Signed, sealed and delivered by Jeff Carter, Jr., Virgil Carter, Rodel Carter, Mrs.Mary Young, Mrs. Homer Dawson, Mrs.Jeff Carter, Sr., Mrs. Minnie Butts, in the presence of, in the county of Washington, State of Georgia.

C. C. Adams

J. A. Harbin N.P.Washington Co.Ga.

Signed, sealed and delivered by Crawford Carter, Mrs. Bertha Renfroe, and Mrs. Sam Turner in the City of Phil., Penn., in the presence of:

J H Shetter (SEAL)
Notary Public,
Commission Expires March 7th, 1937

Jhonie Renfroe

Virge Carter, Admr. L.S.
His Mark
Jeff X Carter Jr. L.S.
Minnie Butts L.S.
M. E. Young L.S.
Lora E Dawson L.S.
Delia Carter L.S.
Rodell Carter L.S.
Crawford Carter L.S.
Bertha Renfroe L.S.
Mrs. Sam Turner L.S.
Lillian Turner L.S.
------------------------L.S.

Fraudulent 'Ennis Deed', January 27, 1933, pg. 2

108

Signed, sealed and delivered by I.V. Scott
in the City of Detroit, Mich.,
in the presence of:

____

____

Recorded October 19th, 1934. Roy H. Duggan, Clerk.

Fraudulent 'Ennis Deed', January 27, 1933, pg. 3

STATE OF GEORGIA, WASHINGTON COUNTY.

THIS INDENTURE, Made the 27th day of January in the year of our Lord, One Thousand Nine Hundred and Thirty-Three, between Jeff Carter, Jr., Virgil Carter, Rodel Carter, Mrs. Mary Young, Mrs. Homer Dawson, Mrs. Jeff Carter, Sr., Mrs. Minnie Butts, all of Washington County, Georgia, and Crawford Carter, Mrs. Bertha Renfroe and Mrs. Sam Turner of Philadelphia, Pennsylvania, and I. V. Scott of Detroit, Michegan, all parties of the first part, and E. N. Ennis of the County of Washington, of the second part,

WITNESSETH, That the said parties of the first part for and in consideration of the sum of One Thousand Four Hundred Seventy-One and 19/100 ($1471.19) Dollars, in hand paid, at and before the sealing and delivery of these presents, the receipt whereof is hereby acknowledged, has granted, bargained, sold, aliened, conveyed and confirmed, and by these presents, does grant, bargain, sell, alien, convey and confirm unto the said party of the second part, his heirs, successors and assigns, all of their undivided interest in the following described tracts of land:

Tract No. 1.: That certain tract in Washington County, containing One Hundred (100) acres, more or less, and known as the Strange Place, lying in the 98th District, G. M., of Washington County, Georgia, being bounded on the north by Mrs. Dr. Graybill, east by Robert Hooks, south by W. J. Cochran, and west by Tom Hodges.

Tract No. 2.: That tract containing Two Hundred (200) acres, known as the Davis Place, being in the 98th District, G. M., Washington County, Ga., and bounded on the north by Tom Hodges, east by Tract No. 1 above described, south by E. N. Ennis, and west by E. N. Ennis.

Tract No. 3.: That tract containing One Hundred (100) acres, more or less, known as the Jim Hooks Place, being place formerly owned by Mrs. Jeff Carter, located in the 98th District, G. M., of Washington County, Georgia, and bounded on the north by Robert Hooks, east by Robert Hooks, south by Sam Gordy and west by W. J. Cochran.

TO HAVE AND TO HOLD, The said bargained premises, with all and singular the rights members and appurtenances thereunto appertaining, to the only proper use, benefit and behoof of the said party of

Fraudulent 'Ennis Deed', January 27, 1933, pg. 1

the second part, his heirs, executors, administrators and assigns, in Fee-Simple: and the said parties of the first part the said bargained premises unto the said party of the second part, his heirs, executors, and administrators and assigns, against the said parties of the first part, their heirs, executors and administrators, and against all and every other person or persons, shall and will warrant and forever defend by virtue of these presents.

THIS CONVEYANCE is intended to operate as provided in Section 3306, 6037 and 3310 of the Code of 1910, in regard to the sales of property to secure debts, and to pass the title of the property described into the said party of the second part, the debt hereby secured being one promissory note for said sum of One Thousand Four Hundred Seventy-One and 19/100 ($1471.19) Dollars, the consideration aforesaid, dated this day and due upon the 15th day of October, 1933, With ten per cent on the principal and interest for Attorney's fees, if incurred in the collection of said note. The said parties of the first part also agree to keep the said property insured during the continuance of this loan and to pay the premiums for insurance when due; and also to pay all taxes on said property when the same shall fall due and before any levy or advertisement of any tax execution thereon; and the said parties of the first part hereby agree that if any of said interest or principal installments are not promptly paid when the same become due (time being hereby expressly made of the essence), of if the parties of the first part shall fail to pay the premiums of insurance or the taxes aforesaid, then the entire principal of said debt shall become due and payable at once, if the party of the second part shall so elect; and the said parties of the first part hereby agree that if the debt to secure which this deed is made, is not promptly paid at maturity according to the tenor and effect of said note, or it any one of said interest or principal installments is not promptly paid when it matures, or if said parties of the first part shall fail to pay the premiums of insurance and taxes afore-

Fraudulent 'Ennis Deed', January 27, 1933, pg. 2

said, then the said party of the second part, his agent or legal representatives or assigns, may, and by these presents, is authorized to, sell at public outcry, before the Courthouse door, in the County of Washington to the highest bidder for cash, all of said property to pay said principal with the interest thereon to the date of sale, and expenses of the proceeding, including Attorney's fees, if incurre of ten per cent. on the amount of the principal and interest due afte advertising the time, place and terms of sale in any newspaper publis ed in said County of Washington once a week for four weeks prior to said day of sale, and it is hereby stipulated that the foregoing powe of sale, being coupled with an interest shall be irrevocable by the death of either party thereto; and the said party of the second part, his agent or legal representatives or assigns, may bid at said sale should they desire, and the said party of the second part, his agent or legal representatives or assigns may make to the purchaser or purchasers of said property good and sufficient titles in Fee-Simple to the same, thereby divesting out of the said parties of the first part all right and equity that they may have in and to said property, and vest ing the same in the purchaser or purchasers aforesaid.

The proceeds of said sale are to be applied first to the payment of said debt and interest, also all taxes and premiums of insurance that may have been paid on said property by the party of the second part, his agent or legal representatives or assigns, and the ex penses of this proceeding, the remainder, if any, paid to the said parties of the first part. The said party of the second part, his agen or legal representatives or assigns, shall be authorized to proceed summarily to put the purchaser or purchasers in possession, the said parties of the first part covenanting and agreeing to surrender the same without let or hindrance of any kind. The method of sale hereinbefore provided for shall be cumulative of the othr remedies allowed by law.

Fraudulent 'Ennis Deed', January 27, 1933, pg. 3

$1471.19 Sandersville, Georgia, January 27,

On or before the 15th day of October, 1933, after date, promise to pay to E. N. Ennis, or order, the sum of One Thousand Fou Hundred Seventy-One and 19/100 ($1471.19) DOLLARS, for value receiv with interest payable from date at the rate of 8 per cent per annum and for the consideration above expressed, we hereby expressly waibe and renounce all homestead and exemption rights in and to all proper owned now or hereinafter acquired by us in so far as we are permitte by law to waive the same, we also agree to pay 10 per cent upon the amount due, as attorney's fees, in the event this note is not paid or or before return day of the court to which suit is brought for its collection, and ten days notice in writing is given to the maker here of of intention to sue the note, and of the term of the court to whic suit will be brought. This note is secured by deed to three (3) tract of land in the 88th District, G. M., Washington County, Georgia, said tracts being known as the Strange Place, Davis Place and Jim Hooks Pla

IN WITNESS WHEREOF, We have hereunto set our hands and affixed our seals, the day and year first above written.

Virgie Carter [illegible] L.S.
Jeff his X mark Carter L.S.
Minnie [illegible] L.S.
M E Young L.S.
Lora [illegible] L.S.
Delia Carter L.S.
[illegible] Carter L.S.
Crawford Carter L.S.
[illegible] L.S.
Lillian Turner L.S.

Fraudulent 'Ennis Deed', January 27, 1933, pg. 4. Forged signatures of Carter heirs.

IN WITNESS WHEREOF, The said parties of the first part have hereunto set their hand, affixed their seals, and delivered these presents, the day and year first above written.

Signed, sealed and delivered by Jeff Carter, Jr., Virgil Carter, Rodel Carter, Mrs. Mary Young, Mrs. Homer Dawson, Mrs. Jeff Carter, Sr., Mrs. Minnie Butts, in the presence of, in the county of Washington, State of Georgia.

C. C. Adams

J. A. Harbin, N. P. Washington Co, Ga.

Virgil Carter, admr. L.

Jeff Carter Jr L.

Minnie Butts L.

M. E. Young L.

Lona E. Dawson L.

Delia Carter L.

Rodell Carter L.

Signed, sealed and delivered by Crawford Carter, Mrs. Bertha Renfroe, and Mrs. Sam Turner in the City of Phil., Penn., in the presence of:

J. H. Skettes

Thomas Renfrow

NOTARY PUBLIC
Commission Expires March 7th, 1937

Crawford Carter L.

Bertha Renfrow L.

Mrs. Sam Turner / Lillian Turner L.

Signed, sealed and delivered by I. V. Scott in the City of Detroit, Mich., in the presence of:

____________ L.

Fraudulent 'Ennis Deed', January 27, 1933, pg. 5. Forged signatures of Carter heirs. Introduced into the Tarbutton Chain of Title in 1984.

STATE OF GEORGIA

COUNTY OF FULTON

AFFIDAVIT OF FORGERY PURSUANT TO O.C.G.A §44-2-23, CURRENT OWNER LOULIE EUGENIA KERNAGHAN TARBUTTON, AS TRUSTEE UNDER DEED RECORDED IN DEED BOOK 6G, PAGE 177 OFFICE OF THE CLERK OF THE SUPERIOR COURT OF WASHINGTON COUNTY, GEORGIA REGARDING DEED TO SECURE DEBT FROM JEFF CARTER, JR., VIRGIL CARTER, RODEL CARTER, MRS. MARY YOUNG, MRS. HOMER DAWSON, MRS. JEFF CARTER, SR., MRS. MINNIE BUTTS, CRAWFORD CARTER, MRS. BERTHA RENFROE AND MRS. SAM TURNER AND I. V. SCOTT, ALL PARTIES OF THE FIRST PART AND E. N. ENNIS, AS PARTY OF THE SECOND PART, RECORDED IN DEED BOOK QQ, PAGE 106, SUPERIOR COURT OF WASHINGTON COUNTY, GEORGIA REGARDING LAND LOCATED IN THE 98TH DISTRICT GMD, WASHINGTON COUNTY, GEORGIA CONSISTING OF 100 ACRES MORE OR LESS PLUS 200 ACRES KNOWN AS THE DAVIS PLACE PLUS 100 ACRES MORE OR LESS KNOWN AS THE JIM BOOKS PLACE

Personally appeared before me the undersigned Notary, an officer duly authorized by law to administer an oath, JOHNNIE DARK RENFROE, who first being sworn states on oath as follows:

I am JOHNNIE DARK RENFROE. I live at 19321 Anglin Street, Detroit, Michigan. I was born in Washington County, Georgia on April 1, 1922. I am now in good health and not suffering under any physical, mental or legal disability which would impair or prevent me from giving this affidavit. I am making this affidavit freely and voluntarily and with the knowledge that it may be recorded on the land records in the office of the Clerk of the Superior Court of Washington County, Georgia or filed in the pleadings of the Civil Action styled as Loulie Eugenia Kernighan Tarbutton as Trustee, etc., vs. Tract of Land in the 98th GM District, Washington County, Georgia; Robert Lee Watkins, Individually and as Attorney in Fact for Timothy Dawson, et.al., and other named defendants, and All the World, defendants, Civil Action No. 5175. I have no financial interest in the outcome of that litigation. I am making this affidavit based on my own personal knowledge.

I have examined the 4 page document which is a Deed to Secure Debt dated January 27, 1933 which is described in the above caption of this affidavit. A copy of that Deed to Secure Debt is attached to this affidavit as Exhibit "A" with pages thereof marked consecutively by separate number.

The signature on page 4 of Exhibit "A", which is the last page of the Deed to Secure Debt, appearing as "JHONI RENFROW" is not my signature. I never signed the attached Deed to Secure Debt and have

Affidavit of Johnnie D. Renfroe, September 17, 1984, page 1.

never seen the document. I was 10 years old in January, 1933 and living in Sandersville, Georgia. I did not go to and was not in Philadelphia, Pennsylvania on or about January 27, 1933. I did not see Crawford Carter, Mrs. Bertha Renfrow and Mrs. Sam Turner in the City of Philadelphia sign this document in my presence.

The correct spelling of my name is Johnnie Dark <u>Renfroe</u>. As a child in 1933 I signed my name as Johnnie Dark Renfroe.

The alleged signature of my name on the attached Deed to Secure Debt is a forgery. I did not authorize anyone to sign my name to the Deed to Secure Debt.

Further, affiant sayeth not.

Johnnie D Renfroe
JOHNNIE DARK RENFROE

Sworn to and subscribed before me this 17th day of September, 1984.

Patricia A. Wise
Notary Public

Notary Public, Georgia, State at Large
My Commission Expires Aug. 8, 1987

Affidavit of Johnnie D. Renfroe, September 17, 1984, page 2.

STATE OF NEW YORK

COUNTY OF ONEIDA

AFFIDAVIT OF FORGERY PURSUANT TO O.C.G.A. §44-2-23, CURRENT OWNER LOULIE EUGENIA KERNIGAN TARBUTTON, AS TRUSTEE UNDER DEED RECORDED IN DEED BOOK 6G, PAGE 177, OFFICE OF THE CLERK OF THE SUPERIOR COURT OF WASHINGTON COUNTY, GEORGIA REGARDING DEED TO SECURE DEBT FROM JEFF CARTER, JR., VIRGIL CARTER, RODEL CARTER, MRS. MARY YOUNG, MRS. HOMER DAWSON, MRS. JEFF CARTER, SR., MRS. MINNIE BUTTS, CRAWFORD CARTER, MRS. BERTHA RENFROE AND MRS. SAM TURNER AND I. V. SCOTT, ALL PARTIES OF THE FIRST PART AND E. N. ENNIS, AS PARTY OF THE SECOND PART, RECORDED IN DEED BOOK QQ, PAGE 106, SUPERIOR COURT OF WASHINGTON COUNTY, GEORGIA REGARDING LAND LOCATED IN THE 98TH DISTRICT GM OF WASHINGTON COUNTY CONSISTING OF 100 ACRES MORE OR LESS PLUS 200 ACRES KNOWN AS THE DAVIS PLACE PLUS 100 ACRES MORE OR LESS KNOWN AS THE JIM HOOKS PLACE

Personally appeared before me, the undersigned Notary, an officer duly authorized by law to administer an oath, Rev. Jessie Butts, who first being sworn states on oath as follows:

I am Rev. Jessie Butts. I was born March 15, 1900. I am almost 85 years old, but I am in good health and not suffering under any physical or mental or legal disability which would impair or prevent me from giving this affidavit. I drive my own car when necessary, and I take care of my own personal and business affairs.

I am making this affidavit freely and voluntarily and with the knowledge that it may be recorded on the land records in the office of the Clerk of the Superior Court of Washington County, Georgia and filed in the pleadings of the Civil Action styled as Tarbutton, as Trustee, etc., et al. vs. 585 acres of land, Blanche C. Holley, as Administrator, etc., Robert Lee Watkins, et al. and All the World, Civil Action File No. 84-403-1-MAC, in the United States District Court for the Middle District of Georgia, Macon Divsion. I am making this affidavit based on my own personal knowledge.

I have examined the four page document which is a copy of the Deed to Secure Debt dated January 27, 1933 from various heirs of Jeff Carter, Deceased to E. N. Ennis. A copy of that Deed to Secure Debt is attached to this affidavit as Exhibit A with pages marked consecutively by separate number.

I have carefully reviewed the signature which purports to be the signature of my former wife, Minnie Butts. She died January 28, 1935. On January 27, 1933 we were married and living in Washington County, Georgia. The signature on the Deed to Secure Debt which purports to be hers is not the true signature of my former wife, Minnie Butts. She could read and write, but her signature was not as fine or done in such a perfect script as the

Affidavit of Jessie Butts, February 11, 1985, page 1.

signature which appears on the document. My former wife had only a six grade education. Further, I do not believe that she signed the document because we always did things together and handled our business jointly. She did not tell me of any loan to E. N. Ennis for which she might have been liable. Further, she did not tell me that she pledged her interest in the Carter homeplace to E. N. Ennis to secure any debt owed to him.

I am completely aware of how her signature should appear and what she might have signed. The signature on the attached document is not hers, and it is not genuine. She would not have signed the document without discussing it with me.

Further, affiant sayeth not.

Rev Jesse Butts

Rev. Jessie Butts

Sworn to and subscribed before me

this 11th day of FEBRUARY 1985

1985.

Clyde Gibson

Notary Public

CLYDE GIBSON
Notary Public, State of New York
Commission Expires Mar. 30, 19 85

Affidavit of Jessie Butts, February 11, 1985, page 2.

E. N. Ennis To Mrs. Fannie Belle Hatch

GEORGIA, WASHINGTON COUNTY

THIS INDENTURE, executed this the 2nd day of March 1936, between E. N. Ennis, as party of the first part, and Mrs. Fannie Belle Hatch, as party of the second part, both of said county and state;

WITNESSETH: That on the 27th day of January 1933, the following named parties, to wit, Virge Carter, Jeff Carter, MinnieButts, M. E. Young, Lora E. Dawson, Delia Carter, Rodell Carter, Crawford Carter, Bertha Renfroe and Lillian Turner, borrowed from E.N. Ennis the sum of $1471.19, executing and delivering as an evidence of their indebtedness a certain promissory note, bearing that date and due on the 15th day of October 1933; and

WHEREAS, there is now due upon said note the sum of $949.13 to this date principal and interest; and

WHEREAS, to secure said note the borrowers named above executed and delivered to said E.N. Ennis a security deed covering the lands hereinafter described, which deed is dated on the 27th day of January 1933 and recorded in the office of the Clerk of the Superior Court of Washington County on the 19th day of October 1934 in Book QQ, page 106, which deed is hereby referred to specifically for all its terms, covenants and conditions; and

WHEREAS, the said E.N. Ennis has this day transferred, and is this day transferring and assigning said promissory note to Mrs. Fannie Belle Hatch in consideration of the amount due thereon, towit, the sum of $949.13, to him in hand paid;

NOW THEREFORE, the premises considered, and in consideration of said named sum, the said E. N. Ennis has this day bargained, granted, sold, aliened, conveyed and confirmed and by these presents does grant, bargain, sell, alien, convey and confirm unto the said Mrs. Fannie Belle Hatch, her heirs and assigns, all the lands set forth and described in the security deed heretofore referred to, held to secure said note, that is to say the lands described as follows:

Tract No. 1: That certain tract in Washington County, Containing One Hundred (100) acres, more or less, and known as the Strange Place, lying in the 98th District G.M., of Washington County, Georgia, being bounded on the North by Mrs. Dr. Graybill; East by Robert Hooks; South by W. J. Cochran; and West by Tom Hodges.

Tract No. 2: That tract containing Two Hundred (200)acres, known as the Davis Place being in the 98th District G. M., Washington County, Ga., and bounded on the North by Tom

Fraudulent Indenture beween E.N. Ennis and Fannie Belle Hatch, March 2, 1936, pg. 1.

204

Hodges; East by Tract No. 1 above described; South by E. N. Ennis; and West by E. N. Ennis.

Tract No. 3: That tract containing One Hundred (100)acres, more or less, known as the Jim Hooks Place, being place formerly owned by Mrs. Jeff Carter, located in the 98th District G. M., of Washington County, Georgia, and bounded on the North by Robert Hooks; East by Robert Hooks; South by Sam Gordy; and West by W. J. Cochran.

TO HAVE AND TO HOLD the said bargained premises for the purpose of securing the note so transferred to the only proper use, benefit and behoof of the said Mrs. Fannie Belle Hatch, her heirs and assigns, in fee simple forever.

And for the consideration aforesaid the said E. N. Ennis hereby assigns to the said Mrs. Fannie Belle Hatch, her personal representative and assigns, any and all rights, powers and privileges conveyed to him, the said E.N. Ennis, by the said named grantors in the security deed aforesaid, so that the said Mrs. Fannie Belle Hatch, under and by virtue of this assignment, shall have, hold, enjoy and exercise any and all rights, power and authority which might have been and could be exercised by the said E. N. Ennis under and by virtue of the provisions of the security deed aforesaid.

And the said E. N. Ennis the said bargained premises unto the said Mrs. Fannie Belle Hatch, her heirs and assigns, shall and will warrant and forever defend the title thereto as against the claims of the said E. N. Ennis and all persons claiming under him.

IN WITNESS WHEREOF, the said E.N. Ennis has hereunto set his hand, affixed his seal and delivered these presents, this the day and year first above written.

Signed, sealed and delivered
in the presence of:

E. W. Jordan — E. N. Ennis (L.S.)

Ruth Burns N. P. W. CO. GA.

Recorded March 2nd, 1936. — Roy H. Duggan, Clerk.

Fraudulent Indenture beween E.N. Ennis and Fannie Belle Hatch, March 2, 1936, pg. 2.

STATE OF GEORGIA, WASHINGTON COUNTY.

KNOW ALL MEN BY THESE PRESENTS:

THAT WE, Robert Hooks Sr., Principal and Mamie Carter Charlie Young; Lora E. Clawson, Jeff Carter Jr., Rodell Carter, Bertha Renfroe, Lillian Turner and Crawford Carter Securities, are held and firmly bound unto the Ordinary of said County, and his successors in office, and assigns, in the just and full sum of Ten Thousand & no/100 Dollars for the payment of which sum to the said Ordinary, and his successors in office, we bind ourselves, our heirs, executors and administrators, in the whole and for the whole sum, jointly and severally, and firmly by these presents.

Sealed with our seals, and dated this 20th *day of* July, 1936

THE CONDITION OF THE ABOVE OBLIGATION IS SUCH, That if the above bound Robert Hooks Sr. Administrator of the estate, real and personal, of Jeff Carter late of said County, deceased, do make a true and perfect inventory of all the estate, both real and personal, of said deceased, which have or shall come into the hands, possession or knowledge of the said Robert Hooks Sr. or the hands or possession of any person or persons, for him and the same so made to exhibit unto the said Ordinary, when he shall be hereunto required; and such Goods, Chattels, Credits, Lands and Tenements, do well and truly administer, according to law, and do make a just and true account of his actings and doing therein, when he shall thereunto be required by the Court; and the balance shall deliver and pay to such person or persons, respectively as they may be entitled to the same by law: And if it shall hereafter appear that any last Will and Testament was made by the deceased, and the same be proven before the Court of Ordinary, and the Executor obtain a certificate of the probate thereof, and said Robert Hooks Sr., in such case, if required, render and deliver up the said Letters of Administration, then this Obligation to be void, else to remain in full force.

Signed, sealed and acknowledged in open court.

Robert Hooks Sr. L.S.
Mamie Carter L.S.
Charlie Young L.S.
Lora E. Clawson L.S.
Jeff Carter Jr. L.S.
Rodell Carter
Bertha Renfroe L.S.
Lillian Turner L.S.
Crawford Carter L.S.

Approved!
Thos. J. Swint, Ordy.

Robert Hooks Sr., Fraudulent Letter of Approval to Adminstrate the Carter Estate, July 20, 1936.

JULY TERM 1936 CONTINUED : ESTATE OF JEFF CARTER

GEORGIA WASHINGTON COUNTY.

TO THE COURT OF ORDINARY OF SAID COUNTY:

The petition of Robert Hooks, Sr., of said County, shows that on the the 24th day of January 1930, one Jeff Carter, of said County, died intestate leaving an estate in this State to be administered.

That on the 5th day of May, 1930, Letters of Administration were granted to Virge Carter, by whom said estate was partially administered.

But on account of the death of Virge Carter, on June 1sy, 1936 there is now no representative of said estate, and there remains yet to be administered part of the same, of the value of Five Thousand & No/100 ------Dollars.

Petitioner has been selected and that he be appointed by a majority of the next of kin to Jeff Carter, and prays the Court, after the usual citation in that behalf, to appoint him as Administrator de bonis non of said estate.

This June 9th, 1936.

Robert Hooks

COURT OF ORDINARY OF WASHINGTON COUNTY.

CHAMBERS 9th day of JUNE 1936.

On reading the application of Robt. Hooks Sr. for Letters of Administration de bonis non on the estate of Jeff Carter, it is ordered that the usual citation issue in his behalf.

Thos. J. Swint, Ordinary

STATE OF GEORGIA, WASHINGTON COUNTY.

TO ALL WHOM IT MAY CONCERN:

Robert Hooks Sr., of said State, having applied for Letters of Administration de bonis non on the estate of Jeff Carter, late of said County, deceased, this is to cite all and singular the heirs and creditors of said deceased to be and appear at the July Term 1936, of the Court of Ordinary of said County, to be held on the first Monday in July next, and show cause, if any they can, why such letters should not be granted.

This June 9th 1936.

Thos. J. Swint, Ordinary

WASHINGTON COURT OF ORDINARY, JULY TERM 1936.

Citation having been duly issued and published, requiring all and singular the creditors and heirs of Jeff Carter, late of said County, deceased, to show cause at the present term of this Court why Letters of Administration de bonis non on Jeff Carter's Estate on said estate should not be granted to Robert Hooks, Sr.; and no valid objection being made in the premises, it is considered that such Letters be granted to said Robert Hooks, Sr. on his giving bond in the sum of Ten Thousand & no/100 Dollars, with The heirs at law of Jeff Carter surety, and taking the oath of office.

Thos. J. Swint, Ordinary

GEORGIA WASHINGTON COUNTY.

We, the undersigned being of the next of kin and being a majority of the next of kin to Jeff Carter, now deceased and Virge Carter, now deceased, both late of said State and County. Said Virge Carter prior to his death was the administrator of the estate of Jeff Carter. We agree and select Robert Hooks, Sr. as administrator de bonis non of the estate of Jeff Carter, Virge Carter departed this life June 1st, 1936, leaving the estate of Jeff Carter not fully administered, and that he be appointed administrator de bonis non of the estate of said Jeff Carter and we ask his appointment.

This 9th day of June, 1936.

Jeff Carter, Jr.

Jeff Carter Estate, Probate Record, pg. 1.

JULY TERM 1936 CONTINUED : ESTATE OF JEFF CARTER CONTINUED

GEORGIA, WASHINGTON COUNTY.

We, the undersigned being of the next of kin and being a majority of the next of kin to Jeff Carter, now deceased and Virge Carter, now deceased, both late of said State and County. Said Virge Carter prior to his death was the administrator of the estate of Jeff Carter, We agree and select Robert Hooks, Sr. as administrator de bonis non of the estate of Jeff Carter, Virge Carter departed this life June 1st, 1936, leaving the estate of Jeff Carter not fully administered, and that he be appointed administrator de bonis non of the estate of said Jeff Carter and we ask his appointment.

This 9th day of June, 1936.

Lova Ella Dawson
Lillie Turner
Bertha Renfroe
Mamie Carter

Jeff Carter Estate, Probate Record, pg. 2.

APRIL TERM 1937 CONTINUED : ESTATE OF JEFF CARTER

GEORGIA WASHINGTON COUNTY.

To The Ordinary of said County.

The petition of Robt Hooks Sr. adm. de bonis Non of the estate of Jeff Carter shows to the court that part of the assets of said estate is farm lands which have been rented to tenants. That said tenant in order to obtain a crop loan from the Governor of the Farm Crediting Administration to be made in 1937, it will be necessary for such Administrator to waive the rent on the following described lands: 262 acres of land in the 90th Dist. G.M. bounded as follows: on the north by Robt. Hooks; on the East by Buffalo Creek and lands of Brook; on the South by lands of Sam Gordon and West by Mrs. Mollie Graybill & Lawson place

Your petitioner further shows that it will be to the best interest of said Estate for the Court to grant an order authorizing such waiver.

Dated: April 10, 1937. Robt. Hooks, Petitioner

IN THE WASHINGTON COUNTY COURT OF ORDINARY.

In the matter of Robert Hooks Sr. Adm. De bonis Non of Jeff Carter's est.

This cause came on this day to be heard upon the petition of Robt. Hooks Sr. Adm. de bonis non of the Estate of Jeff Carter asking permission to waive the lien of the landlord on the following described lands belonging to the foregoing estate in favor of the Governor of the Farm Credit Administration for a crop loan to be made in 1937. 262 acres of land in the 90th Dist. G.M. Washington County. bounded as follows: On the North by Robt. Hooks on the East by Buffalo Creek and lands of Brooks. on the South by lands of Sam Gordon and west by Mrs. Mollie Graybill & Lawson place.

And it satisfactorily appearing to the Court that it is for the best interest of all parties that such authority be granted, it is hereby orderdd, adjudged and decreed that the said Robt. Hooks Sr. Adm. be and he is hereby authorized to execute the aforesaid waiver.

Dated April 10, 1937. Thos. J. Swint, Ordinary

Jeff Carter Estate, Probate Record, pg. 3.

DECEMBER TERM 1937 CONTINUED : ESTATE OF JEFF CARTER

GEORGIA, WASHINGTON COUNTY.

TO THE ORDINARY OF SAID COUNTY:

The Petition of Robert Hooks Sr., as Admr. De Bonis Non of the estate of Jeff Carter deceased, showeth that the estate of said deceased consist of 300 acres of land the same being all the land belonging to the estate of said deceased. bounded as follows: On the west by Luther Ennis; On the south by lands Sam Gordy and Walter Cochran; on the North by Robert Hooks and on the east by Buffalo Creek and lands of Ella Carter's estate. Also a one tenth undivided interest in Ella Carter's estate which consist of One Hundred and four acres more or less and bounded as follows: On the North by Robert Hooks; On the East by Buffalo Creek; On the South by Sam Gordy and on the West by lands of Jeff Carter's estate. and that for the purpose of Paying the debts and making distribution among the heirs it is necessary to sell the said land. Therefore, Petitioner prays an order directing citation to issue and be published as the law requires; and if no good cause be shown to the contrary, your Petitioner be granted Leave to sell said Land.

Robert Hooks, Petitioner.

Washington Court of Ordinary, Nov. Term 1937.

Upon reading the foregoing Petition, it is ordered that citation issue therein and be published as the law requires.

Thos. J. Swint, Ordinary

WASHINGTON COURT OF ORDINARY, DECEMBER TERM, 1937.

The written Petition of Robert Hooks Sr., as Admr. De Bonis Non of the estate of Jeff Carter deceased, praying for leave to sell the land of said deceased, having been duly filed, and it appearing that notice of the same has been published as required by law; that it is necessary for the purpose of paying debts and making distribution among the heirs that said land be sold, and no objection being filed thereto, it is ordered by the Court that the said Robert Hooks Sr. be, and he is hereby granted leave to sell, for the purpose aforesaid, the following described land of said deceased 300 acres of land the same being all the land belonging to the estate of said deceased bounded as follows: On the West by Luther Ennis; On the south by lands of Sam Gordy and Walter Cochran; On the North By Robert Hooks and on the east by Buffalo Creek and lands of Ella Carter's estate. Also a one tenth undivided interest in Ella Carter's estate which consist of one Hundred and four acres more or less and bounded as follows: On the North by Robert Hooks; On the east by Buffalo Creek; On the South by Sam Gordy; and on the west by lands of Jeff Carter's estate.

Thos. J. Swint, Ordinary

Jeff Carter Estate, Probate Record, pg. 4.

GEORGIA, Washington County

THIS INDENTURE, executed this the 7th day of December 1937, between Mrs. Fannie Bell Hatch, as agent and attorney in fact of and for Virge Carter, Jeff Carter, Minnie Butts, M. E. Young, Lora E. Dawson, Delia Carter, Rodell Carter, Crawford Carter, Bertha Renfroe, and Lillian Turner, as parties of the first part, and Mrs. Fannie Belle Hatch, as party of the second part, both of said county and state;

WITNESSETH: That on the 27th day of January 1933, the said Virge Carter, Jeff Carter, Minnie Butts, M. E. Young, Lora E. Dawson, Delia Carter, Rodell Carter, Crawford Carter, Bertha Renfroe, and Lillian Turner did execute and deliver to E. N. Ennis their certain promissory note, which note was secured by a deed to certain land hereinafter described, the said deed of even date with said note, and recorded in the Clerk's office of the Superior Court of Washington County in Book CC, page 106, on the 19th day of October 1934, which deed, its recitals and references, are made expressly a part hereof; and

Whereas, said deed confers a power of sale upon the said E. N. Ennis, his personal representative or assigns, upon default by the said grantors in the payment of principal, and all interest due upon said note; and

Whereas, later, to wit, on the 2nd day of March 1936 E. N. Ennis did transfer and assign to Mrs. Fannie Bell Hatch said described promissory note, the balance thereon as of that date being $949.13, and contemporaneously therewith did execute and deliver to Mrs. Fannie Belle Hatch a deed conveying all of the lands hereinafter described, existing as security for the indebtedness of said named parties to the said E. N. Ennis, in which deed all of the [illegible] rights, and privileges of the said E. N. Ennis were transferred [illegible] to the said Mrs. Fannie Belle Hatch in consideration [illegible] said deed from E. N. Ennis to Mrs. Fannie [illegible]

Fraudulent Indenture of Fannie Belle Hatch, December 7, 1937, pg. 1.

Whereas, the said named makers of the note so transferred and the original grantors in the deed to E. N. Ennis heretofore referred to, failed to pay the note secured by said deed, and have made default in both the principal and interest so secured, and in consequence thereof the power of sale heretofore referred to is operative in the said Mrs. Fannie Belle Hatch, as assignee of the said E. N. Ennis; and

Whereas, further, to wit, the said Mrs. Fannie Belle Hatch, under and by virtue of the power of sale existing in her as such assignee, advertised the said lands for sale at public outcry before the court house door of Washington County, in the City of Sandersville, on the first Tuesday in December 1937, to the highest bidder for cash; and

Whereas, said advertisement was duly published once a week for four weeks in the said Sandersville Progress, said advertisement giving the time and place of sale, together with a recital of all the powers of the said Mrs. Fannie Belle Hatch to make such sale;

Now Therefore, the premises considered, the said Mrs. Fannie Belle Hatch, acting under and by virtue of said power in the aforesaid instrument, exposed said land for sale at public outcry on the first Tuesday in December 1937, before the Court House door of Washington County, when the same was knocked off to her as the highest and best bidder for cash, she being authorized to bid upon said land and purchase the same at such sale, at and for the sum of $500.00;

Now Therefore, in consideration of said sum to her, and as agent and attorney in fact for the aforesaid named parties, she has this day granted, bargained, sold, aliened, conveyed and confirmed and by these presents does grant, bargain, sell, alien, convey and confirm unto herself, personally and individually, as the highest and best bidder, all of the lands referred to in the aforesaid deeds, under which this power is exercised, described as follows:

[illegible] Tract No. 1: That certain tract in Washington County, [illegible] Hundred (100) acres, more or less, and known [illegible] Place, lying in the [illegible] District G. M. of [illegible] Georgia, being bounded on the North by [illegible] Robert [illegible] [illegible]

Fraudulent Indenture of Fannie Belle Hatch, December 7, 1937, pg. 2.

Tract No. 2: That tract containing Two Hundred (200) acres, known as the Davis Place, being in the 98th District G. M., Washington County, Ga., and bounded on the North by Tom Hodges; East by Tract No. 1 above described; South by E. N. Ennis; and West by E. N. Ennis.

Tract No.3: That tract containing One Hundred (100) acres, more or less, known as the Jim Hooks Place, being place formerly owned by Mrs. Jeff Carter, located in the 98th District G. M., of Washington County, Georgia, and bounded on the North by Robert Hooks; East by Robert Hooks; South by Sam Gordy; and West by W. J. Cochran.

TO HAVE AND TO HOLD the aforesaid described tracts or parcels of land, together with all and singular the rights, members and appurtenances thereunto appertaining to the only proper use, benefit and behoof of the said Mrs. Fannie Belle Hatch and in as full and ample a manner as was had and held by the said named parties, as grantors in the original deed to the said E. N. Ennis.

IN WITNESS WHEREOF, the said named parties, Virge Carter, Jeff.Carter, Minnie Butts, M. E. Young, Lora E. Dawson, Delia Carter, Rodell Carter, Crawford Carter, Bertha Renfroe, and Lillian Turner, acting by and through their attorney in fact, Mrs. Fannie Belle Hatch, have hereto set their hands, affixed their seals and executed and delivered these presents, this the day and year first above written.

VIRGE CARTER (L.S.)
JEFF CARTER (L.S.)
MINNIE BUTTS (L.S.)
M. E. YOUNG (L.S.)
LORA E. DAWSON (L.S.)
DELIA CARTER (L.S.)
RODELL CARTER (L.S.)
CRAWFORD CARTER (L.S.)
BERTHA RENFROE (L.S.)
LILLIAN TURNER (L.S.)

By Mrs Fannie Belle Hatch

As Agent and Attorney in Fact for Virge Carter, Jeff Carter and other parties named above

Signed, sealed and delivered in the presence of:

N.P. W. Co. Ga.

Fraudulent Indenture of Fannie Belle Hatch, December 7, 1937, pg. 3.

Mrs. Fannie Belle Hatch TO Robert Hooks Jr.

GEORGIA, Washington County

THIS INDENTURE, executed this 9th day of December 1937, between Mrs. Fannie Belle Hatch, as party of the first part, and Robert Hooks Jr., as party of the second part, both of said county and state;

WITNESSETH: That the said Mrs. Fannie Belle Hatch for and in consideration of the sum of Twelve Hundred Thirty Seven and 59/100 Dollars ($1237.59) to her in hand paid, at and before the sealing and delivery of these presents, the receipt whereof is hereby acknowledged, has granted, bargained, sold, aliened, conveyed and quitclaimed, and by these presents does grant, bargain, sell, alien, convey and quitclaim unto the said Robert Hooks Jr., his heirs and assigns, all of the right, title and interest that the said Mrs. Fannie Belle Hatch has in and to the following described tracts or parcels of land, to wit:

Tract No. 1: That certain tract in Washington County, containing One Hundred (100) acres, more or less, and known as the Strange Place, lying in the 98th District G. M., of Washington County, Georgia, being bounded on the North by Mrs. Dr. Graybill; East by Robert Hooks; South by W. J. Cochran; and West by Tom Hodges.

Tract No. 2: That tract containing Two Hundred (200) acres, known as the Davis Place, being in the 98th District G. M., Washington County, Ga., and bounded on the North by Tom Hodges; East by Tract No. 1 above described; South by E. N. Ennis; and West by E. N. Ennis.

Tract No. 3: That tract containing One Hundred (100) acres, more or less, known as the Jim Hooks place, being place formerly owned by Mrs. Jeff Carter, located in the 98th District G. M., of Washington County, Georgia, and bounded on the North by Robert Hooks; East by Robert Hooks; South by Sam Gordy; and West by W. J. Cochran.

TO HAVE AND TO HOLD the aforesaid described tracts or parcels of land, together with all and singular the rights, members and appurtenances thereunto appertaining to the only proper use, benefit and behoof of the said Robert Hooks, Jr., his heirs and assigns, in fee simple.

And the said Mrs. Fannie Belle Hatch does hereby warrant unto the said Robert Hooks, Jr., the title to said described lots or parcels of land as against herself, and all persons claiming under her, only

In witness Whereof, the said Mrs. Fannie Belle Hatch has hereunto set her hand, affixed her seal and delivered these presents, this the day and year first above written.

Mrs. Fannie Belle Hatch (L. S.)

Signed, sealed and delivered
in the presence of:
G. J. Elkins
E. W. Jordan
N. P. W. C. Ga.

Recorded December 10, 1937 Roy H. Duggan, Clerk.

Fraudulent Warranty Deed, Fannie Belle Hatch to Robert Hooks Jr., December 9, 1937.

5 D-4

GEORGIA, WASHINGTON COUNTY

THIS INDENTURE, executed this 9th day of December 1937, between Mrs. Fannie Belle Hatch, as party of the first part, and Robert Hooks Jr., as party of the second part, both of said county and state;

WITNESSETH: That the said Mrs. Fannie Belle Hatch for and in consideration of the sum of Twelve Hundred & Thirty-Seven & 59/100 Dollars ($1237.59) to her in hand paid, at and before the sealing and delivery of these presents, the receipt whereof is hereby acknowledged, has granted, bargained, sold, aliened, conveyed and quitclaimed, and by these presents does grant, bargain, sell, alien, convey and quitclaim unto the said Robert Hooks Jr., his heirs and assigns, all of the right, title and interest that the said Mrs. Fannie Belle Hatch has in and to the following described tracts or parcels of land, to wit:

> Tract No. 1: That certain tract in Washington County, containing One Hundred (100) acres, more or less, and known as the Strange Place, lying in the 98th District G. M., of Washington County, Georgia, being bounded on the North by Mrs. Dr. Graybill; East by Robert Hooks; South by W. J. Cochran; and West by Tom Hodges.
>
> Tract No. 2: That tract containing Two Hundred (200) acres, known as the Davis Place, being in the 98th District G. M., Washington County, Ga., and bounded on the North by Tom Hodges; East by Tract No. 1 above described; South by E. N. Ennis; and West by E. N. Ennis.
>
> Tract No. 3: That tract containing One Hundred (100) acres, more or less, known as the Jim Hooks place, being place formerly owned by Mrs. Jeff Carter, located in the 98th District G. M., of Washington County, Georgia, and bounded on the North by Robert Hooks; East by Robert Hooks; South by Sam Gordy; and West by W. J. Cochran.

TO HAVE AND TO HOLD the aforesaid described tracts or parcels of land, together with all and singular the rights, members and appurtenances thereunto appertaining to the only proper use, benefit and behoof of the said Robert Hooks Jr., his heirs and assigns, in fee simple.

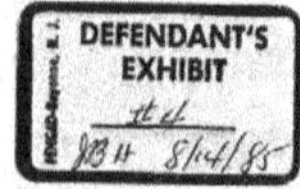

Another Fraudulent, Forged Warranty Deed; Fannie Belle Hatch to Robert Hooks *Jr.*, December 9, 1937, pg. 1.

And the said Mrs. Fannie Belle Hatch does hereby warrant unto the said Robert Hooks Jr., the title to said described lots or parcels of land as against herself, and all persons claiming under her, only.

In witness Whereof, the said Mrs. Fannie Belle Hatch has hereunto set her hand, affixed her seal and delivered these presents, this the day and year first above written.

Mrs Fannie Belle Hatch (L.S.)

Signed, sealed and delivered in the presence of:

J Blann

E. W. Jordan

N. P. W. C. Ga.

Another Fraudulent, Forged Warranty Deed; Fannie Belle Hatch to Robert Hooks *Jr.*, December 9, 1937, pg. 2.

Esther Scott	To	B. J.Tarbutton

STATE OF MICHIGAN,

COUNTY OF WAYNE.

THIS INDENTURE, Made this the 31st day of January, 1938, between Esther Scott, of the County of Wayne, of the first part, and B. J. Tarbutton, of the County of Washington, of the second part,

WITNESSETH, That the said party of the first part, for and in consideration of the sum of One ($1.00) Dollar, in hand paid, at and before the sealing and delivery of these presents, the receipt whereof is hereby acknowledged, has granted, bargained, sold, and conveyed, and by these presents does grant, bargain, sell, and convey, unto the said party of the second part, his heirs and assigns, all of the following described tracts or parcels of land:

TRACT NO. 1. That certain tract in Washington County, containing One Hundred (100) acres, more or less, and known as the Strange Place, lying in the 98th District, G.M., of Washington County, Georgia, being bounded on the North by Mrs. Dr. Graybill; East by Robert Hooks; South by W. J. Cochran; and West by Tom Hodges.

TRACT NO. 2. That tract containing Two Hundred (200) acres, known as the Davis place, being in the 98th District, G. M., Washington County, Georgia, and bounded on the North by Tom Hodges; East by tract no. 1 above described; South by E. N. Ennis; and West by E. N. Ennis.

TRACT NO. 3. That tract containing One Hundred (100) acres, more or less, known as the Jim Hooks place, being place formerly owned by Mrs. Jeff Carter, located in the 98th District, G.M. of Washington County, Georgia, and bounded on the North by Robert Hooks; East by Robert Hooks; South by Sam Gordy; and West by W. J. Cochran.

TO HAVE AND TO HOLD, The said bargained premises, together with all and singular the rights, members and appurtenances thereof, to the same being, belonging or in anywise appertaining to the only proper use, benefit and behoof of B. J. Tarbutton, the said party of the second part, his heirs, executors and administrators in fee simple.

And the said party of the first part, her heirs, executors and administrators, the said bargained premises unto the said party of the second part, his heirs, executors, administrators and assigns, against said party of the first part, her heirs, executors and administrators, and all and every other person or persons shall and will warrant and forever defend by virtue of these presents.

IN WITNESS WHEREOF, The said party of the first part has hereunto set her hand and affixed her seal, the day and year first above written.

Signed, sealed and delivered by Esther Scott, in the County of Wayne, State of Michigan, in the presence of:

Esther Scott L.S.

Charles E Williams
Notary Public Wayne Michigan (N.P.SEAL)
My Commission Expires December 16, 1940

Recorded March 30th, 1938. Roy H. Duggan, Clerk.

Fraudulent Warranty Deed between Esther Carter Scott Hinton and B.J. Tarbutton, January 31, 1938.

STATE OF MICHIGAN,

COUNTY OF Wayne.

THIS INDENTURE, Made this the 31st day of January, 1938, between Esther Scott, of the County of Wayne, of the first part, and B. J. Tarbutton, of the County of Washington, of the second part,

WITNESSETH,

That the said party of the first part, for and in consideration of the sum of One ($1.00) Dollar, in hand paid, at and before the sealing and delivery of these presents, the receipt whereof is hereby acknowledged, has granted, bargained, sold, and conveyed, and by these presents does grant, bargain, sell, and convey, unto the said party of the second part, his heirs and assigns, all of the following described tracts or parcels of land:

TRACT NO. 1. That certain tract in Washington County, containing One Hundred (100) acres, more or less, and known as the Strange Place, lying in the 98th District, G. M., of Washington County, Georgia, being bounded on the North by Mrs. Dr. Graybill; East by Robert Hooks; South by W. J. Cochran; and West by Tom Hodges.

TRACT NO. 2. That tract containing Two Hundred (200) acres, known as the Davis place, being in the 98th District, G. M., Washington County, Georgia, and bounded on the North by Tom Hodges; East by tract no. 1 above described; South by E. N. Ennis; and West by E. N. Ennis

TRACT NO. 3. That tract containing One Hundred (100) acres, more or less, known as the Jim Hooks place, being place formerly owned by Mrs. Jeff Carter, located in the 98th District, G. M. of Washington County, Georgia, and bounded on the North by Robert Hooks; East by Robert Hooks; South by Sam Gordy; and West by W. J. Cochran.

TO HAVE AND TO HOLD, The said bargained premises, together with all and singular the rights, members and appurtenances thereof, to the same being, belonging or in anywise appertaining to the only proper use, benefit and behoof of B. J. Tarbutton, the said party of the second part, his heirs, executors and administrators in fee simple.

Forged Warranty Deed between Esther Carter Scott Hinton and B.J. Tarbutton, January 31, 1938, pg. 1.

And the said party of the first part, her heirs, executors and administrators, the said bargained premises unto the said party of the second part, his heirs, executors, administrators and assigns, against said party of the first part, her heirs, executors and administrators, and all and every other person or persons shall and will warrant and forever defend by virtue of these presents.

IN WITNESS WHEREOF, The said party of the first part has hereunto set her hand and affixed her seal, the day and year first above written.

Esther Scott L.S.

Signed, sealed and delivered by Esther Scott, in the County of Wayne, State of Michigan, in the presence of:

Charles E Williams
Notary Public Wayne Michigan
Maude Williams

My Commission Expires December 16, 1940

Forged Warranty Deed between Esther Carter Scott Hinton to B.J. Tarbutton, January 31, 1938, pg. 2.

STATE OF GEORGIA
WASHINGTON COUNTY
CLERK'S OFFICE, SUPERIOR COURT:
FILED MAR 30 1938 193
4:30 P. M.
Recorded MAR 30 1938 193
Book 3.5. Page 545
Ruby Hartley
Deputy CLERK, S. C. W. C. GA.

GEORGIA, WASHINGTON COUNTY
I hereby certify that the within instrument was filed for record on JUN 21 1984 19__, at 4:55 o'clock P. M.
Was recorded in Deed book 7-Q page 152 on JUN 21 1984
Janie Lindsey Bryan
Clerk S. C. W. Co. Ga.

Forged Warranty Deed between Esther Carter Scott Hinton and B.J. Tarbutton, January 31, 1938, pg. 3.

STATE OF CALIFORNIA

COUNTY OF LOS ANGELES

AFFIDAVIT OF FORGERY PURSUANT TO O.C.G.A §44-2-23, CURRENT OWNER LOULIE EUGENIA KERNIGHAN TARBUTTON, AS TRUSTEE UNDER DEED RECORDED IN DEED BOOK 6G, PAGE 177, OFFICE OF THE CLERK OF THE SUPERIOR COURT OF WASHINGTON COUNTY, GEORGIA REGARDING WARRANTY DEED FROM ESTHER SCOTT TO B. J. TARBUTTON, RECORDED IN DEED BOOK TT, PAGE 545 AND RERECORDED IN DEED BOOK 7Q, PAGE 152, OFFICE OF THE CLERK OF THE SUPERIOR COURT OF WASHINGTON COUNTY, GEORGIA REGARDING LAND LOCATED IN THE 98TH DISTRICT GM OF WASHINGTON COUNTY CONSISTING OF 100 ACRES MORE OR LESS PLUS 200 ACRES KNOWN AS THE DAVIS PLACE PLUS 100 ACRES MORE OR LESS KNOWN AS THE JIM HOOKS PLACE

Personally appeared before me, the undersigned Notary, an officer duly authorized to administer an oath, Esther Scott Hinton, who first being sworn states on oath as follows:

I am Esther Scott Hinton. I live at 1642 Seventh Avenue, Los Angeles, California 90019. I was born in Washington County, Georgia on May 7, 1914. I am a daughter of Jeff Carter, Deceased, by his second wife, Easter Gordy Carter.

I am now in good health and not suffering under any physical, mental or legal disability which would impair or prevent me from giving this affidavit. I am making this affidavit freely and voluntarily and with the knowledge that it may be recorded on the land records in the office of the Clerk of the Superior Court of Washington County, Georgia or filed in the pleadings of the Civil Action styled as Loulie Eugenia Kernighan Tarbutton as Trustee, etc., vs. Tract of Land in 98th GM District, Washington County, Georgia; Robert Lee Watkins, Individually and as Attorney in Fact for Timothy Dawson, et.al., and other named defendants; and All the World, defendants, Civil Action File No. 5175. I am making this affidavit based on my own personal knowledge.

I have examined the 2 page document which is a copy of the warranty deed dated January 31, 1938 which is described in the caption of this affidavit. A copy of that warranty deed is attached to this affidavit as Exhibit "A" with the pages thereof marked consecutively by separate number.

The signature on page 2 of Exhibit "A" appearing as "Esther Scott" is not my signature. I did not sign the original of the warranty deed described herein and I have never seen the original warranty deed. I do not know who signed my name to the original warranty deed described herein. I never authorized anyone to sign my name to the original warranty deed. I have never signed any deeds to the Carter Place which is the land

Affidavit of Esther Scott Hinton, September 21, 1984, page 1.

described in the caption of this affidavit.

I moved to Los Angeles, California on or about February, 1937 and did not return to Michigan until six or seven years later. I was not in Wayne County, Michigan on or about January 31, 1938.

"Esther Scott" was my correct name on or about January, 1938. I later became known as Esther Scott Hinton after a subsequent marriage.

The signature of my name, "Esther Scott" as I was known on or about January, 1938 appearing on the copy of the attached warranty deed, is a forgery.

Further, Affiant sayeth not.

Esther Scott Hinton
Esther Scott Hinton

Sworn to and subscribed before me
this 21 day of September,
1984.

Erwin William Jefferson
Notary Public

OFFICIAL SEAL
Erwin William Jefferson III
NOTARY PUBLIC - CALIFORNIA
LOS ANGELES COUNTY
My Comm. Expires Feb. 2, 1985

Affidavit of Esther Scott Hinton, September 21, 1984, page 2.

Recorded March 30th, 1938. Roy H. Duggan, Clerk.

Robert Hooks,Jr. To B. J. Tarbutton

GEORGIA. WASHINGTON COUNTY.

THIS INDENTURE, Made this the 19th day of February, 1938, between Robert Hooks, Jr. of the County of Washington, of the first part, and B. J. Tarbutton, of the County of Washington of the second part,

WITNESSETH, That the said party of the first part, for and in consideration of the sum of Six hundred & Forty ($640.00) Dollars, in hand paid, at and before the sealing and delivery of these presents the receipt whereof is hereby acknowledged, has granted, bargained, sold, and conveyed, and by these presents does grant, bargain, sell, and convey, unto the said party of the second part, his heirs and assigns, all of the following described tract or parcel of land: Tract No. 1.

That certain tract in Washington, County, Georgia, containing One Hundred (100) acres, more or less, and known as the Strange Place, lying in the 98th District, G.M. of Washington County, Georgia, being bounded on the North by Mrs. Dr. Graybill, East by Robert Hooks, South by W. J. Cochran, and West by Tom Hodges.

Tract No. 2. That tract containing Two Hundred (200) acres known as the Davis place, being in the 98th District, G.M., Washington County, Georgia, and bounded on the North by Tom Hodges, East by Tract No. 1 above described, South by E. N. Ennis, and West by E.N. Ennis.

Tract No. 3. That tract containing One Hundred (100) acres, more or less, known as the Jim Hooks place, being place formerly owned by Mrs. Jeff Carter, located in the 98th District, G.M. of Washington County, Georgia, and bounded on the North by Robert Hooks, East by Robert Hooks, South by Sam Gordy and West by W. J. Cochran.

TO HAVE AND TO HOLD, The said bargained premises, together with all and singular the rights, members and appurtenances thereof, to the same being, belonging or in anywise appertaining to the only proper use, benefit and behoof of B. J. Tarbutton, the said party of the second part, his heirs, executors and administrators in FEE SIMPLE.

And the said party of the first part, his heirs, executors and administrators, the said bargained premises unto the said party of the second part, his heirs, executors, administrators and assigns, against said party of the first part, his heirs, executors and administrators, and all and every other person or persons shall and will warrant and forever defend by virtue of these presents.

IN WITNESS WHEREOF, The said party of the first part has hereunto set his hand and affixed his seal, the day and year first above written.

Signed, sealed and delivered in presence of Robert Hooks Jr L.S.

Terressa G. Franklin

D. E. McMaster N. P. W. CO. GA.

U. S. REVENUE STAMPS $1.00 ATTACHED AND CANCELLED

Recorded March 30th,1938. Roy H. Duggan, Clerk.

Fraudulent Indenture between Robert Hooks Jr. and B.J. Tarbutton, February 19, 1938.

GEORGIA, WASHINGTON COUNTY.

THIS INDENTURE, Made this the 19th day of February, 1938, between Robert Hooks, Jr., of the County of Washington, of the first part, and B. J. Tarbutton, of the County of Washington, of the second part,

WITNESSETH, That the said party of the first part, for and in consideration of the sum of Six hundred & Forty ($640.00) Dollars, in hand paid, at and before the sealing and delivery of these presents, the receipt whereof is hereby acknowledged, has granted, bargained, sold, and conveyed, and by these presents does grant, bargain, sell, and convey, unto the said party of the second part, his heirs and assigns, all of the following described tract or parcel of land:

> Tract No. 1. That certain tract in Washington, County, Georgia, containing One Hundred (100) acres, more or less, and known as the Strange Place, lying in the 98th District, G. M. of Washington County, Georgia, being bounded on the North by Mrs. Dr. Graybill, East by Robert Hooks, South by W. J. Cochran, and West by Tom Hodges.
>
> Tract No. 2. That tract containing Two Hundred (200) acres known as the Davis place, being in the 98th District, G. M., Washington County, Georgia, and bounded on the North by Tom Hodges, East by Tract No. 1 above described, South by E. N. Ennis, and West by E. N. Ennis.
>
> Tract No. 3. That tract containing One Hundred (100) acres, more or less, known as the Jim Hooks place, being place formerly owned by Mrs. Jeff Carter, located in the 98th District, G. M. of Washington County, Georgia, and bounded on the North by Robert Hooks, East by Robert Hooks, South by Sam Gordy and West by W. J. Cochran.

TO HAVE AND TO HOLD, The said bargained premises, together with all and singular the rights, members and appurtenances thereof, to the same being, belonging or in anywise appertaining to the only proper use, benefit and behoof of B. J. Tarbutton, the said party of the second part, his heirs, executors and administrators in FEE SIMPLE.

Fraudulent Indenture between Robert Hooks Jr. and B.J. Tarbutton, February 19, 1938, pg. 1.

And the said party of the first part, his heirs, executors and administrators, the said bargained premises unto the said party of the second part, his heirs, executors, administrators and assigns, against said party of the first part, his heirs, executors and administrators, and all and every other person or persons shall and will warrant and forever defend by virtue of these presents.

IN WITNESS WHEREOF, The said party of the first part has hereunto set his hand and affixed his seal, the day and year first above written.

Robert Hooks Jr. L.S.

Signed, sealed and delivered in presence of:

Teresa T. Franklin

D. E. McMaster

N.P.W.Co. Ga.

Fraudulent Indenture between Robert Hooks Jr. and B.J. Tarbutton, February 19, 1938, pg. 2.

G. P.O. Box 501
Brooklyn, N. Y. 11202
Feb. 17, 1978

Mr. Tarbutton
Sandersville, Ga. 31082 RE: " CARTER PLACE "

Mr. Tarbutton ;

Not having had returned the mailed copy , to you, of my formal request of Jan. 17,1978, by United States Mail, and through Mr. William Duggan - Tax Commissioner Court-house, Sandersville, Georgia, and Mr. Newsom Summerlin, Superior Court Clerk, it is most respectfully taken that you were duly apprised of my layman's attempt through the official authorities of Sandersville, as noted above, to assert my inherited right and lawful return of title to the property a/k/a as the " CARTER PLACE ", and request if you have any intention of filing any resistance or/and response to my official request.

Most respectfully

Virgil Carter

Virgil Carter

TO:Newsom Summerlin, esq.
Clerk , Superior Court
P. O. Box 231
Sandersville, Georgia 31082

Mr. William Duggan
Tax Commissioner- Court-house
Sandersville, Georgia, 31082

Letter from Virge Carter, Jr. to B.J. Tarbutton, February, 17, 1978

The Honorable Judge
Superior Court Washington County
P.O. Box 231
Sandersville, Ga. 31082

Re: " Carter Place " in the 98th G. M. District of Washington County, Ga. "

Sirs;

Whereas I've not received a legal determination from this Honorable Court, of my application to this Honorable Court for a determination on my claims, against the mortgage holders, the Tarbuttons of Sandersville, Georgia, with regards to my lawful rights concerning that tract or parcel of land in Washington County, heretofore known as the "Carter Estate" in the following boundary:

ALL THAT TRACT OR PARCEL OF LAND LYING, SITUATED AND BEING IN THE 98th G. M. DISTRICT OF WASHINGTON COUNTY, GEORGIA, CONTAINING FIVE OR SIX HUNDRED (500 or 600) ACRES, MORE OR LESS, AND BEING BOUND AS FOLLOWS: ON THE NORTH BY LANDS OF ROBERT HOOKS AND LANDS OF LUTHER ENNIS, EAST BY BUFFALO CREEK, SOUTH BY LANDS OF SAM GORDY AND LANDS OF THE ELKINS ESTATE, AND WEST BY LANDS OF ELKINS ESTATE AND LANDS OF LUTHER ENNIS, SAID TRACT OR PARCEL OF LAND BEING KNOWN AS THE "CARTER PLACE" TOGETHER WITH ALL THE , RIGHTS AND PRIVILEGES THEREUNDER BELONGING FOREVER, IN FEE SIMPLE.

this request is renewed, even though I've not been sucessful in my attempts to elicit the competent assistance of an attorney.

Hon. sirs, ~~though~~ even though I'm an indigent, under Governmental and Educational Technology contract and assistance, had my lawful rights been adjudicated or/and should my lawful rights be adjudicated under the here to-fore and present lawful premises, heretofore advanced to this Honorable Court, the land would be alive of agriculture ordevelopment and not robbed and plundered of its resourse and wealth, as the Tarbuttons have did , in their attempts to take the land from this lawful heir, and heretofore, aided by the officials of Sandersville and this Superior Court .

Letter from Virge Carter, Jr., March 2,1979, pg. 1

Therefore, I have this renewed request, and not being attorney, a copy is being sent to the Columbus Legal Aid Society, Inc. P.O. Box 2802, Columbus, Georgia 31902, who have to date refused my requests for assistance.

Most respectfully,

Virgil Carter

Virgil Carter
G.P. O. Box 501
Brooklyn, N. Y. 11202

To:

Managing Attorney
Columbus Legal Aid Society, Inc.
P.O. Box 2802
Columbus, Georgia 31902

Tarbutton ,
Sandersville, Georgia 31082

Mrs Mamie Carter
c/o Mrs Teresa C. Snyder
Brooklyn, N. Y. 11225

Sworn to before me
this 2 day of March 1979
Elliott Moskowitz

ELLIOTT MOSKOWITZ
Commissioner of Deeds
City of New York - No 4-2158
Certificate Filed in Kings County
Commission Expires March 1, 1981

Letter from Virge Carter, Jr., March 2,1979, pg. 2

Testimony of Robert Hooks, Jr. - given to D. E. McMaster, Attorney, on July 16, 1980

M...Robert, hold up your right hand, please. The evidence you shall give in this testimony shall be the truth, the whole truth, and nothing but the truth, so help you, God.-------Give us your name and address and age.

H...My name, Robert Hooks, Jr.

M...Age?

H...Age 72

M...Address?

H...Route 3, Box 75, Sandersville, Georgia.

M...--you reside near what is known as the Carter property?

H...I do.

M...Have you been familiar with the Carter property all of your adult life?

H...I have.

M...At one time, you were the owner of the Carter property?

H...Yes sir, just about two months-----

M...---You knew the Carter property as consisting of three tracts of land?

H...Yes sir.

M...Known as the Strange place, as the Davis place, and the Jim Hooks place?

H...Right.

M...The Jim Hooks place was a part of the land which you now own

H...Right, yes sir.

M...adjoining the Carter property?---The tract of land which you know as the Carter property is the tract of land that was sold at public outcry after being advertised in the <u>Sandersville Progress</u> and purchased by Mrs. Hatch?

H...That's right.

M...This tract then was sold by Mrs. Hatch to you?

H...That's right.

D. E. 'Stick' McMaster interrogates Robert Hooks Jr., July 16, 1980, page 1.

M...On a later date, after you purchased this property from Mrs. Hatch, did you sell the same to Mr. B. J. Tarbutton?

H...Yes sir, it was transferred from me to him.

M...To B. J. Tarbutton?

H...That's right.

M...Being the three tracts of land which you have stated that you knew as the Carter place?

H...That's right, exactly.

M...Have you, in recent years, known or do you now know of any controversy in regard to these three tracts of land? Now, if you do, tell us for this record.

H...Now, for me to know, I don't know any controversy - hearsay is, and you understand - hearsay, there's a lot of it, but I don't know of any.

M...That's all right, go ahead.

H...I had heard that some of the heirs hadn't signed and all of that nature, but

M...To your knowledge, you do not know?

H...Know that. To my knowledge, I don't know it.

M... Robert, you have looked at the deed from E. N. Ennis and the deed from Mrs. Fannie Belle Hatch?

H...Yes sir.

M...And you note that they are not signed by Esther Scott. She didn't sign it?

H...She didn't sign it at the time.

M...At the time?

H...Right.

M...Later, I hand to you a deed dated January 31st, 1938, recorded in Book TT, page 545, from Esther Scott to B. J. Tarbutton conveying the same property which you sold to Mr. Tarbutton?

H...That's right.

M...Robert, there were certain heirs of Jeff Carter dead at the time you bought the property?

H...Yes sir.

M...But, if you remember, these parties died after the execution of the deed to Ennis and Mrs. Hatch.

D. E. 'Stick' McMaster interrogates Robert Hooks Jr., July 16, 1980, page 2.

Testimony of John Barker - given to D. E. McMaster, Attorney, on July 16, 1980

M...Mr. Barker, state your name.

B...John Barker.

M...What is your occupation?

B...Surveyor.

M...Have you had an opportunity to look over what is known as the plats and deeds on the Jeff Carter place now owned by the Tarbuttons?

B...Yes sir.

M...I hand you a drawing of the Jeff Carter place which you furnished to me. Does this include all that you know as being the, the Carter place owned by the Tarbuttons?

B...Yes sir, so far as I know.

M...You know of no contests now as to any lines or any question has been brought to your attention of any contest as to the title?

B...No.

M...O. K.

D. E. 'Stick' McMaster interrogates John Barker, July 16, 1980.

My name is Harry Hollien. I am a Professor of Linguistics, Speech and Criminal Justice at the University of Florida. I am 59 years old and hold degrees from Boston University, B.S. (1949) and MEd. (1951); University of Iowa, M.A. (1953) and Ph.D. (1955).

I am giving this affidavit for use by Defendants in opposition to Plaintiff's Motion for Summary Judgment filed in the above case and for any other lawful purpose.

I was the founding Director of the Institute for Advance Study of Communication Processes at the University of Florida. I am also Senior Consultant to Forensic Communication Associates. This organization consults and gives seminars on tape recorded evidence. My address is P.O. Box 12323, University Station, Gainesville, Florida, 32604-0323.

I attach hereto as Exhibit A 5 pages of my resume which summarizes in detail my academic experience, honors, grants received and worked on, memberships in professional societies, and a catalog of my other professional experience which includes my work on federal government projects, University of Florida projects, as well as professional and editorial projects which I have undertaken in my career. I have written or co-authored numerous articles and papers in my field during my career. I have also been employed as an expert in numerous criminal and civil cases by both Plaintiffs and Defendants and I have given expert testimony at trial in many such cases.

Harry Hollien, Senior Consultant to Forensic Communication Associates, page 1.

I hold myself out as an expert in the area of linguistics, speech and criminal justice with specialty in phonetics science, forensic communication, underwater communication and psychoacoustis. I was employed as an expert on behalf of Defendants in the above case. I am competent to testify laboring under no disability and give my testimony based on personal knowledge. I have no financial or other interest in the outcome of the above case.

The scope of my employment was to examine two tape recordings on standard cassettes and compare them to the transcript of an interview in an attempt to validate or verify the authenticity of the tape recordings and hence the interview. The interview in question was conducted on July 16, 1980. A copy of the interview transcript is attached hereto as Exhibit B.

The two tapes of the interview from which the transcript was prepared were furnished to me on or about September 18, 1985 by Wallace Miller, Jr., attorney for Plaintiffs in the above case.

Upon receipt of a package from Mr. Miller, I opened it in the presence of a witness and examined the two tape cassettes contained therein. Several copies of the tape recordings were made. The tapes received were then placed in a shield non-magnetic box especially designed for safekeeping tape recordings.

Harry Hollien, Senior Consultant to Forensic Communication Associates, page 2.

In my opinion to be valid, a tape recording must satisfy the following criteria: 1) It must not be interrupted, 2) No section can have been removed, and 3) Only the natural sounds that existed during the recording should occur. Only original recordings can be authenticated, however, some tests for authenticity can be carried out on good copies of original tape recordings.

After examining the two tape recordings, I found them to be physically unremarkable. As to the recordings on the tapes themselves, I made three major findings which relate to the question of authenticity of the tape recordings. The first finding is that the interview of Robert Hooks, Jr. as transcribed was actually taken from two tape recordings and not one. The first recording of part of the interview appears near the end of the first tape and lasts about 4 minutes and 20 seconds. The second recording of the interview begins about two-thirds into the second tape and lasts about 5 minutes and 23 seconds. The Hooks interview is followed by an interview of John Barker. In any case, there appear to be two Hooks interviews and it is not possible to determine what is said or not said between them.

Second, I found nearly four dozen instances where modification or tampering could have occurred on the two tapes. Most of these could be identified as innocuous noises, but I was not able to account for two clicks on the first tape or a sharp drop in ambient noise on the second tape.

Harry Hollien, Senior Consultant to Forensic Communication Associates, page 3.

Third, I found that the tape recorder was turned off and then on again on the first tape at counter position 057. This on-off activity indicates a period when the interview was not recorded. Moreover, certain words can be heard on the tape that are not on the transcript. A break of this type indicates that the integrity of the recording has been compromised.

My conclusion is that the fact that the Hooks interview is on two tapes where the recording was turned off and on suggests that the tape recording in question - and hence the interview cannot be authenticated. Morever, it is difficult to assume even that the tape recordings sent to me were originals. I have not previously encountered original tape recordings of this nature where different parts of an interview appear on different parts of two otherwise blank or erased tapes. Because of my findings, I am unable to validate or verify the authenticity of the tape recordings which I received from Wallace Miller, Jr. on behalf of Plaintiffs in the above case.

Further affiant sayeth not.

Harry Hollien PhD
Harry Hollien, Ph.D., Senior Consultant
Forensic Communication Associates

Sworn to and subscribed
before me this 30 day
of October, 1985.

Katherine M. Harley
(Please imprint notary stamp and seal.)
Notary Public, State of Florida
My Commission Expires Sept. 2, 1938
Bonded Thru Troy Fain - Insurance, Inc.

Harry Hollien, Senior Consultant to Forensic Communication Associates, page 4.

August 22, 1980

Mrs. Eloise Gordy
Route 3, Box 78
Sandersville, Georgia 31082

To Whom It May Concern:

This is a note informing you of some facts that I recall while living on the Jeff Carter estate. I can recall hearing my mother, Mrs. Lora Ella Carter Dawson, on several occasions talk about a debt on the family property owed to Ben Tarbutton, Sr. There was an approximate $500.00 debt for mortgage owed to a woman named Annie Bell Hatch. She, for some apparent r reason, could no longer carry this debt. The family of course, couldn't pay it all off. The bill was transferred to Ben Tarbutton, Sr.

The bill was to be paid through the crops raised each year. Cotton was turned over to Mr. Tarbutton every year at harvest. This was presumably paying off the $500.00 debt. But Mr. Tarbutton would never give anyone a receipt. They would ask for receipts but Tarbutton always had excuses. Lied is what he did every time. He would tell them his secretary was not in or come back next week. This went on continously. Mrs. Lora Ella Carter Dawson, one of the heirs, had tried to reason with Tarbutton but he only put her off time and time again.

Letter from Carter Heir, Eloise Dawson Gordy, August 22, 1980, pg. 1

Trips into town were very expensive for Blacks back in the 1940's. Each time they were rejected. Seeing that Tarbutton was trying to steal the land, the family, primarily, the women, hired a lawyer only to have him bought off by Tarbutton. The women tried to settle the matter, but what women could do in the 40's was limited. Black women could not demand receipts. They could only ~~ask for receipts.~~ Getting to town was a problem in itself. It took almost all they had for travel alone.

They then figured it out that Tarbutton, Sr., was maneuvering to take the land. Because year end and year out with the turning over of crops to Tarbutton didn't change the situations. There were five families living on the farm. Each family's crop was going toward the debt on the property. At least that's what they thought. Tarbutton was taking the crops for rent and had really taken the property. My mother then informed my aunt Lillie about the situation. Aunt Lillie made several trips from Philadelphia to try to straighten out the situation. She and my mother would go to Tarbutton's office only to have him make excuses time after time. He didn!t even want to talk to them. He would lie and say that his secretary wasn't in or have his secretary to say that he wasn't in. The family got up money for lawyers only to have them bought off by Tarbutton. Every lawyer the family got was paid off by Tarbutton.

Letter from Carter Heir, Eloise Dawson Gordy, August 22, 1980, pg. 2

Finally, my mother and Aunt Lillie went back to Tarbutton and told him that their land was all they wanted. Tarbutton then came up with a monstrous figuto of $3000.00 and told them that if they could pay $3000.00 they could have their land back. Through some negotiating with M. C. Smith, a local mortician, the money was raised. When they went to Tarbutton to pay the money, he would not accept it---saying that it had to be paid through the farm resources. He had thought that a Black family couldn't raise this kind of money. He resented them more because they raised the money. He resented Aunt Lillie even more because she lived in the North and was in a position to get money. This really crushed my mother and Aunt Lillie. They had worked so hard and sacrificed so much for lawyer fees.

They still looked for a lawyer that Tarbutton wouldn't but off. That was impossible in the 40's. Then in 1950, Tarbutton had the sheriff of Washington County, A. W. Smith, brutally attack my mother, Lora Dawson, and put her household belongings out in the public road and pad locked the door. This inhumane treatment really affected my mother. She was never the same after this. Her land, her home, everything she had and loved had been taked. All of these terrible things that happened caused my mom to have a nervous breakdown. She and Aunt Lillie both died from mental stress because what they loved most was taken from them illegally---their land.

Letter from Carter Heir, Eloise Dawson Gordy, August 22, 1980, pg. 3

I remember an incident that hppened on the place.. One of the tenants had a well for water (as did all the rest of us) asked Mr. Tarbutton to put him a pump for water. This was a manual type. I think it cost approximately $200.00 or $300.00. My mother being the only heir living on the place at the time asked Mr. Tarbutton not to place a pump because they were already struggling to pay him off.. However, he went on and installed the pump. This was another way to burden us---since our only resources was what we made on the farm. There were no other jobs to be had if you were black and lived in the South.

Sincerely,

Eloise Gordy

(Mrs.) Eloise Gordy

Letter from Carter Heir, Eloise Dawson Gordy, August 22, 1980, pg. 4

To wnom it may concern:

Re : Jeff Carter's Place
Sub: Crawford Carter and payment of debt to Mr, Tarbutton

In 1936 I went to Mr. Tarbutton's office and asked to speak to him a young man asked wno are you and what is the nature of your business? I told him that I was Jeff Carters' son and I had come from Philadelphia to talk to Mr. Tarbutton and to make arrangements to pay of the debt on my fathers's place.

He said can't Vergie take care of it here? I told him that I was Jeff Carter's son too and I have a good job in Philadelphia and could borrow the money as soon as I make arrangements with Mr. Tarbutton. He then said Mr. Tarbutton isn't in. As I was leaving the office some one told me the man I was talking to was Mr. Tarbutton's son.

I went a second time and I could tell by the way the people in the office were acting Mr. Tarbutton did not want to talk to me. I went back the third time I knew he was in the office even though he would not talk to me.

I left the next day for Philadelphia and was told when I arrived my brother Vergie had died under mysterious circumstances. My brother Rodell was not a responsible person .

My father told me that Mr. Tarbutton wanted to buy back the land he sold him but my Dad did not want to sell. He always paid his bills when due and would put the rest of his money away. My father did not beleive in borrowing.

Robert Hooks Sr. and my father were never on friendly terms and I believe this is why Robert Hooks Jr. bought and sold the place to Mr. Tarbutton without our knowledge.

Mr father averaged (18) ba;es of cotton a season (9 or 10) bales of his own and (8 or 9) bales from the sharecroppers. After the cotton was baled it was stored until there was a scarity and would they sell it at a higher price. When my father died the Carter heirs continued to turn over bales of cotton to Mr. Tarbutton as payment of debt. He woud not give them a receipt.

Name Crawford Carter

Relationship Son

Sworn to and Subscribed:
Before me this 4th day:
of September A.D. 1980;
Virginia M. Kline

VIRGINIA M. KLINE
Notary Public Phila., Phila. Co.
My Commission Expires Oct. 23, 1983

Letter from Carter Heir, Crawford Carter, September 4, 1980

To whom it may concern

Re: Jef Carter's Place
Sub: Lillie Ruth Carter Turner
payment of debt to Mr. Tarbutton

When my mother Lillie Ruth Carter Turner went to Sandersville Georgia in 1947 there abouts to pay Mr. Tarbutton for debt on her fathers place she had over ($ 300.00) three hundred dollars brorrowed from the Lyons Finance Co. and co-signed by Blanche and Dabney Holley..and three hundred and fifty dollars her brother Crawford Carter had given her.

My mother told us she went to see Mr Tarbutton he took the money and refused to give her a receipt. He told her she came down there to stir up trouble. She told him she came only to give the money she thought was due him.

When she came back to Philadelphia she was so upset she couldnot re-strain her self from tears at the humilation and fear tactics she ex-perienced when she told us what had happened.

Relationships to Jeff Carter

Name Crawford Carter

Relationship Son

Name Blanche Holley

Relationship daughter (grand)

Name Dabney P. Holley

Relationship Grandson in law

Sworn to and Subscribed:
Before me this 4th day:
September A.D. 1980:
Virginia M. Kline

... M. KLINE
Not... Phila. Co.
My Commission Expires Oct. 23, 1983

Letter from Carter Heirs, Crawford Carter and Blanche Holley, September 4, 1980, pg. 1

page 2

Re: Jeff Carter's Place
Sub :Lillie Ruth Carter Turner paymen
of debt to Mr: Tarbutton

Many times my mother went to Sandersville Ga. to negoiate payment of the debt on the Jeff Carter's Place, paid fees to lawyers whom she felt had betrayed her,

" Uncle Robert" Uncle Robert" were the words my mother uttered day and night.Fite months my mother was hospitalized in 79, broken in sprit, and drained mentally ,cried day and night calling the name "Uncle Robert" "unc Robert" The nurses and the other attendents asked who is uncle Robert? He Her uncle whose son some how manage to gain control of her father's estate without the knowledge of the heirs.

My mother passed in March of 1980 and until she lost consciousness Called " Uncle Robert" Uncle Robert".

Relationships to Jeff Carter Grandchildren

Name Blanche Holley

Relationship daughter (grand.)

Name Mildred Moore

Relationship Grand-daughter

Name O'Neal Turner

Relationship Grandson

Sworn to and Subscribed:
Before me this 4th day:
September A.D. 1980:
Virginia M. Kline

VIRGINIA M. KLINE
Notary Public, Phila., Phila. Co.
My Commission Expires Oct. 23, 1983

Letter from Carter Heirs, Crawford Carter and Blanche Holley, September 4, 1980, pg. 2

To whom it may connern

Re: Jeff Carter's Place

Sub: Payment of debt to Mr. Tarbutton

My fatner Jeff Carter Jr. turned over for payment of debt bales of cotton every harvest season to Mr. Tarbutton. He would not give him a receipt.

When my father died in 1939 my mother Gevernia Fisher Carter continued to turn over bales of cotton every harvest season to Mr. Tarbutton for payment of debt qwed on the Jeff Carter's Place

Name Ruby C Nelson Carter

Relationship Grand daughter of Jeff Carter

Sworn to and subscribed before me this 19 day of Sept 80

William Perloff

WILLIAM PERLOFF
Notary Public, Phila., Phila. Co.
My Commission Expires Jan. 30, 1982

Letter from Carter Heir, Ruby Carter Nelson, September 1980

To whom it may concrrn:

Re: Jeff Carters Place
Sub: Mary Carter Young payment of debt
to Mr. Tarbutton

The heirs agreed to turn over crops during the harvest seasons
to Mr. Tarbutton as payment of debt on the Jeff Carters' Place.

I remember my father Charlie Young turned over bales of cotton during the harvest seasons to Mr. Tarbutton as payment of the debt on the Jeff Carters' Place. He never gave my father a receipt for none of the crops turned over to him

Name Lillie Glenn

Relationship Daughter

Name Corene Harris

Relationship Daugter

" to Jeff Carter grand daughters

Sworn to and subscribed before me
this 4th day of Sept 1980

Leslie Edith Francis
LESLIE EDITH FRANCIS
Notary Public, Phila., Phila. Co.
My Commission Expires Sept. 27, 1982

Letter from Carter Heir, Corene Young Harris, September 4, 1980

CHAPTER II

The Kaolin Cartel

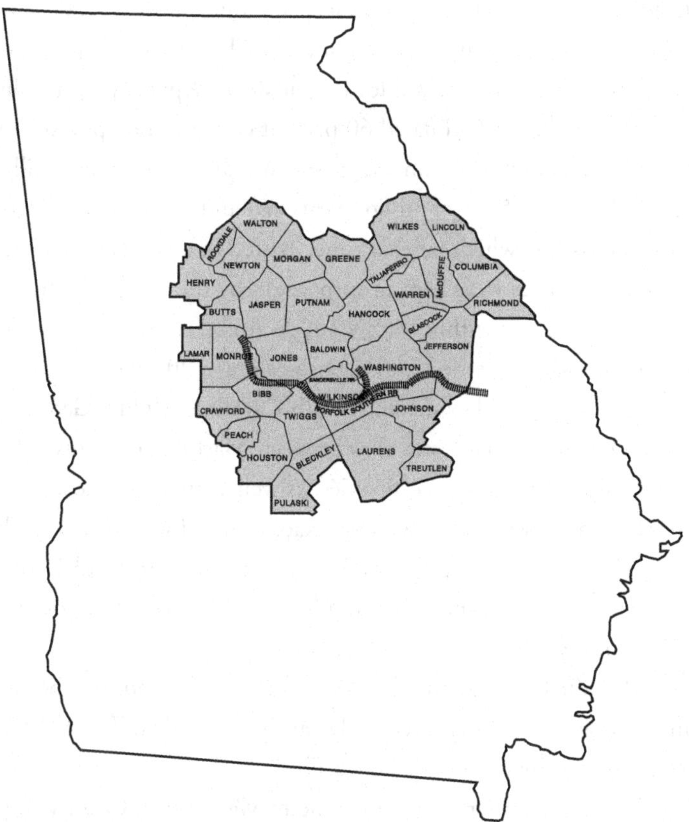

The Kaolin Belt

Because kaolin is not a household term, few people know much about its history or its impact on modern-day industry. To fully appreciate what was taken from the Carter family (in terms of mineral worth beyond land values), some knowledge of the subject, and who the principal players are, is essential.

On May 29, 1874, there was a small news article about kaolin in the *Sandersville Herald* that described the mineral as having "multitudinous uses...hundreds of hogheads of the white earth are annually sent from the kaolin works in South

Carolina". The article went on to list uses for kaolin including notepaper, Northern-Manufactured candy, powdered loafsugar, and Northern flour. The effect kaolin would have on the country's future was unimaginable at this time.

Kaolin, a white chalk often referred to as 'white gold', is vital for making hundreds of products including china, toothpaste, rubber, ceramics, soaps, medicines, porcelain, fire brick, adhesives, cosmetics, paint, kaopectate, mineral wool, and as both filler and finish in the paper industry. It was first mined in China, where it was named, and then in England where it was prized for its brilliance by pottery firms. Nine Middle Georgia counties harbor an estimated 60 percent of the world's purest kaolin reserves.

Geologists conclude that kaolin was originally formed in the foothills of the Appalachian Mountains 50-100 million years ago and was carried down-river until it met the ocean coastline which, at that time, existed in a line across Middle Georgia.

Small kaolin particles were kept in suspension by the energy developed within the steam system. The energy within the system decreased, rivers and streams flowed into lakes and lagoons. Kaolin settled into deposits along a 20-mile-wide belt through Middle Georgia and into Alabama and South Carolina. Middle Georgia's "kaolin belt", as it has become known, stretches between Macon and Augusta. Several of Georgia's biggest kaolin mining companies, as well as many of those under foreign-control, excavate a billion dollars worth of kaolin out of Georgia annually.

In the 1920s, enormous deposits of kaolin were found in Sandersville, Georgia. The influence of the kaolin industry would soon effect every facet of life in Washington County.

After World War II, the kaolin mining and processing industry began to grow rapidly in Washington County, eventually earning the title of "Kaolin Capital of the World" shipping products around the world.

Among the earliest mineralogists to come to Washington County to prospect for chalk was L.U. Campbell, a native of Scranton, Pennsylvania, who brought his family from South Carolina. In 1922, L.U. Campbell took an option on 523 acres of Mack Tucker's land. In 1925, Campbell advised American Standard Clay Company to purchase part of the Tucker farm where they eventually dug a test pit.

The first clays mined in Washington County were hauled by mule and wagon, unprocessed, to be loaded onto rail cars in Tennille and moved to Dry Branch, below Macon, to be analyzed and refined.

In 1927, Edgar Brothers began processing clay after they purchased R.J. Wood's property (known as the Old Irwin Place). They constructed a processing plant in Oconee, built a "blunger" (a heavy container with rotating metal arms which crush lump clay, mix it with water, and form a suspension which can then be pumped), at the Wood mine and pumped the washed clay by pipeline to the Oconee facility. It became the county's first clay refinery. Later, it was purchased by Minerals and Chemicals Corporation, and eventually by Englehard Corporation.

In 1928, a firm called Southern Clays acquired property from E. Pierce Wood. Later, they began mining operations, pumping their clays to Gordon, Georgia, for processing.

Sandersville's first kaolin refinery was built and owned by Champion Paper and Fiber Co., one of the world's leading producers of paper goods.

In 1945, Malcolm S. Burgess leased several mineral properties, obtained a plant site, and began operations as Burgess Washington Clays, Ltd., producing water-washed coating and filler clays primarily for the paper industry. In 1946, he sold the mineral rights and leased the plant to Thiele Kaolin Company. Two years later, Burgess began a calcining business under the name of Burgess Pigment Company, producing calcined kaolin for paint, paper, rubber, and plastics. Owen Etheridge, served as vice president of Burgess and later worked as an official at Thiele. Elmo Beck became the first manager in 1948. Malcolm Burgess, Jr. succeeded his father as president.

In May 1946, Bill Kingman began a washed filler operation that he eventually sold to the Cabet Company of Boston. In 1956, they sold the company to the American subsidiary of the largest kaolin company in the world, English China Clays (ECC).

To illustrate the economic importance of this enterprise to its parent company, Princess Anne of Great Britain visited their plant in 1984. Anglo-American, which began with 23 employees, is a wholly-owned subsidiary of ECC America, Inc (ECCA), which is a wholly-owned subsidiary of English China Clays. Anglo-American Clays Corporation produces the finer grades of water-washed clays and calcined clays, primarily for the paper industry, all over the world.

Ed Grassman owned several clay-related companies, amongst the many business' he owned, including: Georgia Kaolin Company, American Industrial Clays and Yara Engineering. Grassman originally planned to build a plant in the Buffalo Creek basin on American Industrial Clay property, and run a railroad from there, down Buffalo Creek and the Oconee River to Oconee, where it would connect with the Central of Georgia Railroad.

Over the years, Grassman had several conferences with B.J. Tarbutton, owner of the Sandersville Railroad, and eventually agreed that Georgia Kaolin Company would build a pipeline from its mine, to the plateau where they built a plant. Tarbutton built a railroad from Sandersville to the plant on Deepstep Road between Sandersville and Deepstep. In 1958 they shipped the first car of kaolin from the new plant. Kaolin from different properties is pumped and blunged to this plant for processing.

Georgia Kaolin became one of the largest companies of its kind, producing products for ceramics, sanitary ware, paint, adhesives, and today primarily for the paper industries. These operations were sold to and operated by Combustion Engineering after Grassman's death.

Englehard Corporation led in the development of high brightness clays, and a process for calcining clays to make the opacity suitable for the paper industry. They operated a processing plant in Oconee, which was founded by Edgar Brothers. Around 1970, Freeport Kaolin Company (formerly Southern Clays) began mining properties in the area. The company mined, blunged, and cleaned the clay in Oconee, and pumped it to the plant in Gordon, Georgia. This lasted for a few years before being purchased by Englehard.

In 1939, United Clay Mines purchased property on what is now Kaolin Road in Sandersville. They built an air float plant and produced clay primarily for the ceramic trade, and fillers for other trades. A slurrying operation and spray dryer were added, and a large operation was built several miles west of Sandersville on Deepstep Road. In 1963, the unit operated under the name Cyprus Industrial Minerals Company until it was purchased by Heckla Mining Company in 1989.

In 1938, Champion Paper and Fiber built the first air float plant in Sandersville. The same year, Champion purchased a plant site on what is now Kaolin Road. They produced air float filler clays for it's own mills. In the late 1980s, it was sold to Combustion Engineering, and was operated as Sandersville Clay Company, owned by Georgia Kaolin.

In his 1985 book, *Kaolin: A Glacier's Gift to Georgia*, Malcolm S. Burgess, Sr. gave his account of the growth of the kaolin industry. "After starting Burgess-Washington Clays, Ltd., in early 1945, I also took charge of the sales of Burgess-Washington Clays, Ltd. Not having experience in the sale of kaolin I realized, after a while, that it would be worthwhile if we could get a large coated paper company to lease our mines and plant".

W.F. Thiele, chief engineer with a company in Wisconsin Rapids, Wisconsin, showed an interest in Burgess' inquiries. On October 28, 1946, Burgess-Washington

Clays, Ltd. was leased to W.F. Thiele and Associates. W.F. Thiele's son, Paul Thiele, was named manager. The Thieles consummated the deal with Burgess in a long-term contract, with plans to build a pipeline from the mine deposits.

Paul Thiele moved to Washington County to oversee the operation, which became known as Thiele Kaolin Company. In 1970, the company opened a water-wash facility at Reedy Creek, in Jefferson County, Georgia. From this facility, they delivered kaolin to customers in a variety of forms: bagged, bulk or slurry, shipped by truck or railcar to domestic markets, or to ocean ports for shipment overseas.

With the growth of the kaolin industry, came the growth of such trucking companies as Howard Sheppard, Inc., B-H Transfer Company, C.T. Harris, Inc. and Mike McCoy Hauling, Inc., and of service providers such as W.F. Jackson Construction Company.

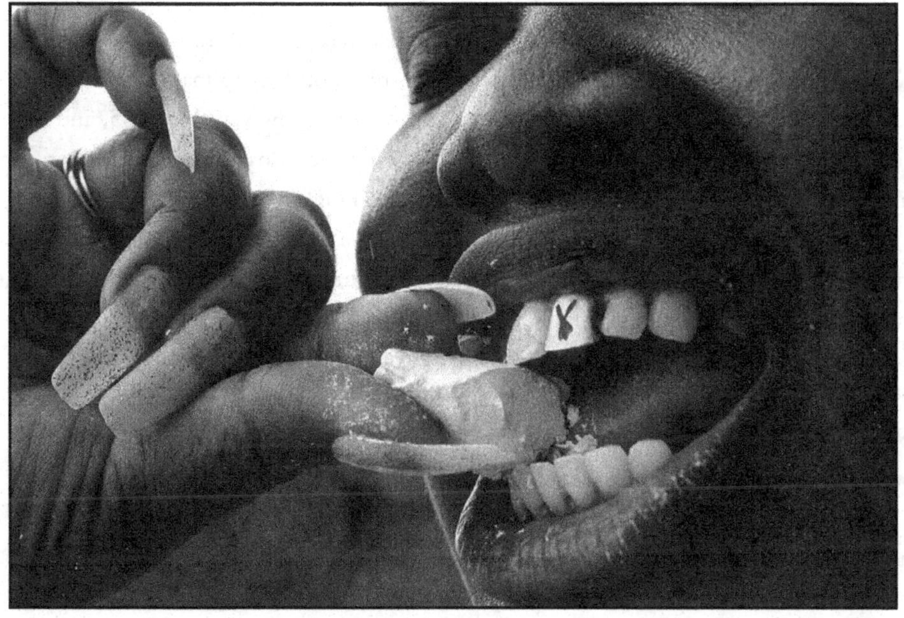

In 1987, Norfolk Southern Railroad reportedly moved 84,873 carloads of kaolin to the Midwest and New England, and to ports of Savannah, where operations were built, and to Charleston for export to South America, Western Europe, the Far East, and several "Third World" countries. Kaolin has been the leading export from Georgia for many years.

Norfolk Southern and the Sandersville Railroad (owned by the Tarbuttons) serve the companies. The latter served the six processing companies on 25 miles of track.

While kaolin also comes from mines in Africa, England, Brazil, China, Australia, and several other countries, some of the world's purest deposits are in Georgia.

The kaolin industry has continuously grown, largely due to the paper industry and the worldwide demand for glossy magazines, catalogues, and other printed material. Thirty percent (30%) of the weight of glossy paper publications such as *National Geographic* is kaolin, very likely, Georgia kaolin.

Its uses, however, do not stop with paper. The paint industry, the second largest user, relies on dry-processed kaolin particles as filler in white cement. It is also used as a catalyst by the petroleum industry. With such a huge demand for kaolin, it is little wonder that the product is valued so highly.

B.J. Tarbutton

Benjamin Tarbutton married Winifred Thigpen in 1823. Both moved to Washington County, Georgia with their families from South Carolina and North Carolina respectively. Benjamin James, their son, was born on May 14, 1885, and was one of twelve children they produced. In 1928, he married Rosa Moore McMaster and later gave birth to sons Benjamin James, Jr. and Hugh McMaster Tarbutton.

As noted earlier, the Tarbutton family has operated as one of Washington County's major political and economical forces for nearly a century. In 1916, the owners of the railroad connecting Sandersville to Tennille, which had fallen on hard times, offered Ben James Tarbutton the option to buy the line if he could operate it successfully. In 1922, B.J. Tarbutton became the new owner and president of the struggling Sandersville Railroad. As planned, the railroad became the vehicle by which Washington County would become the center of the kaolin industry and Tarbutton a powerful force.

With Tarbutton's acquisition of the Sandersville Railroad, he encouraged clay, paper, and paint companies to locate in Middle Georgia. He offered to lay a track from their companies to his railroad, facilitating their kaolin operation. Between the 1930s and 1960s, demand for kaolin nearly quadrupled. Because of Tarbutton's close friendship with Clark Merion of Champion Papers, the company became the first clay plant to locate in Washington County. Tarbutton was also instrumental in bringing Cypress, Burgess, Thiele, and Anglo-American Industrial Clay plants to Washington County. He was referred to as a pioneer in establishing the kaolin industry in Georgia.

Kaolin express: Tank and box cars filled with kaolin snake along the Sandersville Railroad toward the 10-mile line's terminus in Tennille. The railroad, owned by brothers Ben and Hugh Tarbutton, hauls 20,000 tons of kaolin a day.

B.J. Tarbutton opened a wholesale grocery company in 1932, and in October of 1945, Tarbutton Motor Co. displayed a new Ford automobile. There were two cotton warehouses in Sandersville in the 1950s. One owned by the Gilmores and the other by the Tarbuttons. B.J. also owned the Savannah Hotel, sawmills, and numerous farms. He also speculated in the purchase and "acquisition" of land that was suspected and or known to have large kaolin deposits.

B.J. maintained political prestige during this time as well. He acted as mayor of Sandersville (1947-51), a Georgia senator (1947-48), a member of the Georgia House of Representatives (1949-54), and a delegate to the National Democratic Convention (1952,1956). He was also a member of the Jekyll Island Authority, chair of the Washington County Welfare Board, a director of the Savannah and Georgia Chambers of Commerce, and director of the state's biggest bank, Citizens and Southern National Bank. He was a member of the committee that founded Epworth-by-the-Sea, the American Shortline Railroad Association, and the Gulf Life Insurance Company. He was president of Central of Georgia Railway Company (1951-54), the Central of Georgia Motor Transport Company, and the Ocean Steamship Company of Savannah.

The City of Sandersville, the Sandersville Lions and Rotary Clubs, the Tennille Rotary Club, and the Davisboro Chamber of Commerce, declared "Ben J. Tarbutton Day", on March 23, 1951. That evening, a banquet further honored the man they felt had "done more for industrial development in Washington County than any other person".

Some older residents of Sandersville remember him as genial and approachable. Others say he was a "harsh, tyrannical, arrogant racist". This view of him was perhaps strengthened when B.J. brought his friend Governor Eugene Talmadge - the old race baiter, staunch segregationist, and Klan sympathizer - to the grand opening of a kaolin plant. Tarbutton was later a strong supporter of Gene's white supremacist son, Herman, who also was a Georgia governor and senator.

Ben James Tarbutton, Jr., was born in Sandersville March 20, 1930. He married Nancy Rankin in 1964, and the two later had three children. In 1962, B.J. Tarbutton, Jr. became president of the Sandersville Railroad Company. He participated in many of the same political and social organizations as his father. In 1992, he and his brother, Hugh, were the second largest shareholders of Citizens & Southern National Bank, which later became NationsBank.

The Industry

Several conspiracies have been revealed about the kaolin industry. By exercising unethical business practices such as obtaining fraudulent mining contracts, holding excessive reserves out of market, fixing prices and defrauding landowners out of their kaolin rich land, these companies have formed a multi-hundred-billion dollar cartel.

Six companies maintain a pattern of fraud that preserves the industry and maintains its control of the world's principal kaolin deposits. The kaolin cartel shrouds itself in secrecy and few Georgians, or anyone else, know the true value of kaolin.

The Georgia Department of Natural Resources (DNR) and its officials have worked hand-in-hand with kaolin cartel companies to help them accumulate massive reserves. For example, companies may claim to have 100 million tons of kaolin or 50-100 years worth of kaolin, in reserves. They have created a monopoly by grossly understating their true reserve figures.

Deafening silence on kaolin tax

U.S. probes kaolin firms in Georgia

KAOLIN:
Georgia's Lost Inheritance

Kaolin companies pay no severance taxes in Georgia and leave behind deeply scarred land.

State undervalues its kaolin

Bring in the feds to probe kaolin

Mine tax could net millions for state
Kaolin industry opposes the idea

Unlike most states, Georgia has no tax on minerals, and kaolin land is often undervalued for local property taxes

Legislators to probe clay-mine industry

Legislators to study need for mining tax
Kaolin issue prompts House panel probe

During an extensive examination of Georgia's leading mining industry, Journal-Constitution reporters examined tax records, mining permits filed with the state since 1969 and more than 1,000 mineral leases filed since the turn of the century in the seven primary counties of Georgia's kaolin belt.

GOPAC's "charter members," those giving at least $10,000 annually, also include the heads of two companies under federal investigation – Flowers Industries Inc. and Thiele Kaolin Co., both of Georgia.

The companies acquired most of their kaolin reserves through mineral leases. Landowners were enticed into signing leases, knowing nothing about drill reports or the true value of kaolin. Just as misleading, the landowners were convinced they would receive a fair mining royalty and that they would be paid in a reasonable amount of time. The cartel operates by inducing landowners to sign a contract to mine (lease) minerals they have no intention of mining under said contract.

Upon realizing there was a 99 year lease on their minerals and no plan of mining, many white landowners opted to sell their land to yield some profit. Mineral leases are an illegal restraint of trade. These contracts form a vast pool of reserves held captive by these companies.

The bulk of monies generated by this cornering of minerals are not produced by mining them, but by not mining them, and preventing others from mining them as well. The essence of a mineral cartel is absolute, cultivated secrecy about its reserves.

The kaolin industry conspires to fix prices and uses fraud and trickery to either seize land from its rightful owner, or prevents the landowners from receiving a fair price for the valuable white chalk on their land.

The cartel persuades courts, politicians, and other influential persons, of the important economic contribution of the kaolin mining industry to Georgia. In truth, the communities where the greatest mass of these minerals lay are undeveloped and impoverished.

The economic "contribution" to Georgia from minerals actually mined is so tiny as to be economically insignificant. The 4,000 minimum wage jobs that the cartel claims to have provided in Middle Georgia count for nothing. They are used as the excuse for holding those same wage-earners' millions of dollars worth of minerals out of the market, as the Georgia Supreme Court did in the case of *Higgenbottom.*

The money generated both by mining and not-mining the reserves, which include other minerals in addition to kaolin, leaves the U.S. by train, ship; monetarily (by international bank), and where it stays in Georgia, it does so only to attract the interest of influential political bodies. The National Association of Kaolin Landowners' (NAKLo.) investigations revealed that of the nearly $1 billion of mineral wealth extracted yearly from Georgia by mining companies, very little of the money finds its way back into the poor, rural communities from which it is mined.

Minerals held out of the market to control competition are intrinsically valuable because they are not-mined, creating a monopoly of the world's significant kaolin reserves. Fraud is the only way a company could get 2 or 3 billion tons of any mineral. By deceiving landowners about the quality, quantity, and value of minerals on a property, next to nothing is paid for the kaolin.

Kaolin: Industry dominates life in mining counties

Mining companies dig a billion dollars' worth of white clay a year in Georgia. Precious little of the money winds up in Georgians' hands.

Life in kaolin country

Half or more of the world's kaolin is mined in Middle Georgia. Though production of the white clay is worth more than a billion dollars a year, little of the wealth remains in the seven counties that form the heart of kaolin country.

It's poorer than the rest of Georgia

Georgia's No. 1 export

Crowning Miss Kaolin in the 'Kaolin Capital of the World'

WHITE GOLD

Companies 'aren't paying one red cent'

Kaolin companies are target of U.S. anti-trust probe

The kaolin mining companies operating in Georgia are largely foreign-owned and do little value-added processing here in Georgia. The raw material, and the immense wealth and jobs it creates, is shipped out of state, and in most cases overseas.

The state's richest mineral

Six firms dominate kaolin production

Farmers had no way to find out what the clay was really worth

Georgia has one inspector for a billion-dollar industry

Ga. landowners in fight against kaolin industry

Big Georgia kaolin fortunes not going to the landowners

Most mines are foreign-controlled

How a $40,000 farm became $1.4 million worth of white clay

'White gold' turns to dust

Kaolin mining firms proud of track record

The owners are far overseas, and the prices are kept private

Second mistrial declared in suit against kaolin firm

'If those . . . aren't good, no contracts are

To know whether there is chalk on one's land and how much, drilling must be done. It has been nearly impossible for landowners to get drill and testing reports from kaolin companies. The inflated cost of having these reports done independently makes it an economically unfeasible alternative.

Drill reports show the depth and thickness of kaolin and the amount of the mineral in the ground. Companies analyze the chalk for its endowments, such as brightness and viscosity. The price fixed for kaolin is less than the average royalty paid for sand or dirt, which has made the latter more valuable to a kaolin landowner.

Another facet of the cartel's operations is the fraudulent pattern of acts the kaolin companies employ to keep their network from being interrupted by lawsuits or investigation by the Justice Department. This racketeering includes solicitation of poor Black landowners, by lawyers and agents with kaolin interests.

Large amounts of other minerals exist in kaolin, specifically titanium dioxide. Kaolin companies call titanium dioxide (TiO_2) a "contaminant" removed from kaolin in processing. Titanium dioxide is stockpiled or is sold to buyers, principally in Europe, to manipulate the titanium dioxide market, and increase the price of calcined kaolin (which is a substitute for TiO_2 and sells for at least $500 per ton). The alleged "world shortage" of titanium dioxide creates a market where it can sell for upwards of $2,000 per ton.

England's historical exploitation of Africa has existed for over 500 years, with the pillaging and rape of the continent and its people, and the subsequent enslavement of those captives around the world. Even in the 21st century, European and American institutions and corporations continue to profit from the savage exploitation of Africans and their continent, as well as their descendants throughout the Americas and the Caribbean. As in centuries past, the same tactics of intimidation and brute force are used on Black people, who helplessly battle for control of their own land and mineral wealth. Georgia's kaolin cartel is in fact closely connected to, and in some cases dominated by English interests.

Ernest Oppenheimer founded the corporate empire Anglo American Corp. of South Africa, in 1917. The Oppenheimers monopolize the gold, chemicals, steel, clays, banks, platinum, cars, and insurance on six continents, as well as DeBeers Consolidated Mines Ltd., which controls most of the world's diamond trade. This operation is run from a huge mirror-plated, lopsided pyramid that looks like a diamond, in downtown Johannesburg, South Africa. They own 40% of Minerals and Resources Corp. (Minorco), which owns 33% of Engelhard Corp., one of Georgia's biggest kaolin mining companies. In fact, South Africa's apartheid system was significantly fueled by the tremendous political power and economic influence of the Oppenheimers' Anglo American. Market analysts say Anglo American's interest allows it to control Engelhard.

According to David Pallister, London investigative journalist and co-author of the 1988 book *South Africa Inc.: The Oppenheimer Empire,* the Oppenheimers and their corporate image may have presented a face to the world as South Africa's leading white opponents of apartheid. However, the mines on which their wealth rests once provided the economic impetus for some of South Africa's most vicious legislation: the Pass Laws, the Group Areas Act, and the migrant labor system under which thousands of Black men lived like peons in compounds away from their families. With control of Engelhard, the Oppenheimer's, and other such foreign interests, reap the wealth generated by the un-mined kaolin reserves in Georgia, while the Black landowners remain impoverished. With the aid and cooperation of the state's political organs and officers (including courts and attorneys to whom distressed landowners might appeal), these foreign interests can successfully control the state of Georgia's mineral wealth.

The Coup

The Tarbutton's lawyers, Alston & Bird, are one of Atlanta's most prominent law firms and represented many kaolin industry interests, as well as the Sandersville Railroad, and NationsBank. Franklin R. Nix was a partner at the firm and known as an authority on the kaolin industry, real estate, forgery, inheritance, fraud, bankruptcy, securities and the like.

By the early 1980s, a young Black man, Robert Lee Watkins, was already affiliated with a number of kaolin companies. Watkins went into partnership with Frank Nix and Alston & Bird purportedly to help Black landowners seek redress for claims against kaolin companies.

Although communications between the Carter heirs, Kay Young, Katrina Breeding, and the Emergency Land Fund suddenly stopped in 1981, the curtain had been lifted on a multi-billion dollar swindle. Therefore, Robert Lee, as an agent for Tarbutton attorney Nix, solicited the Carter heirs in 1983. For 40 years prior to this time, no attorney dared to take this Black family's case against a white family as powerful as the Tarbuttons; but Mr. Watkins assured the Carters they would "have their day in court" with "representation" by one of Atlanta's most prominent law firms.

The Tarbutton's lawyers, Alston & Bird and Nix could not legally file a lawsuit against their own client in favor of the Carters, as they well knew. The litigation in this case was precipitated by Watkins filing for record, in the Clerk's Office of the Washington County Superior Court, two (2) affidavits unaccompanied by a lawsuit, "in behalf" of the Carter heirs: one dated December 1983, filed on January 25, 1984, and the second dated February 3, 1984. The second affidavit had attached thereto a 190 page sworn statement of Robert Hooks, Jr., which was conducted by Nix and Watkins on January 11, 1984.

Under Nix's instruction, these two (2) affidavits (that were not a part of any lawsuit and were not privileged information in the courthouse), accused the Tarbutton family of fraud and forgery. This instrument allowed the Tarbuttons to sue the Carter family for slander and defamation. The filing of these documents by Frank Nix and Watkins (acting as attorney in fact for the Carter heirs), allowed Loulie Tarbutton to sue the heirs in April 1984. It was at this time that the Carter heirs first became aware that their cousin, Robert Hooks, Jr., neither the administrator nor an heir, allegedly "sold" their land to B.J. Tarbutton, Sr. for the equivalent of $1.85 per acre for at least 803 acres of land.

Subsequently, Loulie Tarbutton amended her complaint. She added as exhibits a fraudulent plat of the property (which did not include a scale or contain the boundaries which should illustrate the 803 acres Jeff Carter owned), photocopies of the nine recorded deeds constituting her "chain of title", as well as the Georgia Kaolin mineral lease. The "surveyed plat" only shows 585 acres to fit her claim, and not the 803 acres of unprobated and Jeff Carter owned when he died.

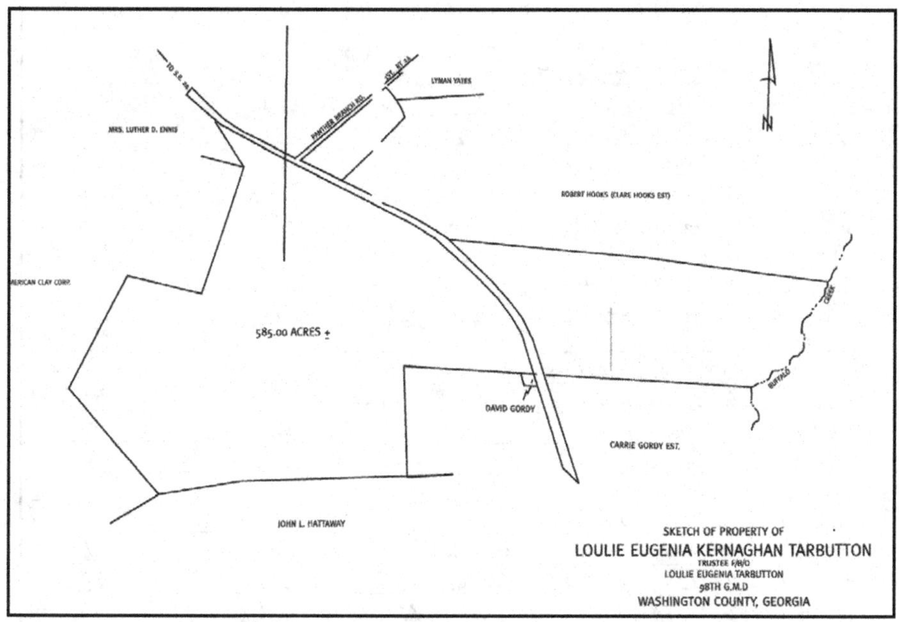

Fraudulent plat of Jeff Carter's Estate, submitted by plaintiff Loulie Tarbutton.

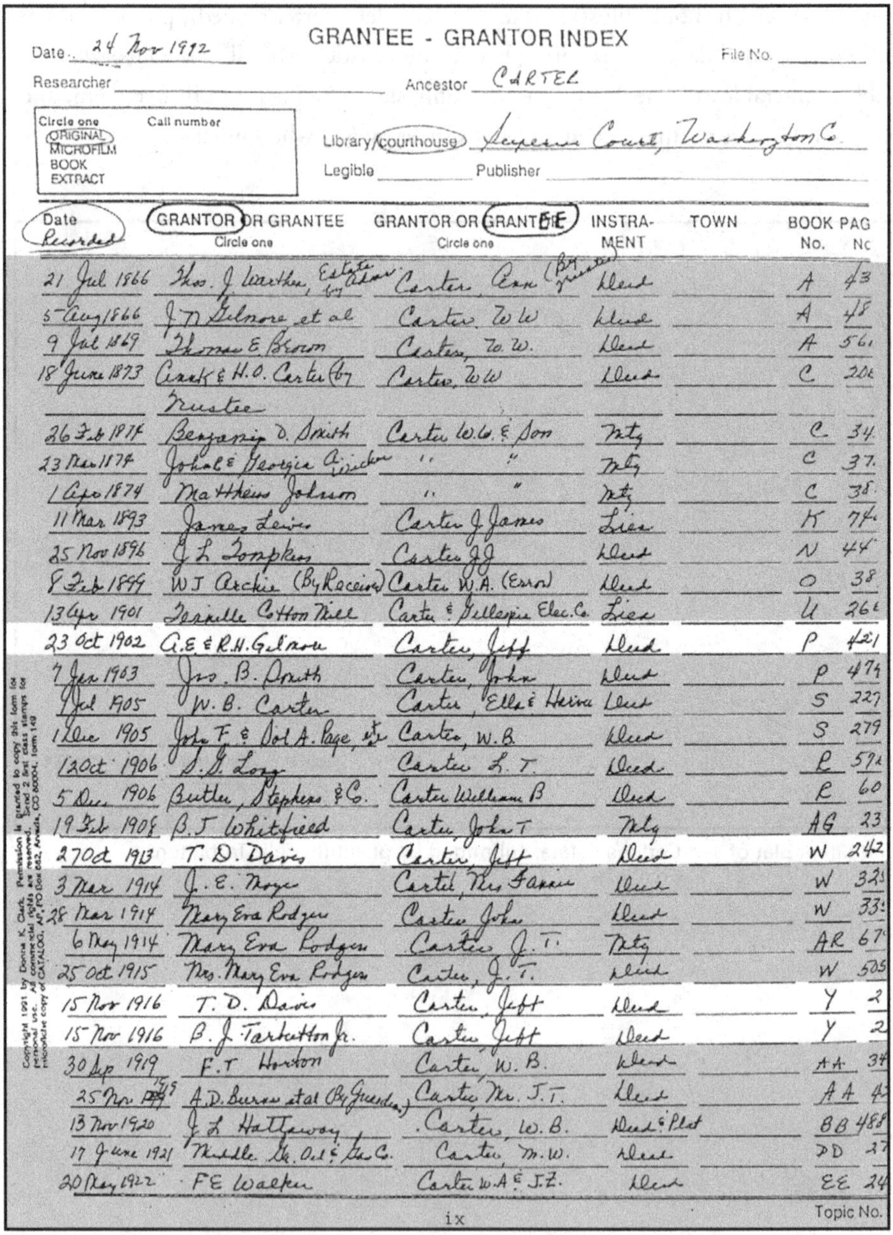

GRANTEE - GRANTOR INDEX

Date: 24 Nov 1992 File No. ______

Researcher ______ Ancestor: CARTEL

Circle one: (ORIGINAL) MICROFILM BOOK EXTRACT — Call number

Library/(courthouse): Superior Court, Washington Co.

Legible ______ Publisher ______

Date (Recorded)	(GRANTOR) OR GRANTEE (Circle one)	GRANTOR OR (GRANTEE) (Circle one)	INSTRA-MENT	TOWN	BOOK No.	PAGE No.
21 Jul 1866	Thos. J. Walker, Estate by Adm	Carter, Ann (By guardian)	Deed		A	43
5 Aug 1866	J N Gilmore et al	Carter, W W	Deed		A	48
9 Jul 1869	Thomas E Brown	Carter, W. W.	Deed		A	56
18 June 1873	Clark & H.O. Carter by Trustee	Carter, W W	Deed		C	20
26 Feb 1874	Benjamin D. Smith	Carter W.W. & Son	Mtg		C	34
23 Mar 1874	John C & Georgia A [illegible]	" "	Mtg		C	37
1 Apr 1874	Matthew Johnson	" "	Mtg		C	38
11 Mar 1893	James Lewis	Carter J James	Lien		K	74
25 Nov 1896	J L Tompkins	Carter J J	Deed		N	44
8 Feb 1899	W J Archie (By Receiver)	Carter W.A. (Exor)	Deed		O	38
13 Apr 1901	Tennille Cotton Mill	Carter & Gillespie Elec. Co.	Lien		U	26
23 Oct 1902	A.E. & R.H. Gilmore	Carter, Jeff	Deed		P	421
7 Jan 1903	Jno. B. Smith	Carter, John	Deed		P	47
9 Jul 1905	W. B. Carter	Carter, Ella & Hiram	Deed		S	227
1 Dec 1905	John F. & Sol A. Page, etc	Carter, W.B.	Deed		S	279
12 Oct 1906	S. G. Long	Carter L. T.	Deed		R	57
5 Dec 1906	Butler, Stephens & Co.	Carter William B	Deed		R	60
19 Feb 1908	B.J Whitfield	Carter, John T	Mtg		AG	23
27 Oct 1913	T. D. Davis	Carter, Jeff	Deed		W	242
3 Mar 1914	J. E. Moye	Carter, Mrs Fannie	Deed		W	32
28 Mar 1914	Mary Eva Rodgers	Carter John	Deed		W	33
6 May 1914	Mary Eva Rodgers	Carter, J. T.	Mtg		AR	67
25 Oct 1915	Mrs. Mary Eva Rodgers	Carter, J. T.	Deed		W	505
15 Nov 1916	T. D. Davis	Carter, Jeff	Deed		Y	2
15 Nov 1916	B. J. Tarbutton Jr.	Carter, Jeff	Deed		Y	2
30 Sep 1919	F.T Horton	Carter, W. B.	Deed		AA	34
25 Nov 1915	A.D. Burrus et al By Guardian	Carter, Mr. J.T.	Deed		AA	4
13 Nov 1920	J L Hattaway	Carter, W. B.	Deed & Plat		BB	488
17 June 1921	Middle Ga. Oil & Gas Co.	Carter, M. W.	Deed		DD	27
20 May 1922	F E Walker	Carter W.A. & J.Z.	Deed		EE	24

ix Topic No.

Jeff Carter, Recorded Deed

On April 19, 1984, Alston & Bird and partner Frank Nix claimed to withdraw from the *Tarbutton* case for "professional and business" reasons. This has been falsely stated in several documents. It was illegal for them to represent the Tarbutton family, and to then solicit the Carter heirs. The conspiracy continued when Frank Nix then selected Roger Moister to "replace" him as attorney for the solicited Carter heirs.

When Loulie Tarbutton sued the Carter heirs and Robert Watkins, Nix appointee Roger Moister acted as counsel for both, and answered her complaint.

Despite the conflict of interest, Frank Nix maintained control of the case. He stayed in constant contact with Watkins and counseled Moister on how to proceed. Nix specifically chose Moister because it would enable him to remain in control of the case. He planned the litigation strategy and told Moister what to do and how to do it.

On February 18, 1992, Moister said, "To be candid with you, the way I see this, looking back, is that unfortunately I think Mr. Nix was operating through me... the case had been investigated, the theories had been formulated, the global plan and the strategy was basically in place and he introduced me to this and then throughout the coming months, Frank was basically steering me on this case. I had no idea that I couldn't get him out of the case. I mean, he not only stayed in the case, he drove me crazy toward the end of it. And I was very upset with it, but I thought that he was going to turn the case over to me, get out of the case, and that was going to be it, but that is not what happened...Nix kept his finger on the pulse of *Tarbutton* from beginning to end, little if anything, was done without his knowledge."

Nix, of course, expected to be compensated for this. He told Moister that he wanted his share of the contingent fee from the Carter heirs (the 33% fee he negotiated for Alston & Bird), to the exclusion, however, of his partners at Alston & Bird. In violation of the American Bar Associations disciplinary rules, Moister agreed to the fee-splitting.

Moister sent Nix a check for $135, payable to Alston & Bird, to reimburse them for expenses incurred in removing *Tarbutton* from the Superior Court of Washington County to the Middle District of Georgia. Nix, however, returned the check and instructed Moister to give him $135 in cash and "to remove from your check ledger any reference thereto".

To cement the burial of the Carter claim, Frank Nix arranged for Robert Watkins to meet with a Charles Williams in Detroit, Michigan around July of 1984. This Charles Williams, however, was not the Charles E. Williams who allegedly notarized the Esther Scott deed to B.J. Tarbutton in 1938. That Williams was a Black lawyer who graduated from the University of Michigan in 1899, and had died in the late

1940s. The Williams whom Watkins met with was white and only 14 years old in 1938 when the deed was executed.

Misconduct Charges Against Two Federal Judges Linger

10-mile railroad put Tarbuttons on track to wealth and power

The Tarbutton brothers—Hugh, left, and Ben, right—fought allegations that their father had forged a 1938 warranty deed.

Waiting for the Kaolin Dust to Settle

Did Judge Have Conflict In Kaolin Cases?
Fitzpatrick Role Questioned In Suits Involving Industry Critic

Judicial Complaint Lingers in 11th Circuit

Fitzpatrick and Owens Exonerated

The following story was created for Williams to tell: In 1938, he and his family were living in Sandersville, Georgia. One day, while mowing B.J. Tarbutton's lawn, Tarbutton called him into his house and had him sign his name on a piece of paper. Tarbutton then "stamped" the paper, gave Williams $5, and told him to leave. If asked whether there were any signatures on the paper when he signed his name, or whether Esther Scott was present, Williams was to say no.

On Saturday, October 13, 1984, Watkins reported to Moister's law office as instructed - Nix was already there. According to Moister, Nix was present "to make sure that it happened about the way that it did". Nix told Watkins to call Williams and they would record the conversation. Afterwards, they drew up the affidavit and Nix had it typed.

One week later, Roger Moister wrote a memo to the *Tarbutton* file containing the notation: "Frank Nix takes fee, R.M [Roger Moister] was front man for case".

Moister said himself, "I mean, we're not talking about a transition period here, we're talking about a refusal to turn a case loose. And as the case progressed, I needed help, I turned to Frank - maybe that was a mistake on my part, but he had the entire theory, he had everything there - ask him one question and you get a lecture. Submit a brief draft, you get a 40 page brief coming back. I mean...he's overbearing".

On February 27, 1985, Loulie Tarbutton moved the district court to enter summary judgment against the Carter heirs on the quiet title aspect of her suit (as opposed to her tort claim against Watkins), to foreclose their claims to the subject property.

On March 22, 1985 Moister responded to the motion, including the perjured affidavit of Charles Williams. At the same time, Moister had Watkins record the affidavit in the public records of Washington County, Georgia to create an additional cloud on Loulie Tarbutton's title.

Loulie Tarbutton's attorney, Wallace Miller, Jr., was a partner in the Macon law firm of Jones, Cork and Miller. He had evidence that Charles Williams was not the notary on the Scott deed, and he gave this information to Moister; he or Watkins (who was practically in daily contact with Nix), then gave it to Nix.

Roger Moister, Robert Watkins, and Gerald Handley (of the firm Lokey and Bowden), traveled to Detroit and met with Williams. On August 8, 1985, Moister, Watkins and Handley deposed Williams in Atlanta at the law offices of Lokey and Bowden. After the deposition concluded, Wallace Miller, Jr. gave Moister copies of public records from Mayfield, Kentucky that he had held in reserve and not shown to Williams during the deposition. These records established that Williams had been in school in Mayfield throughout the time he said he had been in Sandersville, Georgia.

Despite the fact that his witness' perjured testimony had been exposed, Moister, after consulting attorney Hamilton Lokey, instructed the court reporter to transcribe Williams' deposition. Moister and Lokey then presented the perjured deposition to the court in "opposition" to Tarbutton's pending motion for summary judgment.

Adding insult to injury, Judge Fitzpatrick presided over this case despite his previous association with the law firm representing Loulie Tarbutton. Attorney Timothy Adams represented Fitzpatrick as the executor of his father's estate. Adams and Wallace Miller, Jr. (Loulie Tarbutton's attorney), were law partners at Jones, Cork & Miller. Fitzpatrick claimed the conflict of interest "just didn't register" with him. Unsurprisingly, he continued to preside over the case and this conflict existed through August 6, 1986, when Fitzpatrick granted Tarbutton's motion for summary judgment against the Carter heirs.

The Carter family has made consistent efforts to clear title and control of their estate since this controversy arose in 1938. The mere thought of challenging the "debt", and ultimately, the theft of their land was life threatening. There has been no delay, nor lack of courage by the heirs; just lack of success due to unequal protection under the law, the challenge of uncovering the truth, and the inability to find fearless, uncorrupt attorneys and judges.

This, of course, made it absolutely impossible to obtain action from county officials against the Tarbutton family during this time of Jim Crow. The documents that constitute the Tarbutton "chain of title", were manufactured, forged, and intentionally misfiled during this era. The 'good ol' boy' network has annihilated every effort the Carter's have made to reclaim their estate and its assets even today.

As an influential member of this same network, Judge Fitzpatrick issued a summary judgment against the Carter heirs in 1986, concluding there was no legal excuse for the heirs' "46 year delay in asserting their claim". The Carter's, however, did not discover the fraud until 1984 when Loulie Tarbutton filed a lawsuit against them.

Therefore the doctrine of laches, which states a claim must be brought within 7 years from the time fraud was known, should not have been used against the heirs. The issue of time (adverse possession, laches, statute of limitations, etc.), is prejudicial, considering the Tarbutton's "title" to the Carter estate originated in the 1930s when Jim Crow law permitted whites to treat Blacks as second-class citizens, and as such, had no rights.

Therefore, the heirs didn't even have the legal right to "assert their claim", athough they were reduced to sharecropping in effort to clear the fabricated debt. It was common during this period for Black famers to get stuck in a perpetual cycle of illegitimate debt, but were forced to accept or risk death. According to Jim Crow etiquette, it was lethal to challenge a white person or suggest that they were wrong or lying. It is an outrage that Fitzpatrick would insinuate that they could have done otherwise. The law is specifically their "excuse". However, despite apartheid-like Jim Crow laws, Lora Ella, Lillie Ruth, O'Neal, Blanche and Virge Jr. all made valiant attempts to recover the Carter estate. Their efforts displayed stunning courage and admirable will in the face of glaring intimidation, and the ever-present threat of reckless brutality and destruction.

Acting as a co-conspirator/agent in the kaolin cartel, Fitzpatrick went on to suggest that just because the Carters are Black does not prove that a "...white man, B.J. Tarbutton, utilized his stronger position to take advantage of the original Carter heirs at law".

While the following codes do not represent a complete list of professional responsibility, we have noted here those canons that were unquestionably violated by Tarbutton attorneys Alston & Bird, Franklin Nix, Roger Moister, Hamilton Lokey, and Gerald Handley.

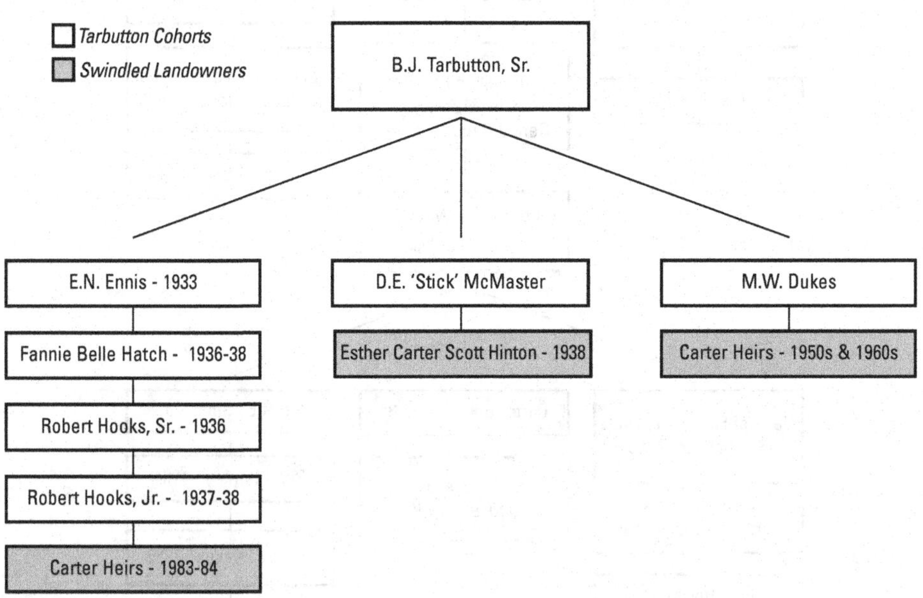

The Tarbutton's Kaolin Industry Syndicate 1930's - 1960's

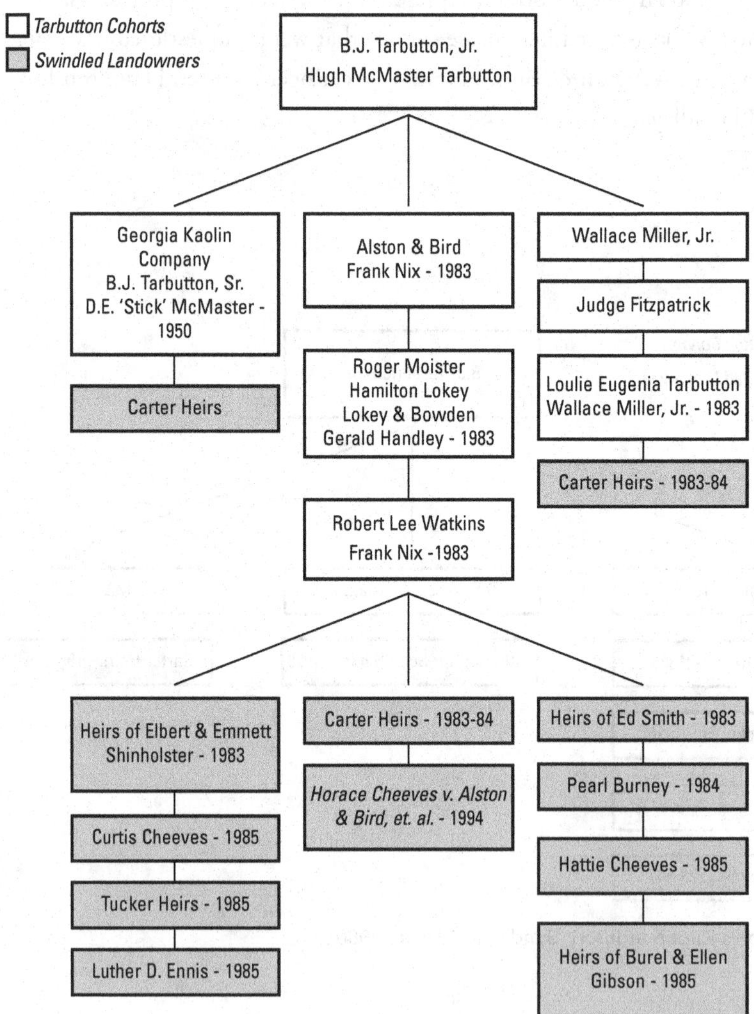

The Tarbutton's Kaolin Industry Syndicate 1950's - 1990's

Model Code of Professional Responsibility: Disciplinary Rules

CANON 1

DR 1-102 Misconduct

A| A lawyer shall not:

1| Violate a Disciplinary Rule.

3| Engage in illegal conduct involving moral turpitude.

4| Engage in conduct involving dishonesty, fraud, deceit, or misrepresentation.

CANON 2

DR 2-107 Division of Fees Among Lawyers

A| A lawyer shall not divide a fee for legal services with another lawyer who is not a partner in or associate of his law firm or law office, unless:

1| The client consents to employment of the other lawyer after a full disclosure that a division of fees will be made.

CANON 5

DR 5-105 Refusing to Accept or Continue Employment if the Interests of Another Client May Impair the Independent Professional Judgment of the Lawyer

B| A lawyer shall not continue multiple employment if the exercise of his independent professional judgment in behalf of a client will be or is likely to be adversely affected by his representation of another client, or if it would be likely to involve him in representing differing interests, except to the extent permitted under DR 5-105(C).

D| If a lawyer is required to decline employment or to withdraw from employment under a Disciplinary Rule, no partner, or associate, or any other lawyer affiliated with him or his firm, may accept or continue such employment.

CANON 6

DR 6-101 Failing to Act Competently.

A| A lawyer shall not:

1| Handle a legal matter which he knows or should know that he is not competent to handle, without associating with him a lawyer who is competent to handle it.

2| Handle a legal matter without preparation adequate in the circumstances.

3| Neglect a legal matter entrusted to him.

DR 6-102 Limiting Liability to Client.

A| A lawyer shall not attempt to exonerate himself from or limit his liability to his client for his personal malpractice.

CANON 7

DR 7-101 Representing a Client Zealously.

A| A lawyer shall not intentionally:

1| Fail to seek the lawful objectives of his client through reasonably available means permitted by law and the Disciplinary Rules, except as provided by DR 7-101(B). A lawyer does not violate this Disciplinary Rule, however, by acceding to reasonable requests of opposing counsel which do not prejudice the rights of his client, by being punctual in fulfilling all professional commitments, by avoiding offensive tactics, or by treating with courtesy and consideration all persons involved in the legal process.

3| Prejudice or damage his client during the course of the professional relationship, except as required under DR 7-102(B)

DR 7-102 Representing a Client Within the Bounds of the Law.

A| In his representation of a client, a lawyer shall not:

4| Knowingly use perjured testimony or false evidence.

5| Knowingly make a false statement of law or fact.

6| Participate in the creation or preservation of evidence when he knows or it is obvious that the evidence is false.

7| Counsel or assist his client in conduct that the lawyer knows to be illegal or fraudulent.

8| Knowingly engage in other illegal conduct or conduct contrary to a Disciplinary Rule.

B| A lawyer who receives information clearly establishing that:

1| His client has, in the course of the representation, perpetrated a fraud upon a person or tribunal shall promptly call upon his client to rectify the same, and if his client refuses or is unable to do so, he shall reveal the fraud to the affected person or tribunal, except when the information is protected as a privileged communication.

2| A person other than his client has perpetrated a fraud upon a tribunal shall promptly reveal the fraud to the tribunal.

DR 7-104 Communicating With One of Adverse Interest.

A| During the course of his representation of a client a lawyer shall not:

1| Communicate or cause another to communicate on the subject of the representation with a party he knows to be represented by a lawyer in that matter unless he has the prior consent of the lawyer representing such other party or is authorized by law to do so.

2| Give advice to a person who is not represented by a lawyer, other than the advice to secure counsel, if the interests of such person are or have a reasonable possibility of being in conflict with the interests of his client.

CANON 9

DR 9-101 Avoiding Even the Appearance of Impropriety.

A| A lawyer shall not accept private employment in a matter upon the merits of which he has acted in a judicial capacity.

TARBUTTON v. ALL THAT TRACT OR PARCEL OF LAND 521
Cite as 641 F.Supp. 521 (M.D.Ga. 1986)

Loulie Eugenia TARBUTTON, As Trustee, etc. Plaintiff and Third-Party Plaintiff in Counterclaim,

v.

ALL THAT TRACT OR PARCEL OF LAND KNOWN AS THE CARTER PLACE, LYING AND BEING IN the 98th GM DISTRICT, WASHINGTON COUNTY, GEORGIA, CONTAINING 585 ACRES, MORE OR LESS, etc; Blanche C. Holley, as Administratrix De Bonis Non of the Estate of Jeff Carter, deceased; Robert Lee Watkins, Individually and as Attorney-in-Fact for Timothy Dawson, et al.; and All The World, Defendants,

v.

Hugh M. TARBUTTON and Ben J. Tarbutton, Jr., Third-Party Defendants in Counterclaim,

Georgia Kaolin Company, Inc., Intervenor as Plaintiff and Defendant in Counterclaim.

Civ. A. No. 84-403-1-MAC.

United States District Court,
M.D. Georgia,
Macon Division.

Aug. 6, 1986.

Possessor of land brought action to quiet title and seeking damages for defamation of title, against heirs at law of estate which initially held title to land. Heirs filed responsive pleadings and counterclaimed for, inter alia, cancellation of recorded deeds in possessor's chain of title and imposition of constructive trust in their favor. Possessor subsequently filed third-party complaints against predecessors in title. Long-term lessee intervened. Possessor and predecessors in title moved for summary judgment on possessor's claim to quiet title, lessor of property moved for summary judgment respecting relief sought in counterclaim, and heirs moved for partial summary judgment respecting their counterclaim. The District Court,

The Tarbutton Case against the Carter Heirs set a precedent, August 6, 1986.

ROGER W. MOISTER, JR., P.C.
ATTORNEY AT LAW
503 CANDLER BUILDING
ATLANTA, GEORGIA 30303
(404) 524-3835

April 16, 1984

Mrs. Mary C. Vincent
335 Rugby Rd.
Brooklyn, New York 11226

Re: Estate of Jeff Carter, Deceased

Dear Mrs. Vincent:

Based on my review of the Estate of Jeff Carter, Deceased, and the claim regarding land owned by him in Washington County, Georgia when he died, I recommend that an Administrator De Bonis Non be appointed through the Probate Court of Washington County, Georgia to complete the administration of this Estate.

Mrs. Blanche C. Holley has agreed to act as Administrator De Bonis Non if appointed. She has been interested and acted over the years in attempts to recover the land of Jeff Carter. She is capable of serving as Administrator. Accordingly, I have prepared a Petition for her to file in the Probate Court of Washington County, Georgia to act as Administrator De Bonis Non. The Court will publish a notice for a hearing to be held June 4, 1984 at 11:00 A.M. in the Probate Court of Washington County, Georgia at which any creditor or heir can show cause why Mrs. Holley should not be appointed.

I would like for you to select Mrs. Holley to serve as Administrator De Bonis Non. Please sign the enclosed selection for Administrator De Bonis Non and return it to me. Additionally, I would like for you to sign and return the enclosed letter which states your reasons for selecting Mrs. Holley. I have prepared a letter addressing certain factors sometimes considered regarding the appointment of administrators in cases like this one. Please sign the letter and the Selection for Administrator De Bonis Non and return them to me by April 23, 1984.

Letter from Roger Moister to Carter Heir Mary Vincent, pg. 1.

I will be working during April and May to get the Administrator De Bonis Non appointed and complete my investigation regarding filing suit. I will let you know whether the Administrator De Bonis Non is appointed in early June.

Please call me if you have any questions. I will keep you advised. Thank you very much.

Yours truly,

Roger Moister

Roger W. Moister, Jr.

New address as of 5/1/84:

1800 Peachtree St. N.W. Suite 508
Atlanta, Georgia 30309-2506
(404) 352-0497

RWMJr/lew

Letter from Roger Moister to Carter Heir Mary Vincent, pg. 2.

ROGER W. MOISTER, JR., P.C.
ATTORNEY AT LAW
PEACHTREE PALISADES WEST
1800 PEACHTREE ROAD, N.W., SUITE 508
ATLANTA, GEORGIA 30309-2506

(404) 352-0497

June 11, 1984

Dear Heir of Jeff Carter, Deceased:

This is a status report to let you know that Mrs. Blanche C. Holley qualified on June 4, 1984 as Administrator De Bonis Non of Jeff Carter, Deceased. I met Mrs. Holley along with Robert Watkins at the Probate Court of Washington County in Sandersville, Georgia when this occurred.

I have filed Pleadings to join Mrs. Holley as Administrator of the Estate in the pending lawsuit regarding title to the property. If the Court permits her to join the case, she will be substituted for the heirs at law of the estate. The claim of the estate respecting title to the land will be prosecuted through her as the real party representing the estate.

I will be keeping you advised periodically regarding this matter.

Yours truly,

Roger Moister

Roger W. Moister, Jr.
Attorney for Estate of
Jeff Carter, Deceased

RWMJr/ejl

Letter from Roger Moister to the Carter Heirs.

ROGER W. MOISTER, JR., P.C.
ATTORNEY AT LAW
PEACHTREE PALISADES WEST
1800 PEACHTREE ROAD, N.W., SUITE 508
ATLANTA, GEORGIA 30309-2506
(404) 352-0497

September 19, 1984

Dear Heir of Jeff Carter (Deceased):

Robert Lee Watkins suggested that I write to you to get some facts needed to prove your case regarding recovery of the land in Washington County, Georgia. Because there are so many heirs of Jeff Carter I am using a form letter to expedite the communication.

One of the issues in the case is whether the heirs of Jeff Carter signed a certain mortgage in January 1933 to encumber the land. I am enclosing a photocopy of the signature page of that mortgage.

I need for you to verify the signature of your parent or ancestor as shown on the enclosed document. Please look at the document very closely and see if the signature shown looks like the real signature of your parent or ancestor.

To simplify your reply, I am enclosing a form which I ask you to complete and mail back to me promptly. The form also requests some other information which may be helpful in trying to verify the signatures of the persons shown on the document.

Please note that there are several questions about Minnie Butts and Crawford Carter. I am asking everyone about the signatures of these two persons because they have no known children to contact now.

Please call me if you have any questions. Thank you very much.

Yours truly,

Roger Moister

Roger W. Moister, Jr.

RWM/cs

Enclosure

Letter from Roger Moister to the Carter Heirs.

Lease

5E-350
recorded 8/10/68

(23)

STATE OF GEORGIA
COUNTY OF WASHINGTON

THIS CONTRACT executed this 7th day of December, 19 50, between

B. J. Tarbutton

of Washington County, Georgia, herein called lessor, and D. E. McMaster, of Washington County, ~~Georgia Kaolin Company, a New Jersey corpora-tion,~~ herein called tenant, witnesseth:

1. In consideration of $ 500.00 cash in hand paid by tenant to lessor, the receipt and sufficiency whereof is hereby acknowledged, and in consideration of the mutual agreements and covenants herein contained, the lessor hereby lets and leases to tenant the following described lands and premises and hereby grants, bargains, sells, and conveys to tenant, subject to the payment of all royalties and minimum guaranteed sums and amounts as hereinafter provided, all the kaolin, bauxite and any and all kinds of ores, metals and minerals in and upon the following described lands and premises and also the exclusive right to drill, prospect for, mine and remove all the kaolin, bauxite, and any and all kinds of ores, metals and minerals in and upon the following described lands and premises to-wit:

All that tract or parcel of land lying, situate and being in the 98th District, G. M., of Washington County, Georgia, containing five hundred (500) acres, more or less, and being bounded on the North by lands of Robert Hooks and lands of Luther Ennis; on the East by Buffalo Creek; on the South by lands of Sam Gordy and lands of Elkins Estate; on the West by Elkins Estate and Luther Ennis.

For the purposes aforesaid and for the purpose of carrying on similar mining operations on other neighboring lands, said tenant shall have full and complete rights of ingress and egress to, from and over all parts of said land, the right to search for said kaolin, bauxite, ores, metals, and minerals, the right to make excavations and pile waste earth on any part of said land, said waste earth being mined on this land or from adjoining lands which may or might be prospected by tenant, the right to use any water in or upon said land, and the right to construct and place upon said land any and all buildings, machinery, roads, railroads and other improvements that may be convenient or proper for said purposes. Said improvements shall remain the property of tenant, who shall have the right to remove the same at any time during the continuance of this contract in force or within sixty days thereafter.

2. All kaolin, bauxite, ores, metals, and minerals removed from said land by tenant during the continuance of this contract in force shall be the property of tenant and tenant shall pay to lessor therefor a royalty of .25 cents for bauxite and .17½ cents for kaolin and any other kind or type of ore, metal, or mineral per ton of 2240 pounds removed from said land by tenant. Payment shall be made on the 20th day of each month for all such kaolin, bauxite, ores, metals and minerals removed during the preceding calendar month. Tenant agrees to keep complete records of all removals and shipments so that lessor may verify such weights. Payments made by tenant under paragraph 3 hereof to make up or complete the minimum guaranteed monthly amounts, shall be credited against amounts due for royalties under paragraph 2. From the gross weight of kaolin or bauxite there shall be allowed a deduction of 22% for moisture. The parties hereto agree that only clay containing more than 53% A12 03 shall be considered bauxite under the terms of this agreement.

Mineral Lease between Georgia Kaolin and B.J. Tarbutton & D. E. 'Stick' McMaster, December 7, 1950, pg. 1.

12/7/51

3. Tenant shall be allowed the exclusive privilege of drilling and prospecting said property until December 7, 19 (which date is hereinafter sometimes referred to as the "specified date") without the payment of any royalties or other sums except the cash consideration paid at the time of the signing of this contract, and tenant shall have the right to terminate this contract at any time on or before the "specified date" by giving notice to lessor at any time on or before the "specified date" of tenant's desire so to terminate this contract; but if said notice is so given and this contract thereby terminated, then within 30 days after said notice and termination, tenant shall pay lessor all royalties, if any, earned or accrued up to the time when said notice is so given and this contract so terminated, (in the event tenant shall have commenced actual mining operations on said land prior to said notice and termination) and also the sum of $5.00, which amounts shall be payable in cash or by check, which sum of $5.00 shall be in addition to the original consideration for this contract or for any extension thereof, and which sum of $5.00 and original consideration and any royalties which may have accrued are by all parties hereto considered and recognized to be ample for all rights, privileges and options acquired by tenant under this contract, including the exclusive privilege of drilling and prospecting said property prior to the "specified date" and the right so to terminate this contract. The effect of giving said notice on or before the "specified date" shall be immediately to cancel and terminate this contract. If, however, this contract is not so terminated by tenant then, in that event, beginning on said "specified date" royalties or a minimum guaranteed amount shall begin to accrue whether or not mining operations shall have actually commenced and should said royalties for any month thereafter during the continuance of this contract in force not amount to as much as 1/12 of 500.00, tenant agrees to pay lessor during the continuance of this contract in force, an amount sufficient with such royalties, if any, as shall have been paid to make 1/12 of 500.00 for each and every month after the said "specified date" and during the continuance of this contract in force, it being hereby agreed, however, that in the event tenant, as the result of actual mining operations, pays lessor as royalties hereunder for any month a sum in excess of 1/12 of $ 500.00, tenant shall be entitled to credit the amount by which each of such payments exceeds 1/12 of $ 500.00 in payment, or toward the payment, of any amount or amounts which may become due at any time hereunder for the purpose of making up of completing the said minimum guaranteed monthly sums or amounts. There shall be no obligation upon tenant to prospect or mine any of said premises, but tenant does assume the obligation to pay a minimum royalty or a minimum guaranteed amount as above specified subject only to all terms and conditions expressed in this contract. All payments called for by this paragraph to make up or complete the said minimum guaranteed monthly sums or amounts, either before or after the commencement of actual mining operations, shall be due and payable annually on the 20th day of January in each year, beginning on the 20th day of January 19 52, and tenant shall be entitled to credit the amount of any and all such payments called for by this paragraph to make up or complete the said minimum guaranteed monthly sums or amounts against any royalties in excess of said minimum guaranteed monthly sums or amounts at any time becoming due hereunder as a result of actual mining operations.

4. At any time, even after the said "specified date," tenant shall have the right to terminate this contract by giving to lessor notice of tenant's desire to terminate this contract, provided, however, that if said notice is given at any time after the said "specified date," said notice shall be a 30-day notice; that is to say, shall be given 30 days before the date on which tenant's desired termination of the contract is to occur and tenant shall in such case pay lessor within 30 days after termination of this contract all royalties and minimum guaranteed amounts earned or accrued up to the date of said termination and in addition thereto the sum of $5.00, which amounts shall be payable in cash or by check, which sum of $5.00 and other said obligations are by all parties hereto considered and recognized to be ample consideration for all rights, privileges and options acquired by tenant under this contract, including said right so to terminate said contract. The effect of giving said notice at any time after the said "specified date" shall be to cancel and terminate this contract immediately upon the expiration of thirty days after said notice is given.

5. The lessor shall return said lands and premises for taxation and pay when due all taxes that shall accrue thereon.

6. Lessor shall, during the continuance of this contract in force, have the right to use and occupy, through himself and/or tenants, any and all of said land, provided such use shall not interfere with the exercise of the rights granted to tenant under this contract. Tenant agrees to pay lessor for any growing crops that shall be destroyed by tenant, provided such crops shall have been planted before notice to lessor that tenant intends, before harvest season, to mine and remove kaolin, bauxite, or any other ore, metal or mineral from the particular land planted to such crops; otherwise tenant shall not be liable for such crops so destroyed.

7. If tenant shall fail to pay as herein provided any amount when due either as a royalty or as a minimum guaranteed amount and shall continue to fail to make such payment for 30 days after written notice thereof shall have been

Mineral Lease between Georgia Kaolin and B.J. Tarbutton & D. E. 'Stick' McMaster, December 7, 1950, pg. 2.

given to tenant by lessor, lessor shall have the right at lessor's option to terminate this contract, which termination shall be effected by an additional written notice to lessor.

8. Any notice required or expressly permitted to be given by either party to the other hereunder shall be in writing and actually delivered in person or by registered United States Mail, return receipt required, to the person to be notified, directed to such person's mailing address indicated at foot hereof, provided, however, that if such notice is sent to such person by letter deposited in the United States Mail properly stamped and directed to such person at such person's mailing address indicated at foot hereof, and so sent by registered mail, personal delivery required and return receipt requested, any receipt or record obtained or made by the Post Office Department of the United States showing or indicating personal delivery of such letter to such person as addressee by any employee, agent or officer of said Post Office Department shall be conclusive upon all parties for the purpose of showing that said letter and notice were properly served upon said addressee in person. In the event of lessor's death, any such notice given by tenant or tenant's successors or assigns may be so given to any one of lessor's heirs or next of kin (whether adult or minors with or without guardian), personal representatives or assigns and in such case it shall not be necessary to serve such notice upon all of the persons above mentioned but the giving of such notice in the manner aforesaid to any one of said persons shall be as fully effective for all intents and purposes as if properly served upon lessor within lessor's lifetime. Should any person or persons, corporation or corporations other than the two original parties hereto now have or hereafter acquire any interest in or title to any of the real estate covered by this contract by purchase, inheritance or otherwise, or now have or hereafter acquire any interest in or title to this contract by transfer, assignment or otherwise, no such person or persons, corporation or corporations shall be entitled to receive any notice required or permitted to be given by one party to the other hereunder unless such person or persons, corporation or corporations other than such original parties shall have previously given to the opposite party written notice of the acquisition of such interest or title and written notice of the address to which any desired notice should be mailed, in the absence of the giving of said last mentioned notice and address, any notice required or expressly permitted hereunder when given by either party hereto only to the other party hereto shall be fully effective for the purpose for which given (provided said purpose is one authorized hereunder) without the necessity of notifying any other person or persons, corporation or corporations; except that if lessor be dead, any notice intended for lessor shall be given to some one of the persons above specified for service in case of lessor's death. If any person at any time entitled to receive any notice required or expressly permitted hereunder should be at the time of the giving of said notice non sui juris or non compos mentis with or without a guardian, the giving of said notice to such person in the manner herein provided shall, nevertheless, be fully effective for the purpose for which given provided said purpose is one authorized hereunder.

9. Tenant's right, title and interest in said kaolin, bauxite, ores, metals and minerals and the rights hereby granted shall continue until this contract is terminated as herein provided and shall then cease and terminate. Upon the termination of this contract, each party shall execute and deliver to the other upon request such instrument in writing as shall be required to cancel this contract of record.

10. The termination of this contract as provided in paragraphs 3, 4, or 7 hereof shall discharge all obligations of tenant under this contract which have not accrued when this contract is so terminated.

11. Lessor warrants the title to said land, kaolin, bauxite, ores, metals and minerals to tenant against the lawful claims of all persons whomsoever, and agrees that in the event tenant's attorneys examine the title to said lands, kaolin, bauxite, ores, metals and minerals and pronounce the same defective, lessor will pay to tenant the reasonable expenses and fees for such title examination and will refund to tenant any and all payments made under the terms of this contract.

12. This contract shall continue in force and effect for a term of 25 years from the date hereof unless sooner terminated as herein provided.

13. Within the time stated in paragraph 12 hereof and for the consideration hereinbefore expressed, the tenant shall have the right and option to extend this contract on the same terms and conditions for an additional term of 25 years from the expiration of the time stated in said paragraph 12, simply by giving notice to the lessor of tenant's intention to extend said contract.

14. The rights, powers, privileges, interest, title and options herein granted shall be held, owned, used and enjoyed not only by the parties hereto but also by their heirs, executors, administrators, successors and assigns, who shall be bound by all obligations herein created in like manner and to the same extent that said obligations bind the parties hereto.

15. Lessor reserves the right to remove from said property any and all timber upon demand of tenant to enable tenant to carry on mining operations and upon such demand lessor will either remove said timber within a reasonable time

Mineral Lease between Georgia Kaolin and B.J. Tarbutton & D. E. 'Stick' McMaster, December 7, 1950, pg. 3.

or abandon the same so that tenant can proceed with any excavations deemed necessary by tenant without any liability for damage to, or destruction of or use of, said timber and such reasonable time is agreed to be sixty days.

16. Tenant shall have the option to purchase the above described land at any time during the continuance of this contract in force, that is to say, during the initial period of this contract or during the continuance of this contract in force by the extension thereof as above provided at and for the sum of $ No Purchase per acre, cash upon delivery of the deed. Should tenant desire to exercise this option to purchase, tenant shall so notify lessor, thereby making this contract into a contract of purchase and sale. Lessor shall convey a good and sufficient fee simple title to said land by warranty deed, free from all liens and incumbrances, within not more than thirty days after notice is given by tenant to lessor of its readiness to close said purchase.

The lessor, his heirs or assigns, in this instrument reserves the right to place across said tract of land at any time he so desires, or at any time his heirs or assigns so desire, a right-of-way for pipe lines, telephone lines, and/or any and other lines of communication; also the right to build across said lands railroads.

By placing of said right-of-ways across said land, it shall in no way interfere with mining operations of tenant, and if said right-of-ways or pipe lines are so placed so that they interfere with the mining operations of tenant, they shall be removed to same other convenient place upon said property.

IN WITNESS WHEREOF, The parties hereto have signed, sealed and delivered these presents in triplicate, each triplicate to be considered an original, the day and year first above written.

Signed, sealed and delivered by
B. J. Tarbutton
in the presence of:
(Seal)
~~Notary Public,~~ Clerk S. C. W. Co. Ga.

B. J. Tarbutton (SEAL)
B. J. Tarbutton
Mailing Address: Sandersville, Georgia

Signed, sealed and delivered by
~~Georgia Kaolin Company~~ D. E. McMaster in the presence of:
(Seal)
~~Notary Public~~ Clerk S. C. W. Co. Ga.

~~GEORGIA KAOLIN COMPANY~~
D. E. McMaster
~~By~~
D E McMaster (SEAL)
Mailing Address
~~433 North Broad Street~~
~~Elizabeth, New Jersey~~
Box 348
Sandersville, Ga.

Assignment

GEORGIA, Washington County.

In consideration of One ($1.00) Dollar, cash in hand paid, and other consideration, I, D. E. McMaster of Washington County, Georgia, do hereby transfer and convey unto the Georgia Kaolin Company, a New Jersey corporation, the within described contract executed December 7, 1950, together with all my rights, powers, privileges and options under the same, and all of my right, title and interest in and to the lands described in same.

Witness my hand and seal, this the 4th day of May, 1954.

D. E. McMaster L.S.

Signed, sealed and delivered
in the presence of:
J. Benton Evans
CLERK, SUPERIOR COURT
WASHINGTON COUNTY, GA.

Mineral Lease between Georgia Kaolin and B.J. Tarbutton & D. E. 'Stick' McMaster, December 7, 1950, pg. 4.

THIS INDENTURE, made this 27th day of December, 1952, between B. J. Tarbutton, Sr., of the first part, and Ben J. Tarbutton, Jr., and Hugh M. Tarbutton, of the second part, all of the County and State aforesaid.

WITNESSES, that the said B. J. Tarbutton, Sr. for and in consideration of the natural love and affection he has for Ben J. Tarbutton, Jr. and Hugh M. Tarbutton, his sons, the said B. J. Tarbutton, Sr. hereby gives, grants and conveys to the said Ben J. Tarbutton, Jr. and Hugh M. Tarbutton, their heirs and assigns, the following described property, to wit:

All that tract or parcel of land lying, situate and being in the 98th G. M. District of Washington County, Georgia, containing five hundred (500) acres, more or less, and being bounded as follows: On the north by lands of Robert Hooks and lands of Luther Ennis; east by Buffalo Creek; south by lands of Sam Gordy and lands of the Elkins Estate; and, west by lands of Elkins Estate and lands of Luther Ennis. Said tract of land being known as the "Carter place",

together with all the rights and privileges thereunto belonging forever, in fee simple.

IN WITNESS WHEREOF, the said B. J. Tarbutton, Sr. hereunto sets his hand and seal, the day and year above written.

Signed, sealed and delivered in the presence of: B. J. Tarbutton Sr. L.S.

William G. Hawkins Jr.

Irwin L. Evans
Judge City Court of Sandersville

Recorded December 29, 1952 Newsom Summerlin, Clerk

Fraudulent Indenture of the stolen Carter Estate from B.J. Tarbutton Sr. "for and in consideration of the natural love and affection he has for" his sons, B.J. Tarbutton Jr. and Hugh McMaster Tarbutton, December 27, 1952.

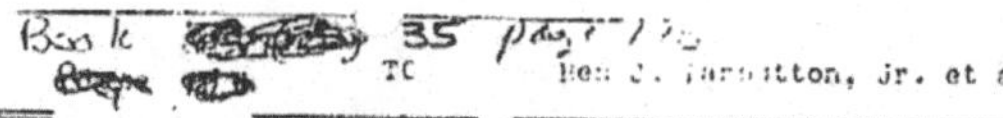

B. J. Tarbutton, Sr. TO Ben J. Tarbutton, Jr. et al

GEORGIA, WASHINGTON COUNTY.

THIS INDENTURE, made this 27th day of December, 1952, between B. J. Tarbutton, Sr., of the first part, and Ben J. Tarbutton, Jr. and Hugh M. Tarbutton, of the second part, all of the County and State aforesaid.

WITNESSES, that the said B. J. Tarbutton, Sr. for and in consideration of the natural love and affection he has for Ben J. Tarbutton, Jr. and Hugh M. Tarbutton, his sons, the said B. J. Tarbutton, Sr. hereby gives, grants and conveys to the said Ben J. Tarbutton, Jr. and Hugh M. Tarbutton, their heirs and assigns, the following described property, to wit:

All that tract or parcel of land lying, situate and being in the 98th G. M. District of Washington County, Georgia, containing five hundred (500) acres, more or less, and being bounded as follows: On the north by lands of Robert Hooks and lands of Luther Ennis; east by Buffalo Creek; south by lands of Sam Gordy and lands of the Elkins Estate; and, west by lands of Elkins Estate and lands of Luther Ennis. Said tract of land being known as the "Carter place",

together with all the rights and privileges thereunto belonging forever, in fee simple.

IN WITNESS WHEREOF, the said B. J. Tarbutton, Sr. hereunto sets his hand and seal, the day and year above written.

Signed, sealed and delivered in the presence of: B. J. Tarbutton Sr. L.S.

William G. Hawkins Jr.

Irwin L. Evans
Judge City Court of Sandersville

Recorded December 29, 1952 Newsom Summerlin, Clerk

Fraudulent Indenture of the stolen Carter Estate from B.J. Tarbutton Sr. "for and in consideration of the natural love and affection he has for" his sons, B.J. Tarbutton Jr. and Hugh McMaster Tarbutton, December 27, 1952.

M. W. DUKES
ATTORNEY AT LAW
SANDERSVILLE, GEORGIA

GEORGIA, WASHINGTON COUNTY.

THIS INDENTURE, Made this 31 day of December, 1975, between Ben J. Tarbutton, Jr., party of the first part, and Hugh M. Tarbutton, party of the second part, both parties of Washington County, Georgia;

WITNESSETH: That the party of the first part, for and in consideration of the sum of Ten ($10.00) Dollars, in hand paid, at and before the sealing and delivery of these presents, the receipt whereof is hereby acknowledged, and for the purpose of the division of certain properties owned by the parties hereto, has granted, bargained, sold, and conveyed, and by these presents does grant, bargain, sell, and convey, unto the said party of the second part, his heirs and assigns, all of the one-half (½) undivided interest of the party of the first part in and to the following described properties, to-wit:

All that tract or parcel of land, known as the Carter Place, lying and being in the 98th G. M. District, Washington County, Georgia, containing 585 acres, more or less, bounded now or formerly as follows: North by property of Robert Hooks and property of Luther Ennis; East by Buffalo Creek; South by property of Sam Gordy and property of the Elkins Estate; and West by property of the Elkins Estate and property of Luther Ennis. The said tract of land is the same conveyed by B. J. Tarbutton to Ben J. Tarbutton, Jr., and Hugh M. Tarbutton, by deed dated December 27, 1952, recorded in Deed Book "3S", Page 193, in the Office of the Clerk of the Superior Court of Washington County, Georgia. Also,

All that tract or parcel of land, known as the Bussell Place, lying and being in the 136th G. M. District, Washington County, Georgia, containing 40 acres, more or less, bounded now or formerly as follows: North by property of Allen Williams; East by property of H. W. Bussell; South by property of Dock Peavy; and West by property of Lamar Brown. Said tract of land is the same conveyed by J. F. Bussell to Ben J. Tarbutton, Jr., and Hugh M. Tarbutton, by warranty deed dated December 16, 1954, recorded in said Clerk's Office in Deed Book "3U", Page 432. Also,

All that tract or parcel of land, lying in the 136th G. M. District, Washington County, Georgia, known as the Blount and Webster Places, containing 450 acres, more or less, bounded now or formerly as follows: North by

Fraudulent Indenture of the stolen Carter Estate from B.J. Tarbutton Sr. to his sons, B.J. Tarbutton Jr. and Hugh McMaster Tarbutton, December 31, 1975, page 1.

hereunto set his hand and affixed his seal, the day and year first above written.

(SEAL)
Ben J. Tarbutton, Jr.

Signed, sealed, and delivered
in the presence of:

Notary Public, Washington County, Georgia

WASHINGTON County, Georgia
Real Estate Transfer Tax
Paid $ - 0 -
Date JAN 2 3 1976
Clerk of Superior Court
Deputy

Recorded JAN 2 3 1976 CLERK

Fraudulent Indenture of the stolen Carter Estate from B.J. Tarbutton Sr. to his sons, B.J. Tarbutton Jr. and Hugh McMaster Tarbutton, December 31, 1975, page 2.

Lawyers Title Insurance Corporation

ATLANTA BRANCH OFFICE

LIMITED

WARRANTY DEED

STATE OF Georgia COUNTY OF Fulton

THIS INDENTURE, Made the 21st day of December , in the year one thousand nine hundred seventy-six , between Hugh M. Tarbutton

of the County of Washington , and State of Georgia, as party or parties of the first part, hereinafter called Grantor, and Loulie Eugenia Kernaghan Tarbutton, as Trustee of Irrevocable Trust for Benefit of Loulie Eugenia Tarbutton under agreement with Hugh McMaster Tarbutton dated December 21, 1976,

as party or parties of the second part, hereinafter called Grantee (the words "Grantor" and "Grantee" to include their respective heirs, successors and assigns where the context requires or permits).

WITNESSETH that: Grantor, for and in consideration of ~~the sum of~~ XXXXXXXX the love and affection which he bears for his daughter Loulie XXXXXXXXXXXX ~~DOLLARS~~ XXXXXXXXXXXXXXXXXXXXXXXXXXXXXXXXXXXXXXXXXXXXXXXXXXXXXXXXXXXXX ~~acknowledged~~, has granted, bargained, sold, aliened, conveyed and confirmed, and by these presents does grant, bargain, sell, alien, convey and confirm unto the said Grantee,

All those tracts or parcels of land lying and being in Washington County, Georgia, and more particularly described in Exhibit "A" attached hereto and made a part hereof.

WASHINGTON County, Georgia
Real Estate Transfer Tax
Paid $ -0-
Date DEC 31 1976
Janie H. Lindsey
Clerk of Superior Court

TO HAVE AND TO HOLD the said tractsor parcelsof land, with all and singular the rights, members and appurtenances thereof, to the same being, belonging, or in anywise appertaining, to the only proper use, benefit and behoof of the said Grantee forever in FEE SIMPLE.

AND THE SAID Grantor will warrant and forever defend the right and title to the above described property unto the said Grantee against the claims of all persons XXXXXXXXXX claiming under Grantor.

IN WITNESS WHEREOF, the Grantor has signed and sealed this deed, the day and year above written.

Signed, sealed and delivered in presence of:

[signature] Unofficial Witness — [signature] Hugh M. Tarbutton (Seal)

(Seal)

[signature] Michael T. Nations, Notary Public — (Seal)

Fraudulent Deed between Hugh McMaster Tarbutton and Loulie Eugenia Kernaghan Tarbutton, as Trustee of Irrevocable Trust for benefit of Loulie Eugenia Tarbutton, December 21, 1976, pg. 1.

All that tract or parcel of land, known as the Carter Place, lying and being in the 98th G. M. District, Washington County, Georgia, containing 535 acres, more or less, bounded now or formerly as follows: North by property of Robert Hooks and property of Luther Ennis; East by Buffalo Creek; South by property of Sam Gordy and property of the Elkins Estate; and West by property of the Elkins Estate and property of Luther Ennis. The said tract of land is the same conveyed by B. J. Tarbutton to Ben J. Tarbutton, Jr., and Hugh M. Tarbutton, by deed dated December 27, 1952, recorded in Deed Book "35", Page 193, in the Office of the Clerk of the Superior Court of Washington County, Georgia.

RECORDED DEC 31 1976 Jamie H. Lindsey, Clerk

Fraudulent Warranty Deed between Hugh McMaster Tarbutton and Loulie Eugenia Kernaghan Tarbutton, as Trustee of Irrevocable Trust for benefit of Loulie Eugenia Tarbutton, December 21, 1976, pg. 2

LAW OFFICES

ALSTON & BIRD

A PARTNERSHIP INCLUDING PROFESSIONAL CORPORATIONS

1200 CITIZENS & SOUTHERN NATIONAL BANK BUILDING
35 BROAD STREET
ATLANTA, GEORGIA 30335
404-586-1500

CABLE: AMGRAM ATLANTA TELEX: 54-2996

WASHINGTON OFFICES
1800 M STREET, N.W., SUITE 1000
WASHINGTON, D.C. 20036
202-223-1300

ATLANTA/GALLERIA OFFICES
100 GALLERIA PARKWAY, SUITE 1200
ATLANTA, GEORGIA 30339
404-955-8400

FRANKLIN R. NIX, P.C.
DIRECT DIAL: 404 586-1556

December 30, 1983

BY HAND DELIVERY

Mr. Timothy Dawson
Mr. Cornelius Dawson
Mr. Homer Dawson
Ms. Elizabeth Whitehead
Ms. Wilhelmina Ross
Ms. Deborah Sparks
Ms. Bertha Young Cheese
Ms. Corrine Harris
Mr. Charlie Young
Ms. Willie Bell Lundy
Ms. Eva J. Tarwick Thomas
Mr. Lucious Renfrow
Mr. Edward Renfrow
Ms. Mamie Carter Butts
Ms. Esther Carter Hinton
Mr. Crawford Carter
Ms. Mamie Carter
Ms. ~~Taereas~~ Carter Snyder
Ms. Ann Carter Green
Ms. Mary Carter Vincent
Ms. Ruth M. Carter Rawlins
Mr. Ennis Carter
Mr. Jeff Carter, III
Ms. Ruby Carter Nelson
Ms. Blanche Holley
Mr. O'Neal Turner
Mr. Samuel Turner, Jr.
Ms. Mildred Turner
Ms. Eloise Dawson Gordy

c/o Ms. Eloise Dawson Gordy
Route 3, Box 78
Sanderville, Georgia 31082

Re: Carter heirs v. Tarbuttons -- Fee Agreement

Ladies and Gentlemen:

This correspondence will serve to confirm our firm's agreement to act as attorney for each of you, as the heirs at law of Jeff Carter, Sr., upon the following terms and conditions:

(1) The scope of our engagement and representation consists of our agreement to prosecute the Carter family's claims against B. J. Tarbutton, Sr., B. J. Tarbutton, Jr., and Hugh M. Tarbutton, and any of their transferees, with respect to all of the lands formerly owned by Jeff Carter, Sr. as of his death in January of 1930. Initially, we envision making formal written demands upon the Tarbuttons for the actual reconveyance of all such lands back to the Carter family. To the extent that our demands on behalf of the Carter family are refused, we envision filing suit against the Tarbuttons, and any of their successors, in the Superior Court of Washington County, Georgia. In such

Fee Agreement between the Tarbuttons' Attorneys, Alston & Bird, Frank Nix, et. al. and the solicited Carter Heirs, December 30, 1983, pg. 1.

ALSTON & BIRD
A PARTNERSHIP INCLUDING PROFESSIONAL CORPORATIONS

litigation we would seek ultimately to cancel all transfers of the subject property made after the death of Jeff Carter, Sr., so as to vest the legal, unencumbered title to all such lands back in the Carter family. Having cleared title to the family's land and revested title in the family, our final goal would be that of selling the mineral rights to the valuable kaolin deposits underlying the subject lands for the best possible price.

(2) My firm has agreed to undertake your legal representation on a contingency fee basis. Though you will ultimately be responsible for reimbursing us for all actual out-of-pocket costs and expenses such as court fees, deposition transcript costs, expert witness fees, etc. we will initially advance such costs and ultimately recover same from the proceeds of any judgment obtained or from the proceeds of any settlement to which all of the Carter family heirs consent.

(3) Upon resolution of your family's claim to the subject lands against the Tarbuttons and their successors, whether through settlement prior to litigation or through litigation of your claims against the Tarbuttons and their successors, my firm's compensation for professional legal services rendered shall be one-third (33-1/3%) of the net amounts received in settlement, recovered by judgment through a trial of your claims, and received from the sale of mineral rights to the family's lands or any portion thereof, said net amount being equal to the gross amount collected in settlement, by judgment, or from a sale of mineral rights, less our firm's out-of-pocket expenses incurred upon your family's behalf.

(4) Upon cancellation of any interest which the Tarbuttons or their successors may have in the family's lands, and upon the revesting of legal, unencumbered title to the subject lands in all of the Carter heirs, whether through settlement prior to litigation, or through a trial of your claims against the Tarbuttons and their successors, our compensation for professional legal services rendered in recovering legal title to the family's lands and in assisting in the sale of the underlying kaolin deposits for the best possible price shall be one-third (33-1/3%) of the total net sales proceeds (i.e., gross sales price less closing costs) received for the sale of the mineral rights to all or any portion of the lands recovered for the family. These fees shall have been earned in their entirety and shall be due and payable upon the entry of a final order vesting title in the subject lands in the Carter family or the execution of any settlement agreement and deeds whereby legal title to the subject lands is restored to the Carter family.

- 2 -

Fee Agreement between the Tarbuttons' Attorneys, Alston & Bird, Frank Nix, et. al. and the solicited Carter Heirs, December 30, 1983, pg. 2.

ALSTON & BIRD

A PARTNERSHIP INCLUDING PROFESSIONAL CORPORATIONS

(5) Actual payment of my firm's one-third (33-1/3%) contingency fee shall be payable as follows:

(a) With respect to any settlement payment, Alston & Bird's contingency fee shall be paid at the settlement closing;

(b) With respect to any judgment obtained on behalf of the Carter family, Alston & Bird's contingency fee shall be paid upon collection of the judgment or any portion thereof; and

(c) With respect to the sale of the family's lands and/or the mineral rights thereto, Alston & Bird's contingency fee shall be paid at the closing of the sale of such lands or mineral rights as to all or any portion of such lands.

(6) Any settlement of your family's claim will, of course, be strictly subject to the unanimous approval of all heirs. Likewise, the actual terms of sale and sales price of the mineral rights for the kaolin deposits underlying the family's lands shall also be strictly subject to the unanimous approval of all heirs.

(7) This fee agreement shall be governed by and construed according to the laws of the State of Georgia.

(8) Finally, though it would appear from our initial investigation of the circumstances and events following the death of Jeff Carter, Sr., that meritorious claims and grounds exist whereby you and your fellow heirs may be able to recover legal title to the family's lands, we cannot guarantee and we have not represented or warranted, nor do we represent nor warrant now, that any particular recovery in this matter can be achieved. Ultimately, the success of our representation may hinge upon matters presently unknown to us, documents in the possession of the Tarbuttons, and upon the consideration given such facts and documents by any jury sitting in judgment on any lawsuit which we may find it necessary to file on your behalf. Equally important is your cooperation and that of every other heir, particularly those heirs who have personal knowledge of events and circumstances directly bearing upon the family's claims.

We count it a privilege to represent the Carter family in this matter and we look forward to working with each of you in the successful resolution of the family's claims.

ALSTON & BIRD

BY: Franklin R. Nix

Franklin R. Nix, Partner

We, the undersigned heirs at law of Jeff Carter, Sr. hereby individually acknowledge that we have read this fee agreement

— 3 —

Fee Agreement between the Tarbuttons' Attorneys, Alston & Bird, Frank Nix, et. al. and the solicited Carter Heirs, December 30, 1983, pg. 3.

ALSTON & BIRD
A PARTNERSHIP INCLUDING PROFESSIONAL CORPORATIONS

letter carefully, that we have addressed any questions we may have had to Mr. Nix in person or by telephone, that he has answered to our satisfaction all of our questions about this representation of the family's claims, and that we have all unanimously retained Alston & Bird to represent us in seeking the recovery of our family's lands from the Tarbuttons, or their successors, upon the terms and conditions stated above.

_______________________________(SEAL)
TIMOTHY DAWSON

Sworn to and subscribed before me this ______ day of ______________, 198__.

____
NOTARY PUBLIC

_______________________________(SEAL)
CORNELIUS DAWSON

Sworn to and subscribed before me this ______ day of ______________, 198__.

____
NOTARY PUBLIC

_______________________________(SEAL)
HOMER DAWSON

Sworn to and subscribed before me this ______ day of ______________, 198__.

____
NOTARY PUBLIC

_______________________________(SEAL)
ELIZABETH WHITEHEAD

Sworn to and subscribed before me this ______ day of ______________, 198__.

____
NOTARY PUBLIC

- 4 -

Fee Agreement between the Tarbuttons' Attorneys, Alston & Bird, Frank Nix, et. al. and the solicited Carter Heirs, December 30, 1983, pg. 4.

AGREEMENT

This Agreement is made and entered into as of the 30th day of December, 1983, between the undersigned heirs at law of Jeff Carter, Sr. (hereinafter "the Heirs"), and Mr. Robert Lee Watkins.

W I T N E S S E T H:

WHEREAS, the Heirs have requested the aid and assistance of Mr. Robert Lee Watkins in asserting claims for the recovery of the family's lands against the Tarbuttons, or their successors, and in the sale of the family's lands and/or the mineral rights thereto upon the successful recovery of the family's lands; and

WHEREAS, Mr. Robert Lee Watkins has already rendered valuable services to the Heirs in investigating the factual basis underlying the Heirs' claims, in obtaining counsel on behalf of the Heirs, and in rendering valuable assistance to the Heirs and their counsel in prosecution of the family's claims against the Tarbuttons and their successors; and

WHEREAS, it is the unanimous desire and intention of all of the undersigned Heirs to compensate Mr. Robert Lee Watkins for all services rendered to date and to be rendered in the future in assisting in the prosecution of the Heirs' claims against the Tarbuttons, or their successors, and the subsequent resale of the family's lands and/or the mineral rights thereto for the best possible price; and

Agreement between Robert Lee Watkins (Tarbutton and Kaolin Industry Agent) and the solicited Carter heirs, December 30, 1983, pg. 1.

WHEREAS, Mr. Robert Lee Watkins has already used his best efforts and hereby agrees to use his best efforts in the future to assist the prosecution of the Heirs' claims and the successful resale of the Heirs' lands and/or the mineral rights thereto to the best of his ability;

NOW, THEREFORE, in consideration of the mutual promises and covenants contained herein, as well as the mutual benefits flowing from one to another under this Agreement, the Heirs and Robert Lee Watkins do hereby solemnly agree as follows:

1.

Robert Lee Watkins hereby solemnly agrees to continue using his best efforts to assist counsel in the recovery of legal title to the family's lands and thereafter to assist the Heirs in the sale of the kaolin underlying the family's lands, either through a sale of the lands themselves or the mineral rights thereto, for the best possible terms.

2.

In consideration for his efforts to date and for all of Mr. Robert Lee Watkins' best efforts in the future on behalf of the Heirs, the undersigned Heirs unanimously agree to pay to Robert Lee Watkins thirteen (13%) percent of the net amount of any monies received in settlement or recovered by judgment through a trial of the family's claims, the net amount of such proceeds being defined as the gross amount of such proceeds less the out-of-pocket expenses and disbursements of Alston & Bird and such out-of-pocket

-2-

Agreement between Robert Lee Watkins (Tarbutton and Kaolin Industry Agent) and the solicited Carter heirs, December 30, 1983, pg. 2.

expenses and disbursements as may be made by Mr. Robert Lee Watkins in the course of rendering the aforesaid services to the Heirs.

3.

In consideration for his efforts to date and for all of Mr. Robert Lee Watkins' best efforts in the future on behalf of the Heirs in the resale of the family's lands and/or the mineral rights thereto, the undersigned Heirs unanimously agree to pay to Robert Lee Watkins thirteen (13%) percent of the total net sales proceeds (i.e., gross sales price less closing costs) received for the sale of the family's lands and/or the mineral rights thereto, or any portion thereof. The amount which the Heirs hereby agree to pay to Robert Lee Watkins for his assistance in the resale of their lands shall have been earned upon the execution by all of the Heirs of a contract for the sale of their lands and/or a contract for the sale of the mineral rights thereto, and the compensation agreed shall be due and payable to Robert Lee Watkins at the closing of the sale of the subject lands and/or the mineral rights thereto.

4.

Specifically, but not by way of limitation, the Heirs and Mr. Robert Lee Watkins hereby specifically agree and confirm that Mr. Robert Lee Watkins shall not be entitled to nor ask for any compensation for exercising the powers of attorney which the Heirs have given Mr. Watkins, but that wholly apart from Mr. Watkins' exercise of any such powers of attorney, he shall be compensated

-3-

Agreement between Robert Lee Watkins (Tarbutton and Kaolin Industry Agent) and the solicited Carter heirs, December 30, 1983, pg. 3.

as agreed above for rendering the services referenced above.

IN WITNESS WHEREOF, the parties have hereunto set their hands and affixed their seals as of December 30, 1983, but upon the actual dates shown below.

______________________________(SEAL)
ROBERT LEE WATKINS

Sworn to and subscribed
before me this ______ day
of ________________, 198__.

____
NOTARY PUBLIC

______________________________(SEAL)
TIMOTHY DAWSON

Sworn to and subscribed
before me this ______ day
of ________________, 198__.

____
NOTARY PUBLIC

______________________________(SEAL)
CORNELIUS DAWSON

Sworn to and subscribed
before me this ______ day
of ________________, 198__.

____
NOTARY PUBLIC

______________________________(SEAL)
HOMER DAWSON

Sworn to and subscribed
before me this ______ day
of ________________, 198__.

____
NOTARY PUBLIC

-4-

Agreement between Robert Lee Watkins (Tarbutton and Kaolin Industry Agent) and the solicited Carter heirs, December 30, 1983, pg. 4.

LAW OFFICES

ALSTON & BIRD

A PARTNERSHIP INCLUDING PROFESSIONAL CORPORATIONS

1200 CITIZENS & SOUTHERN NATIONAL BANK BUILDING
35 BROAD STREET
ATLANTA, GEORGIA 30335
404-586-1500

CABLE: AMGRAM ATLANTA TELEX: 54-2996

WASHINGTON OFFICES
1800 M STREET, N.W., SUITE 1000
WASHINGTON, D.C. 20036
202-223-1300

ATLANTA/GALLERIA OFFICES
100 GALLERIA PARKWAY, SUITE 1200
ATLANTA, GEORGIA 30339
404-955-8400

FRANKLIN R. NIX, P.C.
DIRECT DIAL: 404 586 1556

April 19, 1984

Mr. Timothy Dawson
Mr. Cornelius Dawson
Mr. Homer Dawson
Ms. Elizabeth Whitehead
Ms. Wilhelmina Ross
Ms. Deborah Sparks
Ms. Bertha Young Cheese
Ms. Corrine Harris
Mr. Charlie Young
Ms. Willie Bell Lundy
Ms. Eva J. Tarwick Thomas
Mr. Lucious Renfrow
Mr. Edward Renfrow
Ms. Mamie Carter Butts
Ms. Esther Carter Hinton
Mr. Crawford Carter
Ms. Mamie Carter
Ms. Taereas Carter Snyder
Ms. Ann Carter Green
Ms. Mary Carter Vincent
Ms. Ruth M. Carter Rawlins
Mr. Ennis Carter
Mr. Jeff Carter, III
Ms. Ruby Carter Nelson
Ms. Blanche Holley
Mr. O'Neal Turner
Mr. Samuel Turner, Jr.
Ms. Mildred Turner
Ms. Eloise Dawson Gordy
Ms. Lizzie Carter Dixon

Re: Carter Heirs v. Tarbutton - <u>Withdrawal of Counsel</u>

Ladies & Gentlemen:

Since my last letter of December 30, 1983, confirming the fee agreement under which my firm, Alston & Bird, would represent each of you in attempting to recover your family's land from the Tarbuttons, I have discovered business relationships which will require my firm's withdrawal from your representation. The business relationships to which I make reference are not legal conflicts. My firm does not now and has not in the past represented the Tarbuttons. Unfortunately, however, the largest client of our firm is The Citizens and Southern National Bank, which is the largest bank in the State of Georgia. Two of the largest shareholders in C&S Bank, and two of the most influential directors on the board of directors, are Messrs. Hugh M. Tarbutton and B. J. Tarbutton, Jr. My firm also represents the Sandersville Railroad, which is wholly owned by the Tarbuttons.

Because of these business relationships, the Management Committee of my law firm has decided that we cannot undertake any representation adverse to that of the Tarbuttons individually without jeopardizing our representation of C&S Bank as well as the Sandersville Railroad. Were it strictly a personal decision for me to make, I would much prefer to continue your representation. I am, however, but one of the many partners in my firm and I must bow to the wishes of a majority of my partners and our Management Committee in withdrawing from your representation.

The Tarbuttons' Attorneys (Alston & Bird), 'Withdrawal of Counsel' from the solicited Carter Heirs, April 19, 1984, pg. 1.

ALSTON & BIRD

A PARTNERSHIP INCLUDING PROFESSIONAL CORPORATIONS

I know that the withdrawal of my firm may pose as much of a disappointment to you as it poses to me professionally. Because I believe in the claims of your family to the land in question I wanted to fight for you as long and as hard as I needed to to recover your land.

I want you to know, however, that in withdrawing from your case my firm has not abandoned you. To the contrary, we have felt it our professional obligation to find for you the best counsel available to handle your type of case, indeed to handle it as well as I would had my firm not withdrawn. We have ended our search for such an individual and I am pleased to recommend to you a very fine lawyer and personal friend of mine, Mr. Roger W. Moister, Jr. Mr. Moister is a graduate of Vanderbilt University and the Vanderbilt School of Law, one of the finest law schools in this country. He is a well known and highly respected Atlanta lawyer. He has been practicing as many years as I have and in my professional opinion he will represent you as competently and fight for you as tenaciously as my own firm would have. I have discussed your family's case with him at length and he is willing to represent the family on essentially the same terms and conditions outlined in my prior fee agreement letter of December 30, 1983.

Mr. Robert Watkins and I have discussed your case at length with Mr. Moister. I am sure that Mr. Watkins will share with you his own view that Mr. Moister, being a lawyer of the highest integrity and competence, is one whom Mr. Watkins recommends to you as well. In recommending Mr. Moister to you, I have turned over to him all of my files and other work product which we have developed to date in preparing to file suit to recover the family's land. Mr. Moister has familiarized himself with these materials and is ready to go forward as soon as you retain him.

In summary, though I regret personally my firm's decision to withdraw from your representation, I am pleased that we are able to recommend to you a fine lawyer to take my firm's place. Accordingly, I suggest that each of you act now to approve the appointment of Mrs. Blanche Holley as administrator of the Jeff Carter, Sr. estate and to retain Mr. Moister to handle your representation upon the terms and conditions outlined in his own fee agreement letter.

I will be happy to try to answer any questions which any of you might have in regard to these matters. In the meantime, I recommend Mr. Moister to you and will be hoping in the future that he can obtain favorable results for the Carter family heirs.

Sincerely,

Franklin R. Nix

FRN/dm

The Tarbuttons' Attorneys (Alston & Bird), 'Withdrawal of Counsel' from the solicited Carter Heirs, April 19, 1984, pg. 2.

AFFIDAVIT OF JAMES A. NOLAN, ESQ.

STATE OF GEORGIA

COUNTY OF MORGAN

The undersigned James A. Nolan, having appeared before the undersigned officer who is authorized to administer oaths, the said James A. Nolan, having been first sworn, stated that the following is true and correct to the best of his knowledge and belief.

1.

I am James A. Nolan. I was admitted to the State Bar of Georgia in 1973; my State Bar Number is 545450. I have practiced law in the State of Georgia on a continuing basis from the time I was admitted to the Bar until this date.

2.

I have read the "CANON OF ETHICS" as published by the State Bar of Georgia, and while I do not claim to be an expert on the "CANON OF ETHICS", I believe that I possess a basic understanding as to what conduct constitutes a violation of those "CANONS" so as to constitute legal malpractice.

3.

I have read the attached copy of a Complaint that I understand is to be filed in the Superior Court of Fulton County, Georgia. This copy is marked Exhibit "A" and is incorporated in this Affidavit by reference, and is referred to herein for the purpose of illustration and clarification. As such, it is a necessary part of this Affidavit and this Affidavit is not complete without this

BOOK 12812 PG 692

Affidavit of Document Examiner James Nolan, September 1, 1993, pg.1.

attachment. This Complaint has 16 pages and 57 paragraphs. These pages and paragraphs will be referred to by number.

4.

I have also read various excerpts from the transcript of the trial of the United States of America vs. Robert L. Watkins that was prosecuted in the U. S. District Court in the Middle District of Georgia, as well as excerpts from the various transcripts of the hearing brought by Mr. Watkins before the Eleventh Circuit Court of Appeals involving his complaint against Judges Owens and Fitzpatrick.

Based on the evidence and testimony presented at said trial and hearing, and based on the allegations contained in said Complaint, it is my opinion that said Complaint contains allegations against the Defendants, that if proven in Court would constitute legal malpractice.

5.

The representation of both parties to a controversy, without revealing to both parties the existence of such dual representation, as alleged in Paragraph 24, Page 6 and Paragraph 35, Page 9, is a clear violation of CANONS 6 and 5, and is in my opinion legal malpractice.

6.

The fee splitting arrangement alleged in Paragraph 14, Page 4 is a violation of CANON 2, and is in my opinion legal malpractice.

2

Affidavit of Document Examiner James Nolan, September 1, 1993, pg. 2.

7.

The alleged act of referring a client to an incompetent attorney when the original attorney withdraws from representing the client, as set forth in Paragraph 37, Page 9 and Paragraph 23, Page 6, if proven would be an act of legal malpractice.

8.

The withholding of evidence that would have proven the innocence of a client as alleged in Paragraph 53, Page 13, would be an act of legal malpractice.

9.

I make this Affidavit under oath, after being duly sworn, on the basis of my legal education, experience and personal knowledge of the above-referenced case. This Affidavit is executed for the purpose of being attached to and used in support of Plaintiff's Complaint for Damages for legal malpractice, as required by O.C.G.A., §9-11-9.1.

FURTHER AFFIANT SAYETH NAUGHT.

This 1st day of September 1993.

JAMES A. NOLAN
Georgia Bar No. 545450

Sworn to and subscribed to this 1st day of September, 1993.

Notary Public Notary Public, Morgan County, Georgia My Commission Expires Sept. 18, 1995
My Commission Expires: 9-1-93

3

BOOK 1281 PG 694

Affidavit of Document Examiner James Nolan, September 1, 1993, pg. 3

NAKLo.

In 1984, heirs of Jeff Carter, Sr. from Philadelphia and New York met to appoint an administrator to the Carter Estate. The meeting took place at Blanche Holley's (daughter of Lillie Ruth Carter), home in Philadelphia. It was at this meeting Horace attended with his brother Henry that his involvement in the Carter case began.

Horace's background in consumer advocacy made him immediately suspicious of Robert Lee Watkins, whose scheme was, unfortunately, quite persuasive to many of the Carter heirs. Watkins asked if the purpose of probating an estate was understood. Horace answered yes, henceforth, Robert Lee was curt and hostile towards him. Horace and Theresa Carter Snyder, daughter of Virge and Mamie Carter, found Robert Lee's responses to their questions, defensive and obnoxious. Horace told Theresa he felt it would be unwise to appoint an administrator without further investigating the case.

Appointing an administrator would allow the Tarbutton's, who had maintained control of the estate since the 1930s, to have all of the Carter heirs under one authority. Watkins was vehement about the family's need to appoint an administrator, which lead Horace to question the legality of the Tarbutton's acquisition of the land. There is a historical pattern of Black-owned land being illegally sold, without the knowledge or consent of the heirs. Apprehensive of Watkins, Horace asked O'Neal Turner (Blanche's brother), about going to Sandersville, Georgia to look into the matter. O'Neal discouraged the trip, maintaining Blanche had everything under control.

The meeting perturbed Horace. That evening, he telephoned as many relatives as possible, and attempted to persuade them not to appoint an administrator. Unfortunately, his efforts were unsuccessful.

The following week, Horace flew to Sandersville to investigate the Carter case. It was then that he learned of Loulie Tarbutton's slander and defamation lawsuit against the Carter heirs and Robert Lee Watkins. When he examined the suit, he discovered Robert Lee had filed an affidavit, in "behalf" of the Carter heirs, clouding the Tarbutton's title to the land, without first filing a lawsuit. Horace was also unaware that the heirs had already given Watkins power of attorney, with a 13% contingent fee. On December 30, 1983, Watkins misled the heirs into a fraudulent agreement with the law firm, Alston & Bird, and attorney Frank Nix, alleging they would "represent" the heirs in their effort to regain control of their land. The firm would receive a 33% contingent fee.

4-21-84

Dear Mary,

As promised during our telephone conversation on Monday April 23, 1984, I am am enclosing copies of two agreements, one from Franklin R. Nix and one from Robert L. Watkins both of whom are with the Alston and Bird Law firm in Atlanta Ga. Watkins is an investigator.

I believe you have a copy of the affidavit filed in Washington County Sandersville Ga 1-25-84.

Love,
Blanche

Because of his aversion to Robert Watkins, Frank Nix and Alston & Bird, Horace searched for a different attorney to represent the Carter heirs. For nearly half of a century, the heirs' made several unsuccessful attempts to retain an attorney to help them reclaim their estate from the Tarbutton family. This made the sudden zeal displayed by the prominent Atlanta firm extremely questionable. During his search for an attorney, Horace even contacted Frank Nix and expressed his opinion on Robert Watkins' involvement and Alston & Bird's bungling of the Carter claim. Horace was still unaware, however, of how pivotal a role Nix played in the Tarbutton's victory.

Between 1984 and 1986, Horace was unable to obtain any information beyond Tarbutton's lawsuit against the Carter heirs. The rest of the family seemed equally uninformed.

In 1989, Horace spoke to FBI agent Fred Stofer, at which time he learned that Watkins was going before a grand jury for suborned perjury. He asked Horace what he knew about Watkins' involvement in aiding and abetting the perjured testimony of Charles Williams. He also asked Horace what he thought of Watkins.

Horace responded that after meeting him, he could not imagine Watkins was capable of single-handedly orchestrating such a grand, complex scheme, especially against forces as powerful as the kaolin cartel and the Tarbuttons. Watkins was not an attorney, nor was he scholastically capable of investigating the case and filing the necessary legal briefs. It was evident that he was not working alone. Horace suspected Alston & Bird represented Tarbutton interests, and that they were using Watkins to solicit the Carter heirs to clear the Tarbutton's title to the Carter estate.

Later that year, Blanche and Horace both testified in the grand jury hearing of Robert Lee Watkins in Macon, Georgia. After the hearing, Horace and Blanche began to share information. Horace subsequently contacted the U.S. Attorney General in Georgia to acquire more information.

In 1992, Blanche told Horace that Robert Lee had been sentenced to five years in prison and fined $50,000. The Eleventh Circuit District Court investigated Chief Judge Owens and Judge Fitzpatrick's conduct in *Tarbutton,* as well as other cases in which Robert Lee was involved. Reading the report confirmed Horace's earlier suspicions about Frank Nix, Alston & Bird, and Watkins' conspiracy to clear the Tarbutton's title to the Carter estate, and forever prohibit the heirs from raising the issues of theft, fraud, forgery, and obstruction, again.

Soon after Robert Lee's conviction for suborning perjury, his battle began with Frank Nix for control of cases they once worked on jointly. In a correspondence with one of the landowners, Frank Nix stated, that "if a jury were to give us a verdict of twenty million dollars when your case is tried, Mr. Watkins' share would come to three million dollars - an outrageous sum for someone who has done nothing for you...You can choose to stick by me - a lawyer who has served you faithfully for seven and one-half years - or you can leave yourselves to the mercy of Mr. Watkins, a non-lawyer, a convicted felon and someone who apparently wants to sell you out just to save himself some prison time - regardless of the cost to your family".

During a telephone conversation between Horace and Blanche, she mentioned Lora Ella's grandson, Wendell Dawson, an attorney in Nashville, Tennessee. Horace contacted him around February of 1993, beginning an interaction that often centered around the Jeff Carter estate.

Horace and his cousin, Gloria "Glo" Lord, were discussing the *Cheeves & Gibson* case, when she mentioned another cousin, Michael Cheeves, who was actively involved in it. Nix and Watkins were involved in this case as well, and had made a similar contingent fee arrangement with the Cheeves heirs. The similar pattern of fraud present in both cases gave Horace and Michael plenty to discuss, as they began communicating regularly.

In the case of the heirs of Curtis Cheeves, they were unable to unanimously agree that Frank Nix should take their case. Nix wanted them to merge with the Gibson and Butts' cases. Nix and his attorney, Foy Devine, contacted L. Ray Patterson to arrange an agreement between the three families.

In a proposal, Patterson said, "This situation presents a potential conflict-of-interest for the attorneys and a practical conflict for the families. Mr. Nix and Mr. Devine are confident that these conflicts can be resolved. They feel, however, that an independent lawyer representing the families' mutual best interest can best accomplish a resolution. I will not be trying your cases when they come to trial. My job is figuring out how the families might join together to assure that all three families fairly recover their losses regardless of whose case is first tried".

The threat the lawyers presented to the Cheeves heirs was that funds were limited: the first family's settlement might diminish the others'. In fact, the threat of diminishing funds was just another excuse to coerce heirs into signing their rights away. Nix abandoned the case because some heirs (Gloria "Glo" Lord, Mary "Town" Cheeves Trawick, and others) refused to cooperate. Michael's involvement in the *Cheeves* case ended as well.

Michael told Horace about Charles Seabrook, a journalist for the *Atlanta Journal & Constitution.* Seabrook was writing an investigative report on the kaolin cartel and the landowners they fleece. He said he wanted to fairly report both the landowners' side and the kaolin cartel's side. He participated, however, in propagandizing Watkins' charade that he was helping landowners, and detracted attention from the kaolin cartel's exploitative practices.

Horace immediately contacted Charles Seabrook, curious about the journalist's opinion of the *Tarbutton* case. Seabrook told Horace that Robert Watkins had been released from prison and was living in a halfway house. In February of 1993, Horace contacted Watkins, who told him he had information proving he had been set up to suborn perjury. He also claimed to have volumes of incriminating evidence against Alston & Bird and Frank Nix, which he was willing to share. Within one week, Watkins changed his mind, stating he had given the exclusive story rights to his publisher.

In March of 1993, Horace's cousin Wendell visited him in Philadelphia. Horace and Wendell found the accomplishments of Jeff, Sr. astounding, considering he was a first generation Black man born "free". The two issued a newsletter to Jeff, Sr.'s heirs, briefly explaining his legacy and the brutal eviction of his daughter and grandchildren from his estate. The newsletter also mentioned Seabrook's upcoming series on kaolin and the industry it spawned in Middle District Georgia.

Horace realized after reading Seabrook's article "White Gold", that the fraud and brutality his family experienced was not an isolated incident. The Carter claim differed slightly, primarily due to the large quantity of land lost. It was also set apart by the oppressive psychological torment that took place for over a decade (not to mention an estimated $6,000 worth of cotton delivered to B.J. Tarbutton), and the physical abuse perpetrated on Lora Ella when she was illegally and savagely evicted from her father's estate in 1950. Unfortunately, the kaolin cartel swindled, manipulated, and destroyed many other Black families as well.

It was clear that landowners needed organization to assert their rights. Due to this, Horace established The National Association of Kaolin Landowners (NAKLo.). NAKLo. is a non-profit organization that was formed and registered in Georgia in August 1993. Its mission is to advocate for exploited landowners, particularly those with kaolin.

Through NAKLo.'s investigations, kaolin's historical, multinational, multi-billion dollar value was discovered. The South African-dominated kaolin cartel wields global political influence, and exerts great might in Washington County, Georgia. For instance, the cartel contributes to Democratic and Republican political action committees, in return for exemption from severance tax.

On July 30, 1993, Horace met Watkins at his racetrack in Warner Robins, Georgia. Watkins reiterated he would be unable to share information. Omar Reid, a former tax commissioner and kaolin agent who had assisted Watkins on several kaolin cases, was also present. The two often received more money from their contingent fees, than the landowner received in their entire settlement. The meeting ended with a conversation between Horace and Omar Reid; Watkins had already left the booth. Omar mentioned Robert Lee's intention to sue Alston & Bird and Frank Nix. For Horace, the meeting was a complete disappointment.

STATE OF TENNESSEE
OFFICE OF THE
ATTORNEY GENERAL
450 JAMES ROBERTSON PARKWAY
NASHVILLE, TENNESSEE 37243-0485

May 10, 1993

Letters to the Editor
The Atlanta Constitution
P.O. Box 4689
Atlanta, Georgia 30302

Dear Editor:

Thank you for your extremely informative and comprehensive report on the Middle Georgia kaolin industry. Because I was briefly quoted in the report, I wish to comment further.

It is somewhat ironic that in your lead editorial you refer to the kaolin industry's practices in Georgia as a form of "colonialism". This metaphor is especially appropriate when combined with the fact, as the report asserts, that companies headquartered in South Africa have major interests in several of the kaolin firms operating in the state.

Indeed, it was in context of the racial apartheid policies which were so pervasive in the American South in the decades of the 30's and 40's that in 1950 would allow an affluent, politically powerful white man and an industry to brutally evict my grandmother, Lora Ella Carter Dawson, from a 600 plus acre homestead which she and her siblings inherited from their father, Jeff Carter, Sr. This event so traumatized my grandmother that it is generally believed she suffered a nervous breakdown. While her death certificate in 1966 suggests she expired of natural causes, her family knows that the major reason was a broken heart.

The horror of the memories surrounding the fraudulent loss of the family's land is only exacerbated by the injustice we received in the federal court of Macon in 1986. It was at that time our claims to this homestead, and for lost kaolin and timber profits, were dismissed on summary judgment.

Letter from Wendell Dawson to the *Atlanta Constitution,* pg. 1

Wendell C. Dawson
Letter to the Editor
Page 2

But the report on how Robert Watkins was railroaded into federal prison on an aiding and abetting forgery conviction flowing from the family's litigation against the Tarbuttons, only reaffirms, in our mind, the perception that justice was not dispensed to us. Contributing to this perception is the fact ours was the first case this federal judge ever heard; he failed to disclose to the family's lawyers that the Tarbutton family's lawyers had previously represented the judge's family on a legal matter; and, he admitted in a subsequent proceeding, that his distrust of Watkins predated the Carter litigation.

It is interesting to read that members of the Tarbutton family of Washington County are noted for their civic mindedness. And I'm sure those who have been the recipients of their goodwill are grateful. But no amount of civic "do-gooding" will ever erase the vicious racism that was visited on my grandmother and other family members by the deceased Ben Tarbutton, Sr. With that in mind, it should be easy for others to understand the propriety of many in my family adopting the mantra which those of the Jewish faith promulgated long ago: Never Again.

Sincerely,

Wendell C. Dawson

WENDELL C. DAWSON
Assistant State Attorney General

(615) 333-1779 (H)
741-3514 (O)
741-8151 (FAX)

Letter from Wendell Dawson to the *Atlanta Constitution*, pg. 2

MARCH 1, 1994

ROBERT WATKINS
P.O. BOX 1223
WARNER ROBINS, GA 31099

RE: JEFF CARTER ESTATE
WASHINGTON COUNTY

TO THE CARTER FAMILY,

Ladies and Gentlemen, as a part of my responsibility to the Carter Family by my having held Power of Attorney to all Jeff Carter Heirs, I have a duty to divulge the status of the estate as it stands at this time. Please note the following;

1. Due to my prosecution by the U.S. Government, new evidence has come to light in the Carter Case. It has been determined that Mr. Roger Moister has admitted that he was incompetant to handle the Carter Case. Also Mr. Moister has admitted to other wrong doings in the Carter Case.

This information came to light through the findings of the 11th Circuit Judicial Inquiry which was sent to me at Marianna Florida, by orders of the court in June of 1992.

I am informing you of this because you all may have a valid claim against Mr. Moister and other Attorneys involved for the concealment of fraud and other information.

If you need further information concerning this matter you may call me at (404) 775-2881 or write me at the above address and I will furnish you the documentation and other information that will shed light on this matter.

2. I must also inform you that if you intend to persue this matter you need to contact an attorney no later than May 1994 due to the statue Laws of Georgia.

I wish you all the best of luck.

Sincerely,

Robert L. Watkins

Robert L. Watkins

Letter from Robert Lee Watkins to the Carter Heirs, March 1, 1994

In a letter dated August 16, 1993, Georgia Congresswoman Cynthia McKinney requested someone from Attorney General Janet Reno's office speak with Robert Lee Watkins (to review his material which included files, affidavits, and videotapes). NAKLo. requested a meeting with Congresswoman McKinney when Horace learned of her letter in behalf of Watkins. The meeting was confirmed for Monday, September 27, 1993 at her Washington, DC office.

Wendell Dawson, Michael Cheeves, Charles Seabrook, Adam Renfroe and his son, attended the meeting. NAKLo. correspondent W. Gary Chambers, his son, and their attorney Leo Brown, were also present. Horace gave a general explanation of landowners' struggles. Adam Renfroe and W. Gary Chambers, for instance, were unable to break their mining leases. The kaolin cartel failed to mine their minerals and fairly compensate them. Michael Cheeves represented the struggle of the Curtis Cheeves heirs' against Southern Clays. As with most kaolin cases, fraud, forgery, and deception is intrinsic. The Cheeves heirs were forced to sell their 200-acre estate to Southern Clays, for a minuscule $35,000. Wendell spoke about the Carter heirs' 50 year plight to reclaim their stolen estate from the Tarbutton family.

Congresswoman McKinney was urged to assist in the ongoing battle against the kaolin cartel. Before the meeting ended, she agreed to meet with NAKLo. and local landowners in Milledgeville, Georgia. The date was set for October 12, 1993, when McKinney would be able to meet local landowners and hear their stories.

The following day, newspaper headlines in Georgia, including the *Atlanta Journal & Constitution* read, "McKinney vows aid on kaolin issue. Congresswoman to help landowners against firms." The article states that McKinney pledged help to landowners in Middle Georgia who claim giant international mining corporations intimidate, harass, and cheat them out of millions of dollars worth of kaolin. "I haven't been shy in the past about getting involved in things, and I will not be harassed and intimidated," McKinney said.

The article also quoted Michael Cheeves, who expressed the despair landowners' feel trying to get someone to address their problems. "Anybody who has any power in Middle Georgia seems to be connected to the kaolin companies", he said.

Unfortunately, Horace was hospitalized in Milledgeville the week of the meeting, and had to undergo emergency surgery. He therefore was unable to attend the meeting. Meanwhile, McKinney's assistant for the "kaolin project", Marcy Louza, arranged for Michael Cheeves and W. Gary Chambers to visit radio stations to discuss kaolin-related issues, and their effects on landowners.

For nearly four months, the *Atlanta Journal & Constitution* gave the kaolin issue more coverage than ever. The reapportionment of Cynthia McKinney's district was one of the reasons. In addition, Robert Lee was still involved in several kaolin cases, so he and Frank Nix continued to vie for control of the landowners they once mutually conspired to defraud. Some of the tactics they employed included renewing defective mineral leases and taking land outright.

In January 1994, Horace returned to Georgia for the opening of the state legislature. W. Gary Chambers lobbied on behalf of NAKLo. for a severance tax bill, and a bill to improve reclamation requirements. In addition to lobbying, Horace wanted to organize the landowners that attended the October 12th meeting he missed.

Marcy Louza was the only person who recorded the attendees' names, and she refused to share them with NAKLo. Ms. Louza later "conceded" and gave Horace 3 or 4 names, although an estimated 50 landowners attended the meeting. She was not only uncooperative, but suggested Horace relinquish leadership of NAKLo. to W. Gary Chambers. Naturally he refused. It appeared Ms. Louza was only working for Congresswoman McKinney's case of interest, Robert Lee Watkins. It is suspected by many that Ms. Louza was sent in as an agent for the kaolin cartel.

Horace arranged to meet with Lois Hollingsworth, who attended the October 12th meeting. They met in Milledgeville, at which time he read her complaint and invited her to join NAKLo. Horace was surprised to discover that Ms. Hollingsworth was Robert Lee's cousin. Her story confirmed his suspicions about Robert Lee's credibility. Robert Lee had pilfered his family's land first, following the same pattern of fraud and forgery found in most kaolin-related cases.

When Horace returned to Philadelphia, he compiled a list of names of attendants from the October meeting, along with members who joined during his most recent trip to Georgia. NAKLo.'s premier newsletter outlined a course of direction and included a survey and membership application.

Leader in fight against kaolin firms out of prison

His crime was helping the poor, protesters say

Out of prison, Robert Watkins meets Tuesday with Rep. Cynthia McKinney, a supporter. Watkins will keep fighting Georgia's kaolin industry, which he helped landowners sue.

Landowner turned leader

Head of group opposing kaolin industry never meant to be activist

'Free Robert Watkins,' group shouts at prison

Watkins worked on a contingency basis as an investigator for the Tarbuttons, a family attempting to regain land from a kaolin company through a quiet-title action before Fitzpatrick. *Tarbutton v. Tract of Land*, No. 843-403-1-MAC (641 Fed. Sup. 521) (M.D.Ga. 1986). The perjury charges arise from his having given a key witness in the case a $1,000 cashier's check. Watkins has maintained that the money went to cover travel expenses. But tripped up during a deposition, the witness, Charles E. Williams of Michigan, claimed Watkins had encouraged him to lie.

ATLANTA — A middle Georgia businessman who has fought the big kaolin companies on behalf of small landowners was greeted by Rep. Cynthia McKinney, D-Ga., when he was released from federal prison Tuesday. Robert Lee Watkins, 48, of Warner Robins was released on parole for the second time on a five-year sentence for aiding and abetting perjury in a kaolin-related civil lawsuit in 1990. "I came here today to demonstrate that we remain committed to the issue of Robert Watkins and to fair treatment for everybody in our justice system," McKinney said. The Lithonia lawmaker says there is evidence to suggest Watkins may have been railroaded into prison for fighting the kaolin industry. Her 11th District includes a large part of the land where kaolin — a valuable white clay used in making coated paper — is mined in Georgia. Watkins helped several landowners file lawsuits against the mining companies, which hold leases on thousands of acres of land.

feisty foe of kaolin industry is freed

he was railroaded after irking judges and helping poor, supporters say

In February, Horace flew back to Georgia to work with his daughter Denise Nicole, and her friend Bianca Morris, on the newsletter. Bianca assisted in publishing and editing the three-part series, featuring the Jeff Carter, Sr. story. Horace also established a satellite office for NAKLo. in Atlanta, Georgia.

NAKLo. continued its work on landowners' cases, particularly the Watkins case, and publishing newsletters. Lois Hollingsworth asked Marcy Louza to submit documents concerning the Watkins estate to NAKLo., but her request was not respected. Because Ms. Louza refused to cooperate, Horace drafted a letter to Cynthia McKinney outlining his complaint. Andrea Young (from McKinney's office) responded in a letter dated May 10, 1994, arguing if they shared information with NAKLo., they would be obligated to share information with the kaolin cartel as well.

NAKLo. received a letter from Marcy Louza, dated May 16, 1994, that stated, "…She was working to secure the release of a man being unfairly held in prison based on his work in this area", referring to Robert Lee. However, at the October NAKLo. meeting, Lois Hollingsworth gave Ms. Louza evidence that documents the conspiracy that took place between Robert Lee, Engelhard (kaolin company), agent Robert A. Bragg and others, in the fraudulent sale of the Watkins estate. Marcy Louza, nevertheless, assisted and protected a criminal who had manipulated and defrauded, not only his family, but numerous Black landowners as well.

It is impossible to know the true value of unmined kaolin without drill reports. After being solicited by Robert Lee, many landowners' claims were forever legally buried, largely due to the fact that they did not have access to their drill reports, and therefore, had no way of knowing the value of their chalk. This act of fraud ultimately led to Robert Lee's imprisonment.

Shortly after Seabrook's series ran, Wendell wrote to the editor of the *Atlanta Journal & Constitution,* thanking them for covering the kaolin issue. He also elaborated on the events following the barbaric eviction of his grandmother, Lora Ella Carter Dawson. It was generally believed that the insidious assault on her and her family's estate, which spanned nearly three decades, ultimately caused her breakdown. When she died in 1966, her family felt it was of "a broken heart". In a letter dated May 10, 1993, Wendell stated, "The horror of the memories surrounding the fraudulent loss of the family's land is only exacerbated by the injustice we received in the federal court of Macon in 1986. It was at that time our claims to this homestead, and for lost kaolin and timber profits, were dismissed on summary judgment".

In March of 1994, Wendell notified Horace of a letter Watkins sent. In the letter, Robert Lee states that he “felt it was his duty to divulge the status of the estate at that time”. He said there was “new evidence that Mr. Roger Moister had admitted that he was incompetent to handle the Carter case. Also Mr. Moister admitted to other wrong doings in the Carter case”.

He said this information came to light through the findings of the Eleventh Circuit Judicial Inquiry. It was sent to him by order of the court in June 1992, while he was in prison in Marianna, Florida. He informed the heirs that they might have “a valid claim against Moister and other attorneys involved in the concealment of fraud and other information”. He also offered to furnish documentation and other information that would shed light on the misconduct in *Tarbutton.* He added that if we intended to pursue the matter, we needed to contact an attorney by May 1994, due to Georgia’s statute laws.

Nearly two years had passed before Robert Lee informed the Carter heirs of their time constraints. If he had been acting responsibly, he would have informed the heirs long before his March 1, 1994 letter. In addition, when Horace contacted Robert Lee, he tried to extort $100,000.00 from the Carter heirs for the incriminating information he had offered.

At this point, Horace had less than a month to act. After a discussion with Wendell, and lengthy deliberation, Horace decided to file suit against Alston & Bird, Frank Nix, Roger Moister, Gerald Handley, Robert Lee Watkins, Hamilton Lokey, and Lokey & Bowden. The lawsuit was filed on Friday, April 29, 1994 in Federal District Court in the Middle District of Georgia.

In April 1996, Horace watched a tape of a meeting that featured Robert Lee after his release from prison. Robert Lee had asked Michael to bring together some landowners to update them on “startling” information he uncovered during his incarceration. The Smiths, and the Gibsons attended, along with attorney James Carter (no relation) and journalist Charles Seabrook. Michael’s brother Darryl videotaped the meeting.

Robert Lee told a pitiful story of how his misplaced trust in Frank Nix led to his incarceration. Robert Lee’s cry to the landowners was that the kaolin cartel approached him and instructed him on whom to solicit. The objective was to manipulate landowners to sell their land, or sign or renew a mineral lease. He claimed he only pretended to work for the cartel, but was actually working on behalf of the landowners.

He failed to mention that working with the kaolin cartel's attorneys is no different from working directly with the kaolin companies. Frank Nix had directed Robert Lee just as kaolin companies had. In the end, Nix and Alston & Bird double-crossed him, but Robert Lee also double-crossed many people that he considered dumb, Black landowners.

James Carter praised Robert Lee as his hero and pledged to support him. Despite the existence of incriminating documents, he, Charles Seabrook, and Congresswoman McKinney, continued to support Robert Lee Watkins.

Facts, Not Fiction

Despite the 13th and 14th Amendments to the Constitution, Brown v. Board of Education, and Civil Rights Acts of the 1960s, the right to due process and equal protection under the Constitution remains unavailable to the majority of people of color in the United States. As the supreme law of the land, the Constitution "cannot be abrogated even in part by statute". Judge Fitzpatrick ruled adverse possession, statute of limitations, and laches barred the Carter's claim to their own estate. This is an unconstitutional shield used to protect the many fraudulent violations committed by the Tarbutton's attorneys. Fitzpatrick's prejudiced conclusion that "...there is no legal excuse for defendants' forty-six year delay in asserting their claims. The court's cognizance of the general circumstances of uneducated, rural blacks in the 1930s and 1940s is simply not evidence that a white man, B.J. Tarbuttton, utilized his stronger position to take advantage of the original Carter heirs at law".

The Tarbutton's case against the Carter heirs was significant because it set a precedent, despite the fact that its foundation was built on fraud, forgery, statutes, adverse possession, and laches. The Constitution states that it "is not designed to protect majorities, who can protect themselves, but to preserve and protect the rights of minorities against the arbitrary actions of those in power". The obfuscation of Blacks' constitutional and civil rights in Georgia begins in the probate court. Thomas Swint (the ordinary of the probate court), allowed fraudulent documents and transactions, which permitted the Tarbutton family to illegally acquire the Carter estate, with protection from Georgia's courts. Notwithstanding the documented admissions of fraud and misconduct revealed in the Eleventh Circuit Report and Robert Watkin's lawsuit against his former co-conspirators, the judicial misconduct by the lawyers and judge, was excused.

Judge Sands based his decision in *Horace Cheeves v. Alston & Bird, et al* (hereinafter *Cheeves*) on the adverse possession, statute of limitations, and laches in the fraudulent *Tarbutton* case, as opposed to the fraud, misconduct, and overall malpractice committed by Tarbutton attorneys Alston & Bird, et al, and Jones, Cork & Miller.

On September 14, 1990, Gerald Bard Tjoflat, Chief Judge of the Eleventh Circuit, formed a special "Committee" to investigate claims of misconduct on the part of judges Fitzpatrick and Owens in *Tarbutton,* alleged by Nix. The Committee not only overlooked the judges' misconduct, but also excused Roger Moister's admission of fraud on his part, as well as Frank Nix, Hamilton Lokey and Gerald Handley. Due to his participation on the Committee, Tjoflat should have recused himself from the appellate court ruling of *Cheeves* in 1999. The pattern of fraud and misconduct as committed by the Tarbutton's lawyers and Judge Fitzpatrick in *Tarbutton* is similar to the fraudulent transactions used in other land/mineral-related cases, which tend to end in summary judgment, or the landowners receive an inadequate settlement.

Between 1936-1950, the Carter heir's 13th amendment rights were flagrantly violated. Throughout this period, B.J. Tarbutton and his cohorts forced them into a state of peonage. Life in the Jim Crow south was often dangerous for Blacks. Lynchings and white mob violence provoked real fear in Black communities. The Jim Crow laws were a response to a new reality that required white supremacy to create a rigid legal and institutional basis to retain control over the Black population. What had shifted was not their commitment to white supremacy but the things necessary to preserve it. Nevertheless the Carter family made an earnest effort to clear the fabricated debt.

From 1983 (when the Carter heirs were solicited by the Tarbutton's lawyers), until July 13, 1999 when the United States Court of Appeals decided on Horace's case against them (*Cheeves*), none of Jeff Carter's heirs has received due process. Roger Moister neglected to answer the complaint for four years, Robert Lee failed to answer the complaint altogether, and there was no discovery. Ultimately, Judge Sands' ruling in Cheeves protected the racketeering committed by the Tarbutton's lawyers, barring Horace with the same time statutes named in *Tarbutton,* and concluding there was no remedy.

Every right supposedly available to Blacks as American citizens has been violated - from our human rights, to our constitutional and civil rights. This furtive conduct is ongoing and is systematically protected by the courts, lawyers, and judges. A recent case to illustrate the perpetuation of similar acts of fraud is *Jeffrey T. Lacksen, et al v. Henry Holmes Cheeves, et al,* regarding the estate of Joe Trawick. Henry Cheeves was an heir to his 53 acre estate located in Hancock County, Georgia. Jones, Cork & Miller, the firm that represented Loulie Tarbutton in her case against the Carter heirs, is involved in this kaolin-related case as well, where once again, there is an attempt to defraud the landowners.

Time statutes leave Blacks particularly vulnerable because numerous tragedies occurred when, by law, white citizens did not have to acknowledge the rights of Black citizens. Although Blacks have attained the "legal" right to fight the injustice, it's always, for whatever reason, too late to rectify the damage. Further proof of this judicial prejudice is in the decisions handed down by the courts, from Judge Fitzpatrick to Chief Judge Tjoflat and the appellate court. A remedy for this fifty-year long, arduous, corrupt battle is long overdue.

Reparations will never exist without justice, and our inheritance is a pivotal part of the healing process in our quest for self-determination. We must have the rights and protection necessary to control, mine, and profit from our own land and/or natural resources. Land that has been questionably acquired or outright stolen should be immediately returned to the owners or heirs, along with all profits garnered from it.

One-Eyed Jacks

Kaolin industry agent Robert Lee Watkins, was born June 16, 1945 in Wilkinson County, Georgia. He is the son of Frank Watkins and the grandson of Matty and Robert Watkins, Sr. When Robert Sr. died intestate on March 6, 1955, the Watkins estate consisted of 410 acres of land, more or less, in Wilkinson County. Due to illness, his wife Matty was unable to act as administrator of the family estate, so their eldest son Frank, petitioned the court and was granted administration.

On July 23, 1959, he negotiated a contract between the heirs and Minerals & Chemicals Corp. of America, located in McIntyre, Georgia. Documents state that the tenants were the kaolin company and the owners were the heirs. On July 29, 1960, the lease was terminated. Several months later, on January 11, 1961, Frank died.

On February 2, 1961, his sister Agnes petitioned the court to act as her mother's guardian and administrator of the estate.

Walter Scott and Alex 'Buck' Boone of Boone & Scott, were prominent attorneys in Irwinton, Georgia. They represented three banks at the same time in the same county. They also represented kaolin companies, including Georgia Kaolin, Engelhard Corporation, and M & M Clays.

Buck Boone also acted as an agent for the kaolin industry. Robert Lee alleges that Buck pushed for Agnes' appointment as administrator so that he could control the affairs of the Watkins estate through her. In the July term of 1964, Agnes executed a mineral lease with Thompson-Weinman Company, and was paid $30,000. She distributed the cash amongst the heirs and to the estate's attorney, Boone & Scott. Agnes' role as administrator officially ended around the time of her mother Matty's death in 1966. In a letter dated April 11, 1978, R. Marshall Evans, president of Evans Clay, responded to a letter Agnes sent earlier in the year, offering to sell the Watkins estate.

Sometime around 1980, Robert Lee and Engelhard agent, Robert A. Bragg, joined forces in an apparent conspiracy to gain control of the Watkins estate. Robert Lee convinced his family that the lease on their land, held by Evans Clay, made it worthless for them to hold onto. He argued that Evans Clay had no obligation to mine in their lifetime, and they would therefore never receive any mineral royalties. Without first gaining consent of the court or signatures from the heirs to validate the transaction, Robert Lee assumed the role of receiver with power of attorney to the estate. Robert Lee then falsely led his family members, including his cousins Lois Hollingsworth and Mattie Mae Watkins, to believe his title was valid.

On May 19, 1980, Robert Lee transferred 200 acres more or less of the Watkins estate to Robert A. Bragg for $289,050. According to Lois and her sister Mattie, Engelhard paid Robert Lee $1,000,000 for this fraudulent transaction. Lois and Mattie, however, resisted the sale, which they believed consisted of their entire estate. The probate record states, however, that the Watkins' estate remains in the heirs' title.

Industry Agent

Swindling his family was Robert Lee's rite of passage to becoming an agent for the kaolin industry. Around the time of this "sale", the media claimed Robert Lee "beat the chalk" companies. Because of the publicity he received, Robert Lee gained the trust of Black landowners he had been directed to solicit for their kaolin-rich land. Consistent with other cases Robert Lee participated in, he received a greater profit from the sale than the landowners he claimed to help. This exemplifies how the courts, particularly the probate court, participate in the deception that allows Black landowners to be swindled out of their kaolin-rich land. Too often, Justice's blindfold means Black families cannot get justice at all.

According to Robert Lee, Engelhard paid him $320,000 for "some worthless land", encouraging him to work with them by soliciting mostly Black landowners. As their agent, he was expected to get chalk as cheap as possible, and obtain mineral leases in their behalf. But Robert claims he double-crossed Engelhard by working for the landowners.

The parties that have come to the defense of Robert Lee (the media, newspapers, reporters, lawyers, and a congressperson) have never demonstrated such support for Black landowners who have lost millions if not billions because of deals Watkins led them into.

Robert Lee also operated for the kaolin industry through their attorneys, particularly, Alston & Bird and partner Frank Nix. Watkins and Nix signed agreements with several families including: the Carter heirs (1983), Hattie Cheeves (1985), Pearl Burney (1984), heirs of Elbert and Emmett Shinholster (1983), the heirs of E. D. Smith (1983), the heirs of Burel and Ellen Gibson (1985), Mrs. Luther D. Ennis (1985), Mr. Curtis Cheeves, Sr. (1985), and the Tucker heirs (1985).

E.N. Ennis and nephew Luther Ennis, Fannie Belle Hatch and brother G.J. Elkins, Robert Hooks, Sr. and Jr., D.E. 'Stick' McMaster, and Robert Lee Watkins, were amongst many larcenous, deceptive participants in the kaolin land swindle. In the 1930s and 40s, agents were often white men or relatives. At that time, the agent didn't need a lawyer. They acted as the attorney and dealt directly with a speculator such as B.J. Tarbutton, or a kaolin company.

White agents used fraud, intimidation, conspiracy, and corruption to gain control of land and minerals. When family members acted as agents, it inevitably caused friction within the family. It was the agent's job to tie landowners to a lease or a mining contract. For them, the thought of making large sums of money justified what they were doing - business the "American way", wherein the end justifies the means. Despite the unconscionable exploitation and betrayal inherent in organized crime, acts such as those demonstrated by kaolin agents perpetuate a fascist methodology that has enslaved people of color around the world for centuries.

This also allowed them to gain control of land at the lowest possible rate. The agent's fees came from the speculator or kaolin company, so directly or indirectly; the landowner paid the agent's fees.

In fairness, not all agents, particularly family members, knew the damage they were doing; many were unaware that they were being used. The long-term effect their actions would have on their victims was seldom known.

There is no question that Robert Lee became involved in the kaolin industry when he misled his own family with fraud, intimidation, blackmail, conspiracy, and corruption. The Tarbutton case was groundbreaking and Robert Lee's role in it, as well as his family's case, was pivotal. It served as his apprenticeship to being a kaolin-industry agent in the cartel's quest to accumulate cheap, Black-owned land and minerals.

In the 1980s, Robert Lee became their new agent. He presented himself to families as an investigator, a kaolin expert, and/or a geologist, fighting against the kaolin industry. Robert Lee would request families appoint an administrator when needed, and give him power of attorney. Along with expenses, he would receive a sizeable percentage of whatever the land was sold or leased for, as his fee.

Watkins and the lawyers always profited significantly more than the landowners when there was a settlement. They coerced landowners into selling their land without them knowing its true worth. This mineral conspiracy has existed for more than 60 years in Georgia.

The kaolin industry, aided by their lawyers and judges, legally bury landowners' complaints. It is even easier for the cartel to take land from heirs when the original landowner dies. This is often due to lack of involvement by the heirs in the original negotiations and transactions, coupled with the industry's propensity to use manufactured, forged and misfiled documents, which are rampant in kaolin litigation. The stark reality is that competent legal counsel and/or protection remains unavailable to Black families. Between the lack of information on the part of the heirs, the law's time restraints, and no known "legal" David's to fight the cartel's Goliaths, the heirs are simply unequipped to combat the kaolin cartel's aggressive and furtive nature.

Institutions such as trusts, estates, and foundations are set up for future generations to inherit, establishing a family legacy. When family members die without wills or trusts, the heirs are left in a vulnerable state, easy prey for major corporations such as those that participate in the kaolin industry. It is particularly difficult for Black families, who are vulnerable even with wills. Lawyers and judges in Georgia use the law's time restraints (statutes, laches and adverse possession) and fraudulent documents to allow the cartel to steal Black-owned land and minerals.

Pawns

Lois Hollingsworth is the granddaughter of Robert Watkins, Sr. Lois' mother Rosa, was one of Robert and Matty's seven children. Rosa had four brothers and two sisters respectively: Frank, the father of Robert Lee, Ezekiel, Willie, Robert Jr., Agnes, and Lila.

From 1967 on, Agnes was no longer the receiver of the Watkins estate, although she continued to sell timber, claiming she was doing so to pay taxes. Robert Lee was able to manipulate Agnes because they were both aware that she no longer had the legal authority to make estate decisions.

Around 1980, Lois began to notice Robert Lee was operating as if he had authority over their grandfather's estate. As she recalls, "...he [Robert Lee] got airplanes, and went over the land and see what was under there...ain't nothin' down there. See...he come around telling us the lease is on the land and we ain't never gonna get that land back and we oughta do this and we oughta do that, but I didn't know what was on the land - I didn't even know what was going on cause I wasn't in control - I was thinking that she (Agnes) was still the administrator".

Robert Lee had convinced his family the land was worthless because Evans Clay had a lease on it, and if the family did not sell the land, they would not profit. Although Lois did not want to sell the land, she felt she had no choice.

"Go along with the sale, this the only thing I know. I didn't even know what was the value of nothing", Lois explained. The family was given the impression that they would be selling all of their land to Bragg. The family was unaware that Robert Lee and Robert A. Bragg were actually operating as agents for the Engelhard Corporation.

"They had me all shwood up to them, I'ma tell you the truth", Lois said. "I really didn't even hardly know what was going on. In fact I'ma tell you, after all those years, I said, well Lord, I just don't know how in the world that Robert Lee could of did what he did and I don't know how in the world Engelhard could of did what they did without us signing for them to buy".

Robert Lee brought Robert A. Bragg, "...somebody I never seen before", Lois explained, "You know how he look, brought him over to my Aunt Bea's house, cause Aunt Bea lives right behind me, and we all went over there to sit down and listen…he was talkin' about that lease, that lease, that lease". Lois and her sister Mattie Mae tried to hold out as long as possible, while Robert Lee protested, "We'll all be dead in 80 years...won't none of us be here".

After the "sale" of their family's estate to Engelhard agent Bragg, Lois wondered why Robert Lee received more money than the rest of the heirs. Lois and Mattie Mae could not find anyone to help them uncover what really happened, so Lois, accompanied by her daughter Carolyn, went to Irwinton, Georgia to investigate.

"I was thinking all the land was sold because we were supposed to be selling all the land. But when I went and asked Judge Green, she said, 'What is you talking about?' I said I'm talking about Robert Lee being our administrator and he sold the land and he got all the money."

"She said, 'Wait a minute', so she goes back and she got this big old book with all of the Watkins estates and everything in it, and she said, 'Come here'. So me and my daughter, we went on in where she was at and she said, 'Look at here'. She said, 'Agnes, the administrator-receiver', she got it on record there, 'of this property', and she said Agnes was taken down, '...see, right here, this second Monday, sixth day, in the '67 year'. I was cuttin' a fool, I said, 'No, no, uh huh'. I said, '...we took Agnes down and we put Robert Lee in."

It wasn't until Lois checked the probate record that she discovered the only reference to Robert Watkins was her grandfather. Her cousin, Robert Lee, was never the receiver. He had tricked them into signing papers they thought would appoint him administrator/receiver of the Watkins estate, when in fact they were signing one of the illegal transactions Robert Lee made with agent Bragg. However, there is no record of this transaction in the probate court.

Lois asked Judge Clyde Pain about their case. "He said, Robert Lee ain't nothin...ain't nobody is no nothin over this land. I said, 'Well how did Robert Lee and Bragg sell our land to Engelhard when we ain't signed nothing with Engelhard about our land?' He said, 'Honey let me tell you, your land is still down there'."

The "sale" of 410 acres more or less to Engelhard agent Bragg took place on December 31, 1981. Some time later, Lois' Uncle Robert asked her to accompany him to Irwinton to inquire about a receipt Robert Lee had brought him. "Uncle Robert was curious whether or not there was a record of the transaction at the courthouse".

A woman named Cindy Sloane assisted Lois and her uncle. "Do ya'll want to see what Robert Lee did to ya'll?"

"Did to us, what did he do," Lois asked.

"Do you know ya'll thought ya'll were selling that land to Bragg. Engelhard bought that land from Robert Lee and Bragg".

"I said 'What!'

"She said, 'Come back let me show you'. And she went back there and she showed me where Engelhard had bought that land from Robert Lee and Bragg. See we thought all the land was sold, and she said, 'Look, they bought that land from Robert Lee for one million dollars', and we thought we was selling to Bragg for $289,000. She said, 'Ya'll get ya'll a lawyer'. She gave us a lawyer name down in Albany".

"Me and my uncle and his wife and his sister, we went to Albany. And we gets down there and that's what he told us, he know more about [it] than we did. He said, 'Did Robert Lee tell ya'll that that option he had with Bragg wasn't no good. Cause he ain't make no deal with Agnes'. Denmark Groovy (an attorney and former representative in Macon, Georgia) told Robert Lee that that option he had with Bragg wasn't no good, that wasn't even valid. He let us went on believing that that option with Bragg was some good. Now he told us this because he said, 'See, Agnes was supposed to be administrator and to sell that land, you supposed to went through Agnes to sell it'. But...he didn't go through Agnes to sell it. But in the meantime, the man down in Albany didn't know Agnes wasn't no administrator. Now I went to Denmark Groovy and I called him and I told him I was coming up there to see him. And I went up there...Denmark Groovy said, well way back yonder, Robert Lee come to him and wanted him to fix up some papers to trick us to get our land, and Denmark Groovy said he told Robert Lee, he didn't want no parts of it".

Robert Lee received one million dollars from Engelhard for the collection of his family's signatures on what they believed was an agreement to sell all of their land to Bragg. The sale took place in a building that looked, "like a big old hotel", according to Lois. It was located on First Street in Macon, Georgia, in front of the city auditorium. "They had all our names on all the papers, all what everybody was going to get on that paper. So then they gave everybody their check and even Agnes' check, what she supposed to got, they didn't give it to her because she was in a nursing home. Robert Lee gave it to his two sisters. And I told Clyde Pain over there down the probate judge, he said, 'Wait a minute, she didn't have a power of attorney'".

In 1982, Lois, along with other members of her family, met with Warren C. Grice, the Albany attorney Cindy Sloane referred them to. He was willing to take the case but he wanted $25,000 up front. "There was some more land down there. You see, we find that out after then. We find out some more land was down there, but we didn't know it until we got Grice. Grice went and find out it was some more land down there. But still and yet he carried us crooked, he didn't go straight with us, sho did. And that's when we wanted to prosecute all of them, but no, Grice, he was just, '...No, I'm trying to get ya'll some more money'".

"That man carried us through a loophole...he was going right in the beginning. He really found out everything they had done. Evidently he got down there some way and the way it look like, Engelhard and them paid him off, cause all of a sudden...I'ma tell you, that lawyer did some of everything to us. I did everything I could do but jump on that man and fight him. He told us if we didn't settle, we wasn't going to get nothing, and even the judge (Hunt) told us that. If we didn't agree to that settlement, we wasn't going to get nothing".

Lois and her family had hired Warren C. Grice to sue for the land Robert Lee had illegally "sold" to Engelhard. But the Watkins family was double-crossed again. "That man turn on us like a rattlesnake", Lois said. When Lois and her family went to court on April 2, 1984, their attorney Grice suddenly refused to speak to them and forbade them from speaking as well. This absolute betrayal of an attorney to his client was further aggravated when Judge Willis Hunt, in collusion with Grice (and the kaolin cartel), threatened to put the money in escrow if the heirs didn't accept it. At Hunt's insistence, the Watkins family "sold" their remaining 200 acres (more or less) of land to Engelhard. Several family members, including Robert Lee's brothers and sisters, were paid bribes. Robert Lee was represented by attorney Roy N. Cowart.

"When I gets up there on the stand, he [Hunt] asked me who was I. I told him my name was Lois Hollingsworth. He said, 'Well where is you from'. I said I'm from Twiggs County, Jeffersonville, Georgia. I said one thing I don't like about this here, he made me feel like something is wrong. I said, when Grice get up here and pay my uncle Robert, his two brothers, Collie and Bunyon, all this money here, and I don't think it's right. When Lois confronted Grice about the bribes he paid her family, he told her, 'This is my money, and I can do what I want a do with it'".

Equal Protection?

In 1993, Congresswoman Cynthia McKinney vowed her support to kaolin landowners. Her office assigned Marcy Louza to handle such issues. Mckinney's office, as well as the media, (including Charles Seabrook's series on kaolin in the Atlanta Journal & Constitution that same year) gave Robert Lee generous support. However, when Lois sought the assistance of Marcy Louza, her family's loss, a treacherous result of their hero Robert Lee, was ignored.

The Double-Cross

The Eleventh Circuit Judicial Inquiry documents some of the judicial misconduct that occurred in the Tarbutton case, including the judges' awareness of Robert Lee's involvement in solicitation, fraud and suborned perjury. In April of 1989, Robert Lee was charged and indicted of "inducing, aiding and abetting" the perjury of Charles Williams in the Tarbutton case. His partnership with Frank Nix also dissolved during this time. In a letter dated August 4, 1992 to the heirs of Curtis Cheeves (a case Robert Lee and Nix jointly "represented"), Nix stated:

"Recently Mr. Watkins persuaded his own aunts, uncles and cousins in another kaolin case to fire the lawyers who had worked on the case for four years. He then led the family to two lawyers who don't know the first thing about that case or kaolin litigation in general. If he is willing to do this to his own relatives just to get himself out of prison, God only knows what he will try to do to your family and me."

The relatives Nix refers to in the above mentioned letter are the Cobbs family. They lost their land as well.

Saruge

"...He (marster) says now Billy you preachah, git me de Bible and he reads, Thou shall not steal, den he handed Billy de Bible and sayed read dis. [H]e shore hates to, but Marster makes him do it, den he shore tares loose on Billy bout stealin. [F]inally Billy says now marster I can show you in de Bible where I did not steal. [H]e tells Billy to find it and Billy finds it and reads, "You shall reap when you laborth."
— **Jeff Calhoun,** enslaved preacher

Psychiatry's Betrayal

The Citizens Commission on Human Rights published, "Creating Racism: Psychiatry's Betrayal in the Guise of Help". The publication is based on documentation and evidence amassed over several decades on the subject of psychiatric violations of human rights, which "clearly show calculated psychiatric attacks on blacks and minority racial and religious groups, all of which have helped to create the troubled world we live in," says Jan Eastgate, International President of the organization.

Eastgate believes psychiatry "consciously used pseudo-scientific terminology and experimentation to secure a fraudulently obtained position of authority on the subject of the human psyche. It is a problem masquerading as a solution. The result has been escalating crime, a rise in violence, an epidemic of drug abuse, plummeting education standards, religious intolerance, a widespread decline in morals, the collapse of the family unit and racism. In fact, every area of society in which psychiatry claims authority and influence has only become worse as a result of its presence and influence. Persistent statistics are there to make this an easily demonstrable fact."

Nazi Conspiracy: Psychiatry & Racism

In 1869, Francis Galton first coined the term "eugenics" in his book Hereditary Genius. The term came from the Greek "eugenes", meaning "good in stock." Galton claimed that judicious mating could "give more suitable races or strains of blood a better chance of prevailing speedily over the less suitable."

Among the "less suitable" to Galton was the African. Earlier, after spending two years in South Africa, Galton wrote another book entitled Tropical South Africa. One of the African tribes he studied was the Damaras, of whom he wrote, "These savages court slavery...You engage one of them as a servant, and you find that he considers himself as your property, so that you become the owner of a slave. They have no independence about them, generally speaking, but follow a master as a spaniel would."

In summary, the theory of eugenics posed that defective persons procreated more rapidly and bred more readily than normal, the result being that society was flooded with inferior and unproductive people. In 1870, psychologist Herbert Spencer took Galton's theme further by coining the term, "survival of the fittest," a phrase frequently and incorrectly attributed to Charles Darwin. Spencer believed many people were unfit and worthy only of a quick death, while selective breeding of the fittest could bring about a superior race.

In 1887, G. Stanley Hall, founder of the American Journal of Psychology and first president of the American Psychological Association, theorized that Africans, Indians and Chinese were members of "adolescent races" in a stage of "incomplete growth." As such, this justified psychiatry and psychology's intervention to save them from the "liabilities and dangers" of freedom.

These concepts spread quickly around the world. Eugenics societies sprang up in all the "civilized" countries, including England and the United States, and their members included many of societies "best and brightest".

Director of the Kaiser Wilhelm Institute of Anthropology, Human Heredity, and Eugenics in Berlin, psychiatrist Eugen Fischer urged the annihilation of "Negro" children. Fischer theorized that Blacks were devoid of value and useless for employment other than for "manual crafts."

Ernest Rudin, a psychiatrist at Munich University, chief architect of the Nazis' racial hygiene program and SS chief Heinrich Himmler drew up Germany's 1933 sterilization law, which called for the sterilization of all Jews and "colored" German children. Psychiatry's racial purity law implementing segregation was also introduced. Doctors in the United States applauded Germany's sterilization program. Their own sterilization programs had started in 1905 with more than 15,000 performed in the US by December 1931.

Dr. Lorthrop Stoddard, director of the US Birth Control League, wrote books that contained blatant racist remarks about Blacks. Margaret Sanger, a eugenicist and the Founder of Planned Parenthood of America, argued in 1939 for plans to stop the growth of Black babies in the US. To cover up her plan to "exterminate the Negro population," she suggested that Black ministers be infiltrated and that "three or four" of them with "engaging personalities" be hired to preach throughout the South that sterilization was a solution to poverty. Approaching Blacks "through a religious appeal," she said, would be the "most successful educational approach."

The common thread to psychiatry's "scientific" justification for sterilization, brutal surgery, and other human rights violations was that IQ regulated behavior and status.

By the 1920s this was absolute dogma: IQ was congenital, inherited, and thus unchanging. In this way, the systematic social crippling of certain races could be carried out, if not by violent psychiatric treatments, then by denying them proper education, employment and other cultural advantages.

Around the same period, a prominent "expert" in IQ testing, psychologist Lewis Terman, used his tests to claim that 83 percent of Jews were "feebleminded," that children of the poor could never be educated, and that Mexicans, Indians and Blacks "should never be allowed to reproduce."

The tendency of those who find it difficult to face such evil is to think that since those days we have entered more enlightened times. Unfortunately, this is just wishful thinking.

Similar theories have been peddled in more recent times. In 1958, Audrey Shuey, author of the book Psychology and Life, wrote that IQ test scores "inevitably point to the presence of native [genetic] differences between Negroes and whites..."

This propaganda continues, even as recently as 1994 with Murray and Hernstein's book, The Bell Curve, claiming that Blacks do worse than whites in intelligence tests, are "genetically disabled", and therefore cannot cope with the demands of contemporary American society.

Through the bogus "scientifically tested and proven" concepts of "low IQ" and "racial inferiority," psychiatry has given legitimacy to 20th century mental slavery, racism and white supremacy.

How else can normally intelligent people automatically believe such obvious nonsense? But these beliefs have been advanced for such a long period of time, many people, whether they care to admit it or not, truly do believe it on some level.

However, this is nothing new. Only a century ago, "modern science" was used to justify the enslavement of Black people.

Psychiatric Oppression

When Africans were torn from their continent, country, family, and home, and shackled into "slavery", science stood ready to define any disobedience or insubordination as a "mental illness."

As early as 1851, Samuel A. Cartwright, a prominent Louisiana Physician, published an essay entitled "Report on the disease and physical peculiarities of the Negro race" in the "New Orleans and Surgical Journal." Cartwright claimed to have discovered two mental diseases peculiar to Blacks, which he believed, justified their enslavement. These were called "Drapetomania" and "dysaesthesia Aethiopis."

The first term came from drapetes, a run-away slave, and mania, meaning mad or crazy. Cartwright claimed that this "disease" caused Blacks to have an uncontrollable urge to run away from their "masters". The "treatment" for this "illness" was "whipping the devil out of them."

Dysaesthesia Aethiopis supposedly affected both mind and body. The diagnosable signs included disobedience, answering disrespectfully and refusing to work. The "cure" was to put the person to some kind of hard labor, which apparently sent "vitalized blood to the brain to give liberty to the mind."

Much "scientific" and statistical rhetoric was used to justify slavery. One 1840 census "proved" that Blacks living under "unnatural conditions of freedom" in the North were more prone to insanity. Dr. Edward Jarvis, a specialist in mental disorders, used this to conclude that slavery shielded Blacks from "some of the liabilities and dangers of active self-direction." The census was later found to be a racist facade in that many of the northern towns credited with mentally deranged Blacks had no Black inhabitants at all.

In 1797, the "father" of American psychiatry, Dr. Benjamin Rush -

whose face today still adorns the seal of the American Psychiatric Association - declared that the color of Blacks was caused by a rare, congenital disease called "Negritude" which derived from leprosy. In an address to the American Philosophical Society, Rush said that the only evidence of a "cure" was when the skin color turned white.

Using "disease" as the reason for segregation, Rush drew the conclusion that "Whites should not tyrannize over [Blacks], for their disease should entitle them to a double portion of humanity. However, by the same token, whites should not intermarry with them, for this would tend to infect posterity with the 'disorder'...attempts must be made to cure the disease."

Renowned author and professor emeritus of psychiatry, Dr. Thomas Szasz, wrote in his book, The Manufacture of Madness, "With this theory, Rush made the Black a medically safe domestic, while at the same time called for his sexual segregation as carrier of a dread hereditary disease. Here, then, was an early model of the perfect medical concept of illness - one that helps the physician and the society he serves, while justifying social maltreatment as medical prophylaxis [protection from disease]."

Since the late 1800s, psychiatry's reasoning for "protecting" Blacks from their own "disease" has had a common thread: that the color of skin somehow determines IQ and signals inferiority, and that those with "low" IQ need to be protected from themselves, as well as segregated from the population at large.

In addition to what has already been outlined here about IQ, US eugenics advocate Dr. Paul Popenoe, published the findings of his study, entitled "Intelligence and Race - a Review of the Results of the Army Intelligence Tests - The Negro in 1918." With astounding arrogance, he fabricated and propagated the idea that the IQ of Blacks was determined by the amount of "white blood" they had. The lighter skinned the Black was, the higher his IQ, and the Blacker he was, the lower the IQ.

Popenoe concluded, "...the Negroes' low mental estate is irremediable... The Negro is mentally, therefore eugenically, inferior to the white race. All treatment of the Negro...must take into account this fundamental fact."

Psychiatric "treatment" of Blacks has included some of the most barbaric experiments ever carried out in the name of "scientific" research, and continues today. In the 1950s in New Orleans, Black prisoners were used for psychosurgery experiments, which involved electrodes being implanted into the brain. The experiments were conducted by psychiatrist Dr. Robert Heath from Tulane University and an Australian psychiatrist, Dr. Harry Bailey, who boasted in a lecture to nurses 20 years later that the two psychiatrists had used Blacks because it was "cheaper to use Niggers than cats because they were everywhere and cheap experimental animals."

Heath had also been funded by the Central Intelligence Agency (CIA) to carry out drug experiments, which included LSD and a drug called bulbocapnine, which in large doses produced "catatonia and stupor." Heath tested the drug on Black prisoners at the Louisiana State Penitentiary. According to one memo, the CIA sought information as to whether the drug could cause "loss of speech, loss of sensitivity to pain, loss of memory, loss of will power and an increase in toxicity in persons with a weak type of central nervous system."

At the National Institute of Mental Health Addiction Research Center in Kentucky in the mid-1950s, drug addicted Blacks were given LSD. Seven of them were kept hallucinating for 77 consecutive days. At this same center, healthy Black men were still being used as test subjects almost 10 years later, this time for an experimental drug, BZ - 100 times more powerful than LSD.

This follows a long psychiatric tradition of using, for experimental purposes, the incarcerated, the dispossessed and others who have no voice.

Community Mental Health-Under the Guise of Help

When the Community Mental Health Centers Act was passed in 1963, centers and programs were established and initially funded by the National Institute of Mental Health (NIMH), a funding agency for psychiatric and psychological research. The founder and director of NIMH was Dr. Robert Felix, the same man who was involved in the CIA-funded LSD experiments on Blacks in Kentucky.

It is little wonder then that while the stated purpose of these "health" centers was "a bold new approach" to freeing people from psychiatric treatment in institutions, the reality was that it became an easy way to addict thousands of people to psychiatric drugs.

In effect, then, they became legal, drug pushing agencies: 55 percent of people using a Community Mental Health Center (CMHC) receive powerful psychotropic (mind-altering) drugs; at least 45 percent are given tranquilizers. Medical studies since the 1960s have proven that these psychiatric drugs create violent and aggressive behavior.

And government at every level joined the program. Statistics showed that Blacks were twice as likely as whites to enter Community Mental Health Centers through referrals from social agencies.

The statistics show that after admission to a CMHC, patient arrest rates for criminal activities are nearly double the rate of the general population. While psychiatrists may claim that this is only natural, as these are people who were troubled in the first place, the fact they always neglect to mention is that this only points to the total failure of what they call "treatment."

The Violence Initiative

For years, NIMH has funded one of the most covert and destructive programs in the oppression of Blacks. It has gone by many names, the most recent being the "Violence Initiative."

The stage was set in the wake of the 1960s, when Dr. Ernst Rodin, head of the neurology department of the Lafayette Clinic in Detroit, delivered a speech to fellow psychosurgeons and psychiatrists. Rodin, a strong proponent of the control of violence through the use of psychosurgery, said that "medical technology" should be applied to solve the problems of riots in Black ghettos. Rodin equated "dumb young males who riot" to oxen.

Psychiatrist Louis Jolyon West, former head of the University of California Los Angeles' Neuropsychiatric Institute (NPI), did not disregard this "wisdom". In relation to "riots" in the Black section of Los Angeles in the 1960s, West stated that it was tied to genetic or racial factors, that those prone to such violence were young Black urban males, and something had to be done about it.

Of course, West and his associates at NPI had a proposal. They recommended that violent offenders be treated with psychosurgery and castration. Rather than resort to the violence of physical castration, West suggested that a chemical, cyproterone acetate, be ingested to produce the same effect.

This chemical appeared again in 1973, when West proposed the establishment of a Center for the Study and Reduction of Violence, which as the name implied, would be designed for the experimental study and treatment of violence.

In one of West's planned violence studies, he proposed to use two high schools chosen for their location in primarily "minority" neighborhoods - one Black and one Chicano.

West's planned studies also targeted women, children, and prisoners, as well as autistic or retarded children. Examples of West's treatments included implanting electronic monitoring, or "homing" devices, in the brain.

In 1974, CCHR and other concerned citizens who saw this for what it was, fascism and attempted genocide launched statewide protests. Among psychiatrists, however, these ideas seldom die; they are merely born again under another name.

In 1983, the Duke University Medical Center in North Carolina was given almost three-quarters of a million dollars to research the aggressive "behavior patterns" of Black children living in high crime risk areas.

Then, in 1992, psychiatrist Frederick Goodwin, a director of the institute overseeing NIMH, went so far as to compare Black youth living in inner cities with "hyperaggressive" and "hypersexual" monkeys in a jungle. The NIMH attempted to launch a "National Violence Initiative" which they stated was for "disease prevention." This would use psychiatrists to determine, through "biological markers," which children were likely to develop criminal behavior. Black and Hispanic children, in particular, were to be the targets.

As the Chicago Tribune reported in 1993, the NIMH program claimed to "raise the hope that violent behavior eventually can be curbed by manipulating the chemical and genetic keys to aggression...anti-violence medications conceivably could be given, perhaps forcibly, to people with abnormal levels."

Dr. Seth Farber, director of the group, Network Against Coercive Psychiatry, stated at the time, "Just like the Nazis...what [psychiatrists] want to do is scapegoat African American youth, put them on drugs and take away the rights of their parents. It is an outrageous, racist and oppressive plan."

According to a report by the African American Coalition for Justice in Social Policy, entitled "National Institute of Mental Health - The experiment on African Americans Continues," NIMH's psychiatric research and the growth of the community mental health network parallel the increasing statistics of crime and violence among African Americans. Spokesperson for the Coalition, Dr. William Tutman stated, "NIMH's studies tend to put the Black community under the microscope and form the basis of social programs that are then implemented into African American neighborhoods to their detriment."

The Coalition reported a 2,900 percent increase in drug abuse violations arrests for African American adolescents under the age of 18 between 1965 and 1989, almost five times higher than the arrest for whites.

It is not surprising then that US prisons are filled with Black males (with more prisons being built), and that NIMH-funded studies are still attempting to find a genetic basis to criminality, aggression and juvenile delinquency in the Black community.

Mind Control

The future of any race is largely dependent upon the care, education, and nurturing of its children. The family, being the most influential community in a child's life, should instill the significance of heritage and culture. The absence of familial and cultural values assures a sense of inferiority and self-loathing. The resulting devastation is rampant throughout our families/communities.

A five-year study funded by the US National Institute of Mental Health (NIMH), recommended that the school curriculum should be designed to "bend the student to the realities of society" and to "promote mental health as...a means of altering culture."

The 1963, Community Mental Health Centers Act provided the impetus that psychiatrists and psychologists needed to greatly expand their involvement in schools. Thus, the number of psychologists in schools increased more than seven-fold between 1963 and 1993, from 3,000 to 22,000. Coincidentally, since then SAT scores have steadily declined.

In 1965, the US Elementary and Secondary Education Act established "special education," a lucrative psychiatric program that now costs the taxpayer around $31 billion a year. Children who "qualify" for these classes are diagnosed "mentally retarded," "seriously emotionally disturbed" or "learning disabled." Through this, psychiatry has been able to turn education *into a "medical" problem with catastrophic results. Seven out of ten special education students drop out, "age out" (reach their 22nd birthday), are expelled, or leave school with unearned diplomas. Only a relative handful actually completes a standard high school curriculum of any kind.*

In 1968, three years after the U.S. Elementary and Secondary Education Act was passed, broadening the definition of "handicapped" to include "mental disturbance," and giving psychiatry the green light for wholesale assessment, labeling and drugging of schoolchildren, the second edition of the Diagnostic and Statistical Manual of Mental Disorders (DSM) was published. In it appeared a whole new category called "Behavior Disorders of Childhood and Adolescence."

In 1975, the individuals with Disabilities Education Act (IDEA) was passed providing "special education" classes for children with "learning disabilities." Within two years, the number of children labeled as having a "Learning Disorder" (LD) had reached more than 782,000. This figure soared to 1.9 million in 1989 and by 1996, it had reached 2.6 million.

This, despite Kevin P. Dwyer, assistant executive director at the National Association of School Psychologists in the U.S., admitting that the way "learning disorders" are diagnosed is "not a science." "We're not sophisticated enough to do a perfect diagnosis," he candidly admitted.

In 1987, "Attention Deficit Hyperactivity Disorder" (ADHD) was literally voted into existence by the American Psychiatric Association (APA). Within one year, 500,000 children in the U.S. alone were diagnosed with this affliction created by a vote – a show of hands.

Black, Hispanic, and Native American children are significantly over-represented in special education. According to 1992 statistics, Native Americans were almost twice, and Blacks more than twice as likely to be labeled as "retarded" compared with whites.

Federal government financial incentives added fuel to an already well-established fire. In 1990, the doors were opened to a lucrative cash welfare program to low-income parents whose children were diagnosed with "ADHD." A family could get more than $450 a month for each "ADHD" child. The impact was telling. In 1989, children citing mental impairment that included "ADHD," made up only five percent of all disabled kids on the program. That *figure rose to nearly 25 percent by 1995. To obtain the payout, some parents actually coached their children to do poorly in school and to "act weirdly."*

In 1991, eligibility rules changed for federal education grants, providing schools with $400 in annual grant money for each child diagnosed with "ADHD." The same year, the Department of Education formally recognized "ADHD" as a handicap and directed all state education officers to establish procedures to screen and identify "ADHD" children and provide them with special educational and psychological services. The number of children diagnosed with this "malady" soared again. By 1997, the number of children being labeled as having "ADHD" had risen alarmingly to 4.4 million

Dr. Fred A. Baughman, Jr. a California pediatric neurologist says that the frequency with which "learning disorders" and "ADHD" are diagnosed in schools "...is proportional to the presence and influence within the schools of mind/brain behavioral diagnosticians, testers, and therapists."

American schools spend a combined $1 billion a year on psychologists who work full-time to diagnose students. As of 1996, $15 billion was being spent annually in the U.S. on the diagnosis, treatment and study of these so-called "disorders."

By being diagnosed as emotionally disturbed or educationally retarded, these children are often given hazardous and addictive amphetamine-like drugs, usually Ritalin (methylphenidate), or the central nervous system stimulant, Cylert (pemoline), known to create suicidal and violent behavior. The newer antidepressants, the Selective Serotonin Reuptake Inhibitors (SSRIs), are also increasingly in vogue.

With more than four million American children alone fraudulently labeled as having Attention Deficit Disorder (ADD), Attention Deficit Hyperactivity Disorder (ADHD), Conduct Disorder (CD), Serious Reading Disorder (SRD), Serious Emotional Disorder (SED), and Learning Disorder (LD), psychiatrists are allowed to create a generation of drug addicts.

Ritalin's manufacturer admits it is a drug of dependency. In the U.S., production of Ritalin increased by 665 percent between 1985 and 1995, with a 500 percent increase since 1990. In some classrooms, up to 20 percent of the students are taking the drug. A further 909,000 children and adolescents between the ages of six and 18 are on antidepressant drugs such as SSRIs. Already on the market is peppermint-flavored Prozac as an added incentive for children. Ritalin may also prime children for drug abuse in later life. Scientists report that Ritalin affects the brain like cocaine does, thereby establishing the strong risk of later addiction. A study of California adolescents diagnosed with "ADHD" found that, as adults, those treated with Ritalin as children were three times more likely to use cocaine.

Ritalin is often illegally used by drug addicts in combination with other drugs. Corresponding with this, the number of methylphenidate-related emergency room cases for 10 to 14 year olds in the U.S. has multiplied tenfold since 1990 and, in 1995 reached the level of cocaine-related emergencies for the same age group. In view of all this, it is not surprising that suicide among children and teenagers has skyrocketed. The suicide rate among Black males between the ages of 15 and 19, for example, has risen 219 percent since 1964. Until recently, the proliferation of street drugs has tended to be seen as a phenomenon in itself. However, as more young users of psychiatry's prescription drugs move on to illicit drug use, the link between the two becomes increasingly obvious. Still, what is seldom seen, let alone discussed, is the founding role played by psychiatrists and psychologists in the creation of the chaotic street drug culture itself.

In 1930, 80 percent of Blacks over the age of 14 could read. By 1990, after more than 25 years of "special education," only 56 percent of Blacks over the age of 14 could read.

The Effects of Psychological Warfare

The effects of centuries of psychological tyranny are evident in individuals, families and communities. We have been so debilitated that we are forced to depend on those who have terrorized and oppressed us. The psychology used on people of color throughout the diaspora has created the same symptoms attributed to battered women. "Stockholm Syndrome" is when a person that has been abused feels they have contributed in some way to the treatment they receive(d). Based on their diminished perception of themself, an abused person often feels inferior to their abuser; that they are somehow not "good enough", whether it be intellectually, physically, socially, financially, or racially, amongst other things. As a result of whatever deficiency they perceive themselves as having, they feel fortunate or relieved, so to speak, that their abuser tolerates them, loves them on some level, or has "rescued" them from something "worse". They might feel their way of life is better than what it would be had it not been for their abuser.

The term "Stockholm Syndrome" stems from a 1973 case where a woman held hostage at a bank in Stockholm, Sweden became so emotionally attached to one of the robbers, that she broke her engagement to another man and remained faithful to her former captor during his prison term. According to psychologists, the abused bond to their abusers as a means to endure violence. Unconscious identification with the aggressor is also one of the symptoms of the persecution syndrome. The most notorious instance came when heiress Patty Hearst was kidnapped by the Symbionese Liberation Army, and after some months, re-christened herself "Tanya" and joined their ranks..She shouted, "Get down or I'll blow your motherfucking heads off," while robbing a San Francisco bank with fellow S.L.A. members in April, 1974.

Various tactics can be employed to degrade the character and integrity of a person. By consistently diminishing someone, or a group (verbally, physically, socially, by law, and/or by disregarding their existence altogether), they will begin to question who they are and what they're worth. After enduring such a psychological assault, invariably, those people will no longer love themselves. This fosters an unhealthy relationship between the abuser and the abused, the oppressor and the oppressed, the "supremacist" and the "minority". People who know themselves love themselves. Love cannot be given or shared without first experiencing it within. Love is most clearly expressed through actions, not words. If knowing and loving oneself is the root of being able to give love, than anyone without a grounded sense of self is vulnerable to the mind control (antagonism, degradation, and manipulation) inherent in abuse. Almost without fail, a person who doesn't love themself will feel what they interpret as great passion, love, and/or loyalty for the person (or people) who has tormented them the most. Loneliness, hopelessness, and desperation, are often feelings that accompany an abused psyche in regards to their abuser. Notwithstanding the horrific tendencies and practices of an abuser/oppressor/supremacist, everyone must take responsibility for their participation in an abusive relationship. Once the damage has been assessed, it is necessary that one look at their role in a situation and determine how they can remove themself from the equation, so that, to whatever degree the crisis persists, it does so without their involvement or cooperation. Failure to disrupt and/or cease involvement in unhealthy, abusive patterns creates a cyclical condition known as co-dependence.

Overseers lived on de plantation. No dey wasn't poor whites. All Marse Sam's overseers was good men. Dey lived wid deir families, and Marse's folks 'sociated wid dem, too. Dey had good houses to live in. Dey built better dan ours was. Marse didn't 'low dem to whip de slaves, but dey made us keep straight. If any whipping had to be done, Marse done it, but he didn't have to do much. He didn't hurt 'em bad, den, jes' git a big hickry and lay on a few. He would say if dat nigger didn't walk de chalk, he would put him on de block and settle him. Dat was usually enough, 'cause Marse mean't dat thing and all de niggers know'd it...

Slaves started to work by de time dey was old enough to tote water and pick up chips to start fires wid. Some of dem started to work in de fields when dey about ten, but most of 'em was older. Lawd, Marse Sam must have had more dan a dozen house niggers. It took a lot of work to keep things in and 'round de house in good shape. Cose most of de slaves was jes' field hands, but some of dem was picked out fer special duties.

...Marse have a hundred head of hogs in de smokehouse at one time. Never seen so much pork in my life. We sho lived in fine fashion in hog killing time, cose de meats was cured and us had some all de year. Yes sir, Marse ration out everybody some every week...

Didn't wear much clothes in summer 'cause we didn't need much, but all de grown niggers had shoes. Lawd, I wore many pair of Marse Lyntt's boots, I means sho 'nuff good boots. Marse had his own shoemakers, so twan't no use us gwine widout. Had better clothes fer Sunday. Most de washing was done on Saturday afternoons, and we be all setting purty fer Sunday. Cold weather we was dressed warm, and we had plenty bed kivvers, too. Cose all slaves didn't have it as good as Marse Sam's did. Lawd, I is seed lil' naked niggers setting on de rail fences like pa'cel of buzzards; but Marse Sam's niggers never had to go dat way

— **George Fleming,** enslaved in South Carolina

...Iffen a nigger run away and dey cotch him, or does he come back 'cause he hongry, I seed Uncle Jake stretch him out on de ground and tie he hands and feet to posts so he can't move none. Den he git de piece of iron what he call de "slut" and what is like a block of wood with little holes in it, and fill de holes up with tallow and put dat iron in de fire till de grease sizzlin'

hot and hold it over de pore nigger's back and let dat hot grease drap on he hide. Den he take de bullwhip and whip up and down, and after all dat throw de pore nigger in de stockhouse and chain him up a couple days with nothin' to eat. My papa carry de grease scars on he back till he die.

...And even does your stomach be full, and does you have plenty clothes, dat bullwhip on your bare hide make you forgit de good part, and dat's de truth
— **Sarah Ford,** enslaved in Texas

Sarah Ford

Despite the strength and fortitude Africans and their descendants exhibited by surviving generations of psychological, emotional, and physical brutality, the scars continue to run deep. Further, the manipulation of the economic, political, psychological, and social structure of this society has no redeeming value to oppressed people. Therefore, a thorough strategy must be initiated to rehabilitate our internal and external value system. For the sake of our children and future generations, we cannot continue in our unhealthy state of consciousness. We must heal!

> *I had such a hard time in slavery. Them white folks was slashing me and whipping me and putting me in the buck, till I don't want to hear nothin' about it...*
>
> *The first work I ever did was nursing the white children. My old mis' called me in the house and told me that she wanted me to take care of her children and from then till freedom came, I stayed in the house nursing...I never did work in the fields much. My old mars said I was too damned slow.*
>
> *They carried me out to the field one evening. He never did show me nor tell me how to handle it and when I found myself, he had knocked me down. When I got up, he didn't tell me what to do, but when I picked up my things and started droppin' the seeds ag'in, he picked up a pine root and killed me off with it. When I come to, he took me up to the house and told his wife he didn't want me into the fields because I was too damned slow.*
>
> *My mars used to throw me in a buck and whip me. He would put my hands together and tie them. Then he would make me squat down. Then he would run a stick through behind my knees and in front of my elbows. My knees was up against my chest. My hands was tied together just in front of my shins. The stick between my arms and my knees held me in a squat. That's what they called a buck. You could stand up an' you couldn't git your feet out. You couldn't do nothin' but just squat there and take what he put on you. You couldn't move no way at all. Just try to. You just fall over on one side and have to stay there till you turned over by him.*
>
> *He would whip me on one side till that was sore and full of blood and then he would whip me on the other side till that was all tore up. I got a scar big as the place my old mis' hit me. She took a bull whip once - the bull whip had a piece of iron in the handle of it - and she got mad. She was so mad she took the whip and hit me over the head with the butt end of it, and the blood flew. It run all down my back and dripped off my heels. But I wasn't dassent to stop to do nothin' about it. Old ugly thing! The devil's got her right now! They never rubbed no salt nor nothin' in your back. They didn't need to*
>
> — **Ella Wilson,** enslaved in Louisiana

Master had over a hundred head of cows and most of the time me and Violet, another house girl, did all the milking. We was up before five and by five we better be in that cow pen. We better milk all of them cows too or they'd bull-whip us. But we didn't allus do it. Them calves got lots of that milk. One mon'nin Master cotched me letting one of the calves do the "milking." It was cold and snow was on the ground and I was barefooted. Master says, "I'll let you off this time." But that don't mean he was allus good to us, cause them cows had more feeling for us than they did. Several times Master would say to Mistress that it was cold and bad and hadn't she better try to find some old shoes for us. Mistress say, "Them Niggers don't need no shoes, they better get out of here to that cow pen."

— **Katie Darling,** enslaved in Texas

Katie Darling

The text below is reprinted from The Black Arcade Liberation Library; 1970; recompiled and re-edited by Kenneth T. Spann. It is an introduction to a frightening treatise that indicates, perhaps better than anything or anyone else can, the necessity for us to reexamine our own lives in light of our history, our present, and certainly our future. If we do not study our past and our present, we cannot hope to mold our own future.

> *The following treatise, to the knowledgeable, will be the missing link that has been sought to explain how we were put into the condition that we find ourselves in today. It confirms the fact that the slave-holder tried to leave nothing to chance when it came to his property; his slaves. It demonstrates, how out of necessity, the slave holder had to derive a system for perpetuating his cash crop, the slave, while at the same time insulating himself from retribution by his unique property.*
>
> *A careful analysis of the following "handbook" will hopefully change the ignorant among our people who say "Why study slavery?" Those narrow-minded people will be shown that the condition of our people today is due to a scientific and psychological blue print for the perpetuation of the mental condition that allowed slavery to flourish. The slaveholder was keenly aware of the breeding principles of his livestock and the following treatise demonstrates that he thoroughly used those principles on his human live stock as well, the African Slave, and added a debilitating psychological component as well.*
>
> *It was the interest and business of slaveholders to study human nature, and the slave nature in particular, with a view to practical results, and many of them attained astonishing proficiency in this direction. They had to deal not with earth, wood, and stone, but with men, and by every regard they had, for their own safety and prosperity, the need to know the material on which they were to work.*
>
> *Conscious of the injustice and wrong they were every hour perpetuating and knowing what they themselves would do if they were the victims of such wrongs. They were constantly looking for the first signs of the dreaded retribution. They watched, therefore, with skilled and practiced eyes, and learned to read, with great accuracy, the state of mind and heart of the slave, through his stable face. Unusual sobriety, apparent abstraction, sullenness, and indifference, indeed any mood out of the common way afforded ground for suspicion and inquiry. "Let's Make A Slave' is a study of the scientific process of man breaking and slave making. It describes the rationale and results of the Anglo Saxon's ideas and methods of insuring the master/slave relationship."*
>
> — **Frederick Douglas,** former "slave"

Frederick Douglas

Before you read the following treatise, understand the language and thoughts of the author, Willie Lynch, were commonplace at the time this was written. It was not a matter of what to call a person of color, or how to treat him or her, but how to get the most out of a "slave" and keep the "slave" humble and willing to do as s/he was told. That may change your perspective as you read along.

The psychological, mental and spiritual assault perpetrated on Blacks has caused severe damage on individuals, families and communities, as anticipated by the treatise. Regardless of whether or not Willie Lynch existed, as some have argued, there is no doubt that these practices have been utilized successfully for centuries to perpetuate the manipulation and economic control of Black people.

It should be noted that we are merely reprinting this for the historical perspective it provides. One cannot change any misspellings or unusual grammar when supplying quoted material.

"Let's Make a Slave"

The Origin and Development of a Social Being Called "The Negro", by Willie Lynch

Let us make a slave. What do we need? First of all we need a black nigger man, a pregnant nigger woman and her baby nigger boy. Second, we will use the same basic principle that we use in breaking a horse, combined with some more sustaining factors. We reduce them from their natural state in nature; whereas nature provides them with the natural capacity to take care of their needs and the needs of their offspring, we break that natural string of independence from them and thereby create a dependency state so that we may be able to get from them useful production for our business and pleasure.

Cardinal Principles for Making a Negro

For fear that our future generations may not understand the principles of breaking both horses and men, we lay down the art. For, if we are to sustain our basic economy we must break both of the beasts together, the nigger and the horse. We understand that short range planning in economics results in periodic economic chaos, so that, to avoid turmoil in the economy, it requires us to have breadth and depth in long range comprehensive planning, articulating both skill and sharp perception. We lay down the following principles for long range comprehensive economic planning:

- *Both horse and niggers are no good to the economy in the wild or natural.*
- *Both must be broken and tied together for orderly production.*
- *For orderly futures, special and particular attention must be paid to the female and the youngest offspring.*
- *Both must be crossbred to produce a variety and division of labor.*
- *Both must be taught to respond to a peculiar new language.*
- *Psychological and physical instruction of containment must be created for both.*

We hold the above six cardinals as truths to be self-evident, based upon the following discourse concerning the economics of breaking and tying the horse and nigger together...all inclusive of the six principles laid down above. NOTE: Neither principles alone will suffice for good economics. All principles must be employed for the orderly good of the nation. Accordingly, both a wild horse and a wild or natural nigger is dangerous even if captured, for they will have the tendency to seek their customary freedom, and, in doing so, might kill you in your sleep. You cannot rest. They sleep while you are awake and are awake while you are asleep. They are dangerous near the family house and it requires too much labor to watch them away from the house. Above all you cannot get them to work in this natural state. Hence, both the horse and the nigger must be broken, that is break them from one form of mental life to another, keep the body and take the mind. In other words, break the will to resist.

Now the breaking process is the same for the horse and the nigger, only slightly varying in degrees. But as we said before, You must keep your eye focused on the female and the offspring of the horse and the nigger. A brief discourse in offspring development will shed light on the key to sound economic principles. Pay little attention to the generation of original breaking but concentrate on future generations. Therefore, if you break the female, she will break the offspring in its early years of development and, when the offspring is old enough to work, she will deliver it up to you. For her normal female protective tendencies will have been lost in the original breaking process. For example, take the case of the wild stud horse, a female horse and an already infant horse and compare the breaking process with two captured nigger males in their natural state, a pregnant nigger woman with her infant offspring. Take the stud horse, break him for limited containment. Completely break the female horse until she becomes very gentle whereas you or anybody can ride her in comfort. Breed the mare and the stud until you have the desired offspring. Then you can turn the stud to freedom until you need him again. Train the female horse whereby she will eat out of your hand, and she will train the infant horse to eat out of your hand also.

When it comes to breaking the uncivilized nigger, use the same process, but vary the degree and step up the pressure so as to do a complete reversal of the mind. Take the meanest and most restless nigger, strip him of his clothes in front of the remaining male niggers, the female, and the nigger infant, tar and feather him, tie each leg to a different horse faced in opposite directions, set him afire and beat both horses to pull him apart in front of the remaining niggers. The next step is to take a bullwhip and beat the remaining nigger male to the point of death in front of the female and the infant. Don't kill him. But put the fear of God in him, for he can be useful for future breeding.

The Breaking Process of the African Woman

Take the female and run a series of tests on her to see if she will submit to your desires willingly. Test her in every way, because she is the most important factor for good economics. If she shows any signs of resistance in submitting completely to your will, do not hesitate to use the bull whip on her to extract that last bit of bitch out of her. Take care not to kill her, for in doing so, you spoil good economics. When in complete submission, she will train her offspring in the early years to submit to labor when they become of age. Understanding is the best thing. Therefore, we shall go deeper into this area of the subject matter concerning what we have produced here in this breaking of the female nigger. We have reversed the relationships. In her natural uncivilized state she would have a strong dependency on the uncivilized nigger male, and she would have a limited protective dependency toward her independent male offspring and would raise female offspring to be dependent like her. Nature had provided for this type of balance. We reversed nature by burning and pulling one civilized nigger apart and bull whipping the other to the point of death - all in her presence. By her being left alone, unprotected, with the male image destroyed, the ordeal caused her to move from her psychological dependent state to a frozen independent state. In this frozen psychological state of independence she will raise her male and female offspring in reversed roles. For fear of the young male's life she will psychologically train him to be mentally weak and dependent but physically strong. Because she has become psychologically independent, she will train her female offspring to be psychologically independent as well. What have you got? You've got the nigger woman out front and the nigger man behind and scared. This is a perfect situation for sound sleep and economics. Before the breaking process, we had to be alert and on guard at all times. Now we can sleep soundly, for out of frozen fear, his woman stands guard for us. He cannot get past her early infant slave molding process. He is a good tool, now ready to be tied to the horse at a tender age. By the time a nigger boy reaches the age of sixteen, he is soundly broken in and ready for a long life of sound and efficient work and the reproduction of a unit of good labor force.

Continually, through the breaking of uncivilized savage niggers, by throwing the nigger female savage into a frozen psychological state of independency, by killing the protective male image, and by creating a submissive dependent mind of the nigger male slave, we have created an orbiting cycle that turns on its own axis forever, unless a phenomenon occurs and re-shifts the positions of the male and female savages. We show what we mean by example. We breed two nigger males with two nigger females. Then we take the nigger males away from them and keep them moving and working. Say the nigger female bears a nigger female and the other bears a nigger male. Both nigger females, being without influence of the nigger male image, frozen with an independent psychology, will raise their offspring into reverse positions. The one with the female offspring will teach her to be like herself, independent and negotiable (we negotiate with her, through her, by her, and negotiate her at will). The one with the nigger male offspring, she being frozen with a subconscious fear for his life, will raise him to be mentally dependent and weak, but physically strong...in other words, body over mind. Now, in a few years when these two offspring become fertile for early reproduction, we will mate and breed them and continue the cycle. That is good, sound, and long range comprehensive planning.

Warning: Possible Interloping Negatives

Earlier, we talked about the non-economic good of the horse and the nigger in their wild or natural state; we talked out the principle of breaking and tying them together for orderly production, furthermore, we talked about paying particular attention to the female savage and her offspring for orderly future planning; then more recently we stated that, by reversing the positions of the male and the female savages we had created an orbiting cycle that turns on its own axis forever, unless phenomenon occurred, and re-shifted the positions of the male and female savages.

Our experts warned us about the possibility of this phenomenon occurring, for they say that the mind has a strong drive to correct and re-correct itself over a period of time if it can touch some substantial original historical base; and they advised us that the best way to deal with this phenomenon is to shave off the brute's mental history and create a multiplicity of phenomenon or illusions so that each illusion will twirl in its own orbit, something akin to floating balls in a vacuum. This creation of a multiplicity of phenomenon or illusions entails the principles of crossbreeding the nigger and the horse as we stated above, the purpose of which is to create a diversified division of labor. The results of which is the severance of the points of original beginning's for each spherical illusion. Since we feel that the subject matter may get more complicated as we proceed in laying down our economic plan concerning the purpose, reason, and effect of cross-breeding horses and niggers, we shall lay down the following definitional terms for future generations.

- *Orbiting cycle means a thing turning in a given pattern.*
- *Axis means upon which or around which a body turns.*
- *Phenomenon means something beyond ordinary conception and inspires awe and wonder.*
- *Multiplicity means a great number.*
- *Sphere means a globe.*
- *Cross-breeding a horse means taking a horse and breeding it with an ass and you get a dumb backward ass, longheaded mule that is not reproductive nor productive by itself.*
- *Cross-breeding niggers means taking so many drops of good white blood and putting them into as many nigger women as possible, varying the drops by the various tones that you want, and then letting them breed with each other until the circle of colors appear as you desire.*

What this means is this: Put the niggers and the horse in the breeding pot, mix some asses and some good white blood and what do you get? You got a multiplicity of colors of ass backwards, unusual niggers, running, tied to backwards ass longheaded mules, the one productive of itself, the other sterile. (The one constant, the other dying. We keep the nigger constant for we may replace the mule for another tool) both mule and nigger tied to each other, neither knowing where the other came from and neither productive for itself, nor without each other.

Controlled Language

Cross-breeding completed, for further severance from their original beginning, we must completely annihilate the mother tongue of both the nigger and the new mule and institute a new language that involves the new life's work of both. You know, language is a peculiar institution. It leads to the heart of a people. The more a foreigner knows about the language of another country the more he is able to move through all levels of that society. Therefore, if the foreigner is an enemy of the country, to the extent that he knows the body of the language, to that extent is the country vulnerable to attack or invasion of a foreign culture. For example, you take a slave, if you teach him all about your language, he will know all your secrets, and he is then no more a slave, for you can't fool him any longer and having a fool is one of the basic ingredients of and incidents to the making of the slavery system.

For example, if you told a slave that he must perform in getting out "our crops" and he knows the language well, he would know that "our crops" didn't mean "our" crops, and the slavery system would break down, for he would relate on the basis of what "our crops" really meant. So you have to be careful in setting up the new language for the slave who would soon be in your house, talking to you as "man to man" and that is death to our economic system. In addition, the definition of words or terms are only a minute part of the process. Values are created and transported by communication through the body of the language. A total society has many interconnected value systems. All these values in the society have bridges of language to connect them for orderly working in the society. But for these language bridges, these many value systems would sharply clash and cause internal strife or civil war, the degree of conflict being determined by the magnitude of the issues or relative opposing strength in whatever form. For example, if you put a slave in a hog pen and train him to live there and incorporate in him to value it as a way of life completely, the biggest problem you would have out of him is that he would worry you about provision to keep the hog pen clean, or partially clean, or he might not worry you at all. On the other hand, if you put this same slave in the same hog pen and make a slip and incorporate something in his language whereby he comes to value a house more than he does his hog pen, you got a problem. He will soon be in your house.

Deep in the Mind of a Slave

"Let's Make a Slave," the text by Willie Lynch, reflects the mentality of the captors and their keen awareness of the importance of family and history. By removing these crucial references, even future generations of both races would believe the caste society that exists where enslaved Africans were held, is normal and just. The guidelines detailed in the treatise, described by its author as an "art", were designed to keep the body and take the mind of a "slave", and break their will to resist to avoid turmoil in the economy. Emphasis was placed on the offspring of enslaved women, which was essential in the process of "breaking" the family. It was the "slave-master's" belief that because of their heinous, torturous attacks on enslaved men, (deliberately committed in front of women and children), they would thereafter have a "submissive, dependent mind". These indelible images would traumatize women and her children, causing her to alter traditional methods of rearing boys and girls. "Slave-masters" also rationalized raping enslaved women, calculating the economic profits the offspring would bring, while simultaneously furthering their cause by creating another division amongst the captives.

The present status of people of color throughout the diaspora (economically, psychologically, spiritually, etc.), stems unmistakably from centuries of enslavement succeeded by Jim Crow, a racial caste system of de facto and de jure segregation. The legacy of oppression remains with us to this day. "Slave-masters" have been replaced with institutionalized racism/white supremacy. The inevitable outcome of relentless degradation has created a general state of co-dependence amongst the masses. Many people of African descent across the Diaspora suffer from what psychiatrists refer to as the "Stockholm Syndrome", a state that many persons held in hostage like situations develop, where there is self-loathing and a sense of empathy, gratitude and/or affection for their "slave-master"/abuser/oppressor/captor.

Internal and External Values

In 1966, historian and philosopher Dr. Maulana (mah-oo-lah-nah) Karenga (kah-ren-gah) created Kwanzaa to uplift the spirits of African Americans. It celebrates the seven fundamental principles of the Nguzo Saba: Umoja (unity); Kujichagulia (Self-Determination); Ujima (Collective Work and Responsibility); Ujamaa (Cooperative Economics); Nia (Purpose); Kuumba (Creativity); Imani (Faith).

These principles could ideally be utilized if individuals and families incorporated them into their days, weeks, and months, so that it is a way of life instead of a once a year celebration.

The word "MATAH" was created to describe "a segment of people of African descent who know that it is important to Give and Buy Black." The MATAH Network believes "True Freedom will be reached when we have healthy families, and when we practice the principles of Kwanzaa on a daily basis."

Umoja - Unity

God is the spiritual center of all individuals. Families are made up of individuals. The survival of a family unit (mother, father, children), depends on the establishment of a firm internal and external value system that stresses love of self, health, truth, family, spirituality, history and culture, education, and economic independence. In effort to counter the systematic, psychological oppression and social engineering the Black family has endured, individuals must undergo a training process that teaches them the importance of not participating in the practice of separating or distinguishing themselves from others based on complexion, hair texture, eye color, intelligence/level of education, class, occupation, residence, size, sex, height, or age.

Kujichagulia - Self-Determination

Ultimately our goal is to discontinue contributions to people, institutions, and industries that do not offer equal exchanges, and instead establish our own family/community institutions. Individuals, families, and communities would benefit because dependency on outside sources is reduced, and a more balanced relationship is fostered. The family unit has the greatest possibility of accomplishing this goal of self-sufficiency. By countering existing institutions with ones that are family/community-owned and operated, we can heal the wounds that presently infest our communities.

Ujamaa - Cooperative Economics

A Federal credit union is a member-owned cooperative organized to promote thrift among its members and to make loans to its members from these accumulated savings. It is not in business for profit, but for service. Thus, it is a unique financial institution. It is also a corporation chartered, supervised and insured by the Federal Government through the National Credit Union Administration (NCUA). Credit unions encourage their members to accumulate savings out of income as a means of building economic security for themselves and their families. In addition, credit unions provide consumer and, in some cases, car and home mortgage loans. With these and other benefits, credit unions help their members help themselves to a greater degree of financial stability.

We can begin by establishing a credit union as an economic base that would fulfill the goals and objectives of committed family/members. (Example: Berry Gordy, Jr. was able to start Motown Records, in Detroit, Michigan using money from his family's credit union).

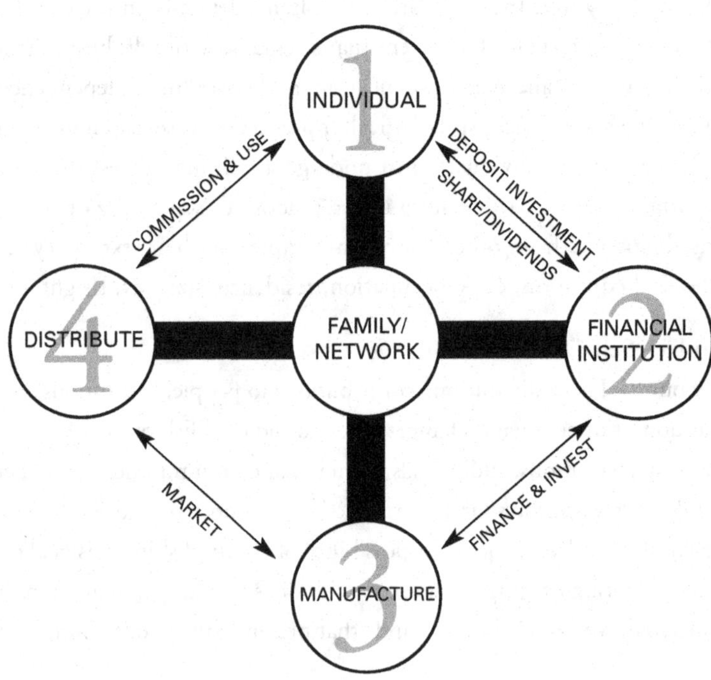

Cooperative Economics Chart

Individual
Makes a pledge to participate

Family/Network
Plans agenda and goals

– **Committees**

Product Committee (research & development); Financial Committee; Historical & Genealogical Research Committee; Education / Rites of Passage Committee (student tutorials / home schooling); Reunion Committee; Health Committee (holistic healthcare and products), etc.

Financial Institution - Credit Union
Individual purchases shares; members receive dividends and voting rights; consumer & personal loans, insurance, scholarship fund, tutorial, and other investments (i.e. products)

– **Board of Directors**

Elected by shareholders to give direction to the Network

Manufacture, Market & Distribute
From natural resources to consumer products (i.e. pure water, soap, vitamins / herbs, hair & body care); marketing the operation similar to Shaklee, Amway, Avon, etc.

– **Commission**

Return to individual

Ujima - Collective Work
Family reunions are the perfect vehicle to annually meet and for family committees to report and conduct business. They should consist of representatives from each family unit. Committees would be established to activate the following (others added as needed):

Historical & Genealogical Research Committee:

– Gather photographs, video
– Search for documents, diaries, letters, wills, trusts, etc., which offer information about our ancestors
– Maintain updated records on family history

– Publish a revised genealogy book regularly
– Establish genealogical societies

Legal Research Committee:
– How to probate family estates
– Estate planning (wills, trusts, realty, etc.)
– Constitutional law
– International law

Anti-Defamation Committee:
– Collect data
– Dispense information
– Document institutional racism (i.e. corporations, media, personalities)
– Catalogue cases (police brutality, hate groups, etc.)
– Respond to attacks made against people of African Descent (city, state, country, diaspora)

Education / Rites of Passage Committee:
– Develop a system of apprenticeship, as well as tutorials, to target youth development academically and culturally (Example: d'zert club)
– Knowing at least four generations of your ancestry
– Understanding the value of saving
– How to always invest in yourself

Reunion Committee:
– Organize economic and social events

Volunteer Committee:
– Family/Community organization

A Board of Directors organizes representatives from each committee and all branches of the family, (i.e. Carter, Cheeves, Trawick, Gordy, Butts, Boyer, etc.) to facilitate a more unified effort. To unveil whom our ancestors are and locate our living family members; we must establish a DNA mapping program. This will help us establish a genealogical database for people of African descent.

The Debt

> *SARUGE: To raise up and restore that which is in ruin; to repair that which is damaged; to rejoin that which is severed; to replenish that which is depleted or lacking; to strengthen that which is weak; to right that which is wrong; to make secure that which is insecure or undeveloped*

Jim Crow laws were grounded in two powerful trends in American intellectual life after 1890: the new social sciences, such as anthropology, determined "scientifically" that Blacks were inherently inferior to whites, while historians drew a nostalgic picture of slavery as a benevolent, peaceful, honorable time. Black families passed along their own memories of enslavement and Reconstruction, which obviously conflicted with the white version of history.

In *Remembering Jim Crow,* a special report from American RadioWorks, several southern whites were interviewed to get their perspective on Jim Crow, and what it was like to grow up in a culture where there was simply no question, Blacks were inferior and treated as such.

Mary Laveaux, who asked not to use her real name, lived her entire 91 years in Iberia Parish (a bayou in southern Louisiana), and belonged to one of the old plantation families. She was raised by a Black nanny and surrounded by Black tenants on her family's plantation. She says the Black people who worked for her family were poor, but happy. For example, she says Blacks chose to sit in the back of the bus because "It was just part of their, they understood that it looks like. I don't think that the white people were cruel to them and made them do that...All the black people who lived in a small town like this, they knew everybody knew everybody else. Except we didn't know the colored peoples that well but I think they all knew the white people...And looked up to the white people I'll tell you...Because they knew that's where there bread was buttered. You know the white people helped them. Gave them work and everything...But they felt that was part of them...The white people I think were good to them...And their way of life, I think they were happier than the white people. Because nothing worried them, you know? Some white people, they were worried of sometimes about losing their land or trying to make things go, you know, they were the leaders. But the Black people, nothing bothered them."

Leonard Barrow, a retired fighter pilot, returned to New Iberia after a long military career. He comes from a plantar family that always had close contact with

Blacks, first as "slave owners", then as employers, always as superiors. "Well, my name is Barrow. Leonard Barrow, Jr. And my connection with New Iberia is I was born here in 1917 on East Main Street. It was very segregated without a doubt. From the time I grew up, you had white folks and black folks. And basically the black folks worked for the white folks. They sort of lived in their part of town and we lived in our part of town...I guess if you didn't grow up here it would be difficult to understand, it was two separate worlds. You know, you just didn't become part of their world, you didn't go into their houses, they worked in your house, but it was just the way it was, it had always been that way...God, there was a fellow who worked for my father for a number of years in the rice field and we ran into each other one day and boy he came and threw his arms around me you know it uh...now this is another funny thing, you wouldn't have dreamed of shaking hands back in those days...The blacks definitely lived at a much lower standard. Much lower. Many of the houses didn't have running water, many of the houses didn't have electricity, heat was rudimentary, of course nobody had air conditioning."

When Barrow was asked if whites openly questioned the way things were, he responded, "Certainly not! Heavens no! Why? Why would they have questioned? I mean, this is the way it was. You grew up, you know it's kinda like, I'm a Catholic because my parents were Catholics. Never questioned why. That's the way it was...[and Blacks] knew their place."

Barrow says he never got a chance to enjoy the comforts of being from the "plantation gentry". "I didn't inherit enough to buy my wife's Oldsmobile when my folks finally died, but my grandparents' grandparents had three plantations over on the Mississippi river. I don't know how many slaves they had. They were awful nice, you know you'd go hunting, 'Boy, clean those ducks', you know 'Skin that deer' uh, 'Shine my shoes,' I believe I could have gone for that. Yeah I think you could have too."

Henry Dauterive is from the "plantar aristocracy". He had a "handyman, chauffeur, aide-de-camp, whatever, who worked for my father and he often sat in the kitchen waiting his orders and I loved him to death. He taught me how to ride a bicycle, he taught me how to shoot a gun. And, so I ran in the kitchen at age seven and I jumped in his lap and I kissed him on the mouth. Well he sat there and then he tried to explain to me that I couldn't do this. He tried to say, 'You can't kiss black folks.' It just puzzled me...When I was 16, I went off to Tulane to college, and the world became much, much larger and I came back and I had the temerity to tell my grandfather that it was possible for a black person to be as smart as a white person. Now that was also crossing the line. He knew that they were inferior, he knew that they were servants, he knew that they were ignorant and dirty and diseased and everything. He was not happy...I don't want to sound as though I were something really good. Because I recognized this and perhaps cared a little bit more, but it was only a little bit more...It is an attitude that the whites have that the black is inferior. I am not at all sure that they're wrong. Today even. I'm not at all sure. In fact, I tend in that direction to think it, because I've watched it now with interest for so many years."

Henry says that a lifetime of observing Blacks, as legal clients and employees, has convinced him he was naive at 16 to think Black people could be as smart as whites. As Henry sees it, Blacks are inherently less intelligent and less motivated than whites.

Deanne and Smitty Landry feel that people who call attention to past discrimination are just prolonging the problem. "I think that when we were growing up we did have the attitude that they are happy, they are getting along, and you know why should we care about them or sense the injustice and uh unfairness in the way that they were treated...I draw the line in the belief that we should not look at the past and create a sense of paranoia over what has happened; I think that the blacks...I think that we should, you know, put that behind us and then say 'Okay, you are what you make of yourself now, you're given, we have given you all the opportunities you can have, do not belabor the question of what happened in the past, and how bad it is and we should give you things.' I think that is a psychologically defeating attitude...You need retribution because of all of this, well I don't think that that's, that's healthy," says Smitty.

"It didn't happen to them actually it happened to their ancestors", added Deanne.

A Different Opinion

Stanley Mark, program director of the Asian American Legal Defense and Education Fund, supports Black redress. "I really believe that the African-American community deserves reparations. One thing I learned from the experience in the movement for redress for Japanese-Americans is that they were able to establish a very close connection between what the government did back in the '40s to the actual crime and injuries that people suffer today. And if there is a way to link that up in a concrete way, then it will be very successful."

According to David H. Swinton, a Harvard-trained economist and president of historically Black Benedict College in Columbia, South Carolina, the link has been made. "The connection between the current status of somebody or the current wealth of somebody, and the future status, the way it turns out, is the way the economic system works. If you practice slavery, discrimination, racism, or any of those things for some period of time, it does have an impact on the future well being of that group. It's not enough to just stop doing those things. Once you get behind in ownership of capital, the normal processes of the economy will keep you behind forever." He defines capital as human capital, things that enable one to earn money, such as education and professional experience, and physical capital, assets such as financial holdings and ownership.

"The main consequence for future generations of current discrimination or past discrimination is that it reduces the capital of accumulation. If it is desirable to equalize the status of the races in the future, then there must be some make up, some compensation, some reparations, whatever you want to call it, for the capital that these groups were prevented from accumulating. Otherwise, the past will continue to perpetuate itself throughout the future."

Group of Blacks Presses the Case for Reparations for Slavery

Reparations sought for slaves' descendants

Slave descendent sues IRS

Convention calls for reparations for slavery

Slavery reparations sought

20,000 Blacks Seek Tax Rebates, Citing Old Law

Leaders want payments for the years African Americans were kept in bondage.

Reparations proponents pushing for Japanese-style lawsuit against government by year's end

Prejudice, Ignorance Obstacles to Reparations for Slavery

Reparations: An issue of justice

U.S. Tax Agency Rejects Thousands of Blacks' Reparation Claims

For Howard Winant, a white Temple University sociologist, reparations goes to the root of U.S. racial problems. "On the moral level, this country absolutely as a nation owes African-Americans an apology for one of the most serious violations of human rights that has existed in recorded history, in fact, in all history, recorded and unrecorded," he said in an interview on National Public Radio.

In the November 2000 issue of ELLE magazine, actress Gwyneth Paltrow declared: "I'll tell you what's appalling to me...that no reparations have been made to black people in this country. There's this whole culture at such a disadvantage, and we put them in this situation. We don't fund the schools in the inner city, we have no health care...If I were African-American, I'd be furious. I'm furious now, and I'm not even black! If I were, I would definitely be an activist..."

> *No'm, I nebbah knowed whut it wah t' rest. I jes wok all de time f'om mawnin' till late at night. I had t' do ebbathin' dey wah t' do on de outside. Wok in de field, chop wood, hoe cawn, till sometime I feels lak mah back sholy break. I done ebbathin' 'cept split rails. Yo' know, dey split rails back in dem days. Well, I nevah did split no rails.*
>
> *Ole Marse strop us good effen we did anythin' he didn' lak. Sometime he get hes dandah up an' den we dassent look roun' at him. Else he tie yo' hands afoah yo' body an' whup yo', jes lak yo' a mule. Lawdy, honey, I's tuk a thousand lashins in mah day. Sometimes mah poah ole body be soah foah a week.*
>
> *Ole Hoss he send us niggahs out in any kine ob weathah, rain o' snow, it nebbah mattah. We had t' go t' de mountings, cut wood an' drag it down t' de house. Many de time we come in wif ouh cloes stuck t'ouh poah ole cold bodies, but 'twarn't no use t' try t' git 'em dry. Ef de Ole Boss o' de Ole Missie see us dey yell: "Git on out ob heah yo' black thin', an' git yo' wok outen de way!" An' Lawdy, honey, we knowed t' git, else we git de lash. Dey did'n cah how ole o' how young yo' wah, yo' nebbah too big t' git de lash.*
>
> *De rich white folks nebbah did no wok; dey had da'kies t' do it foah dem. In de summah we had t' wok outdoo's, in de wintah in de house. I had t' ceard an' spin till ten o'clock. Nebbah git much rest, had t' git up at foah de nex' mawnin' an' sta't agin. Didn' get much t' eat, nuthah, jes a lil' cawn bread an' 'lasses. Lawdy, honey, yo' cain't know whut a time I had. All cold n'hungry. No'm, I aint tellin' no lies. It de gospel truf. It sho is.*
>
> —**Sarah Gudger,** *enslaved in North Carolina*

Sarah Gudger

The compensation program for victims of Nazi prosecution included the declaration of Israel as a state in 1948, (six months after the United Nations voted for the partition of Palestine), and forged on 8,020 square miles of land, some of which was occupied. In 1952, Germany began giving reparations to survivors of the Jewish Holocaust; by 1980, the amount totaled $58 billion in today's dollars.

In 1971, the United States gave Alaskan natives 44 million acres of land through the Alaska Native Claims Settlement Act and nearly $1 billion dollars. In 1976, Australia gave its indigenous Aborigines more than 96,000 square miles of land because it had been taken from them during European settlements in the 18th and 19th centuries. In 1980, Canada compensated Japanese-Canadians with $230 million for World War II internment and indigenous peoples with 673,000 square kilometers of land after 13 years of negotiations over land treaty claims.

In 1985, the Sioux of South Dakota were paid $105 million by the United States government; the Seminoles of Florida, $12.3 million; and the Chippewas of Wisconsin, $31 million.

In 1995, Austria promised Jewish Holocaust survivors $25 million. In 1997, Iraq began paying $300 million for every $1 billion in oil revenue to victims of the 1990 Kuwait invasion, according to terms arranged by the U.N. Security Council. The 1988 Civil Liberties Act provided a formal apology and $20,000 to Japanese-American survivors of World War II internment camps, totaling more than $1 billion. In August of 1997, Latin Americans of Japanese descent who were deported to the United States during World War II and also interned, filed a class-action suit in Los Angeles Federal District Court requesting the same compensation as Japanese-Americans.

It is estimated that the number of Africans who died during the Middle Passage alone range from 60 to 100 million! By comparison, about 120,000 Japanese-Americans were incarcerated during World War II, and six million Jews died in their holocaust. N'COBRA, The National Coalition of Blacks for Reparations in America, is an umbrella organization established in 1989. It is an "all volunteer alliance of activists and organizations dedicated to winning the long overdue debt owed to African people in the U.S. and abroad."

Proposed Remedies

POWERNOMICS®

Dr. Claud Anderson, is president of PowerNomics Corporation of America, a corporation that is involved in major business development, primarily in inner cities, across the country. The word PowerNomics® represents a social-political-economic package of principles and strategies developed by Dr. Anderson to help make Black America a more self-sufficient and competitive group. His latest book, PowerNomics®: The National Plan to Empower Black America sets forth a five year national plan in education, economics, and politics, and outlines a new role for Black religious organizations. His ideas have begun to ignite a national movement of reform among blacks.

Dr. Anderson has drawn the nation's attention to the advantages of redeveloping and industrializing black communities. Dr. Anderson has begun a seafood factory project aimed at urban locations in the United States.

Widely recognized as one of America's most influential intellectuals and authors, Dr. Anderson has popularized Black history. His book, Black Labor, White Wealth: A Search for Power and Economic Justice, is the foundation for the solutions, principles, and activities proposed in PowerNomics®: The National Plan.

Dr. Anderson has a broad and varied base of experiences spanning education, business, federal and state politics and successful social reform. During integration, he served as State Coordinator of Education for Governor Reubin Askew of Florida. While serving in that capacity, he founded the State Action Council, a coalition of black leaders for political action in Florida. Dr. Anderson, appointed by former president Jimmy Carter, served as Assistant Secretary in the U.S. Department of Commerce where he headed the Coastal Plains Regional Commission and funded and directed economic development activities for governors in the Southeastern states. He was executive director of two economic development corporations for the city of Miami, Florida. As special assistant to the 1988 Democratic Convention, he awarded 37% of the contracts to blacks, a record that has not been reached or broken.

The Harvest Institute

The Harvest Institute is a non-profit, tax exempt research, educational, policy and advocacy organization located in Washington, D.C. and founded in 1993. Their mission is to engage in activities that lead to a Black America that is self-sufficient and competitive as a group within the next decade.

All activities of The Harvest Institute:

- Are based upon the books, Black Labor, White Wealth: A Search for Power and Economic Justice and PowerNomics: The National Plan to Empower Black America by Dr. Claud Anderson, founder of the Institute.
- Are dedicated to implementing as much of the PowerNomics National Plan as possible.
- Encourage others to use the principles of PowerNomics as a guide to their activities so that, even though individuals or groups may be operating separately, their work contributes to achieving the PowerNomics vision of a Black America that is self-sufficient and competitive.
- Are based upon the PowerNomics principle that Blacks must aggregate, pool their resources, and build independent communities before allying with competing groups.

"In the 21st century, the only people that will survive and prosper are the people who own and control resources...Since we [African-Americans] don't own and control anything, there are major forces that are going to push us into an underclass structure. Black people have been locked into the lowest level of a real life monopoly game," he said.

Anderson feels the only two problems blacks have in America are "the maldistribution of wealth in the hands of the white society and the inappropriate behavior of black people."

"You got to get away from the dreams...A vision tells you where you are and where you want to go to correct those problems. The next thing you do is that you must change your paradigm. A paradigm is how you see things. The issue in America is not integration [or] segregation. The issue is congregation and assimilation, pulling your resources together into a pile, [this] is called functional pluralism. Integration means disintegration. Integration is nothing but a weaker form of segregation. You were stronger when you were segregated than you are integrated. We are the only people in this country that don't have any community...A community is where you store your wealth and values. I want my people to have the same rights as everybody else."

MATAH

MATAH is an African Centered Economic Solidarity Movement. The movement consists of members who seek and are committed to the TRUE FREEDOM of people of African descent, who know that practicing a race-fist philosophy is the key to the upliftment of people of African descent, and who refuse to have that spirit within them crushed. The organization which coordinates this movement is the MATAH NETWORK, an African owned and operated business organization. It identifies products and services that are created and manufactured by people of African descent, and makes those products and services available to the MATAH. The larger MATAH Network community has three purposes:

– To organize the MATAH
– To raise our African consciousness
– To redirect our consumer spending power

In 1999, Black America generated $530 billion in income. The MATAH Network intends to capture an additional 5% of those Black consumer dollars. The Network wants to discontinue giving "95% of our money to the very people who despise us and finance our oppression...even worse, throughout the course of human history, people of African descent are the ONLY people to consciously finance the future oppression of their own children. That is, the decisions we make now affect the lives of future generations."

THE BLACK MANIFESTO

James Forman interrupted one Sunday morning service in May 1969, at Riverside Church in New York City, addressing himself "to the White Christian Churches and the Jewish Synagogues in the United States of America and All other Racist Institutions." He read a Black Manifesto who demanded that the churches and synagogues pay $500 million as "a beginning of the reparations due us as people, who have been exploited and degraded, brutalized, killed and persecuted."

The amount demanded by the Manifesto, which was adopted by the National Black Economic Development Conference before Forman's action was taken, was to be used to establish a Southern land bank, publishing and printing industries, four audio-visual networks, a research skills center, a training center for teaching skills in community organizations, a Black labor strike and defense fund, a Black university, and several other institutions. To achieve its objectives, the Manifesto called "for the total disruption of selected church-sponsored agencies" by the seizure of their offices, to be held "in trusteeship until our demands are met." It went on to assert that churches and synagogues were only the first targets, and that similar demands would be addressed to private business and the federal government.

Representative John Conyers (D-Michigan) originally unveiled the "Commission to Study Reparation Proposals for African Americans Act", H.R. 40 in 1989 (now House Bill 531). The bill does not actually mandate reparations for African-Americans, but according to the bill's summary, is "to acknowledge the fundamental injustice, cruelty, brutality and inhumanity of slavery in the United States and the 13 colonies between 1619 and 1865 and to establish a commission to examine the institution of slavery, subsequent de jure and de facto racial and economic discrimination against African-Americans, and the impact of these forces on living African-Americans, to make recommendations to the Congress on appropriate remedies, and for other purposes."

The Conyer's bill only proposes a study, followed by a written report and recommendations, which could include a formal apology from the United States for the horrors of slavery. Making amends or giving satisfaction for a wrong or injury, as reparations is defined, is a standard practice in international law. The United Nations negotiates it and the International Court of Justice orders it. Some Nations even give it without prodding from foreign governments or institutions.

FORTY ACRES AND A MULE

If we are to heal, past transgressions must be addressed. In the April 1993 issue of Essence magazine, for example, contributor L.G. Sherrod declares:

> *...There should be no doubt in our minds about whether or not the U.S. Government owes us reparations – our '40 acres and a mule", plus interest. Reparation payments are a well-established principle of international law. It generally involves payment by one nation for damages and harm it causes to people of another. No question, massive damages and harm have been inflicted on us since 1619, when we first hit these shores.*
>
> *Congress tries to atone in 1866, when the Radical Republicans passed a law requiring that Confederate property be confiscated to provide 40 acres of land and a mule to the 4 million former slaves left at the end of the Civil War with no education, no homes, no land, and no money. However, this bill was vetoed by Andrew Johnson, who became president after Abraham Lincoln was assassinated.*
>
> *Since then the United States has consistently and arrogantly ignored the claim for payment of reparations to the descendants of the millions of slaves who were forced to work without pay for 246 years. Based on estimates made by scholars, our 40 acres and a mule would be valued at $300 - $500 billion dollars today.*
>
> *We must demand compensation for the outrageous economic violence perpetrated on us during slavery. We must move on collecting the tax owed to us as a result of the "separate but equal" policy, which made racial discrimination the law of the land. Although the Supreme Court's ruling reduced us to second-class citizens, we did not get any tax breaks to offset the loss of our basic rights and constitutional privileges.*
>
> *The Government also owes African-Americans a tax rebate for the 60 years of segregation and Jim Crow that followed slavery. Although we were consigned by law to second-class citizenship then, we were still forced to pay first-class taxes and poll taxes on property, purchases, income, and a host of other transactions.*
>
> *All we got for our tax dollars were whites-only public facilities; political disenfranchisement; segregated and inferior schools; ghetto housing; barriers to employment, occupations and business ownership; inequity in income; in*

a nutshell, poverty, permanent inequality, and the economic and social marginality we experience today.

Germany paid billions in reparations to European countries after its defeat in World War I and was forced to pay billions more in reparations to Israel for killing millions of Jews during World War II. Japan and the smaller Axis powers also had to pay reparations after World War II. The U. S. Government has paid reparations to several Native-American groups for numerous land frauds. More recently, Iraq was assessed billions in reparations for invading Kuwait.

In 1988, Congress approved $20,000 apiece to approximately 60,000 Japanese Americans who were evacuated, relocated, or interned in concentration camps during World War II. But despite this, the reparations bill drafted by John Conyers, Jr. (D-Mich.), which merely calls for establishing a committee to study the impact of slavery on African-Americans and recommend remedies, can't even get to the House floor for a vote!

We need to bombard Congress with letters, petitions, and phone calls, demanding not only our long overdue reparations, but reparations to sub-Saharan African countries as well, which can best be paid in the form of forgiveness of the outstanding debt obligations that have crippled their economies.

BLACK PEOPLE HAVE LONG FOUGHT FOR FORTY ACRES & A MULE

Dr. Imari A. Obadele is a full time political science professor at Prairie View A & M University. He is a member of the National Conference of Black Political Scientists, and acts as a national officer of the Provisional Government of the Republic of New Afrika (PGRNA). He has authored two textbooks, along with several other works, including a 1993 article detailing the grueling, yet consistent fight for reparations. He makes reference to the pending release of a book on reparations, written by Christopher Alston, a respected researcher who documented and chronicled numerous facts about the movement.

Dr. Obadele notes that some of the 5,000 Blacks who fought on the American side during the Revolutionary War, fought not only because of the promise of freedom, but for reparations.

Historian Benjamin Quarles and others have pointed out that several thousand Black soldiers and sailors fought on the British side during the

Revolutionary War for the promise of freedom and land, a form of reparations. Some of them settled in West Afrika, helping to build the state of Sierra Leone. The promise of land and the desire to keep the Americans from reducing them to slaves induced free Black people in Spanish Florida to fight with the British against the Americans in the War of 1812.

In his book on reparations, Christopher Alston also describes the formation of the Ex-Slaves Bounty and Reparations Society by several Black men and women. This organization of more than 100,000 members fought for just compensation – forty acres and a mule – between 1875 and 1986. The hostility of the executive branch of the government in the United States to the demand for reparations resulted in a number of the leaders of the Ex-Slaves Bounty and Reparations Society being sent to jail on trumped up charges of fraud. These hateful actions of the U.S. government presaged the similar fate of the great Marcus Garvey. He too would be wrongfully jailed for his work of repatriation – return to Afrika – which is also a reparations demand (since those who kidnapped us from Afrika should pay for the return and resettlement of those of us who choose this option).

Black people, however, did not allow the repression of the United States to quiet their demands for reparations. Queen Mother Moore, now 94 years old, has been a leader in the call for reparations for most of her adult life. Robert Brock of California has labored in the same vineyards for nearly thirty years. The Nation of Islam has long made the demand for reparations, publishing this demand regularly in the Nation's first national newspaper, Muhammad Speaks. In 1968, the Provisional Government of the Republic of New Afrika collected thousands of signatures on petitions demanding $10,000 per person and five states for an independent New Afrikan nation-state. Dorothy Lewis of Maryland, founder of the Black Reparations Commission, has published two informative books on reparations. The African People's Socialist Party, through its African National Reparations Organization, has held reparations hearings in several cities for at least a half a decade.

Black elected officials have also made the demand. In 1988, Massachusetts state Senator Bill Owens introduced a reparations bill in that state's legislature. Black state legislators in Louisiana succeeded in 1990 in passing a *resolution demanding U.S. Congressional action on a preliminary reparations bill introduced by Congressman John Conyers. In Detroit, Raymond Jenkins was chiefly responsible for the passage of reparations resolutions by the Detroit Common Council and the Wayne County Board of Supervisors in the Spring of 1989, calling for $40 million for an educational fund.*

The National Coalition of Blacks for Reparations in America, N'COBRA, is striving to create a national united front for all of those groups and individuals working to achieve reparations, so that our present demand for the interest-accumulated "forty acres and a mule" will be successful. The reparations struggle may be a long one, but if We work together in an organized, consistent way, victory is certain!

PG-RNA

The Provisional Government of the Republic of New Afrika (North America) filed a complaint in 1995 against the United States of America for "Egregious Violations of the Human Rights of Afrikans Born in America Who are Descendants of Persons Held as Slaves All Contrary to the Solemn Commitments of the United States Under the International Covenant on Civil and Political Rights".

Leaders of PG-RNA, supported by officers of the National Conference of Black Lawyers, the National Black United Front, the New Afrikan Peoples Organization and others, demonstrated in Washington, D.C. on April 2, 1994. "Black Nation Day" was designed to "make U.S. President Bill Clinton and Congress face and act upon a Black agenda", which included:

A $44 Billion down-payment on the Billions owed as reparations for slavery and post slavery discrimination and trauma

The immediate establishment of a fund, of no less than five billion dollars in this Fiscal Year, with increasing annual amounts for the next ten years (preferably under the control of the popularly elected leadership of a national coalition of Afrikans in America), for the purpose of providing a friendly development bank to assist New Afrikan merchants and Community Cooperatives in economic development.

The immediate establishment of a billion dollar fund, directed and controlled by a national commission of organizations established by the democratically elected officers of a coalition of Black organizations in America, to distribute these token reparations to churches, community groups, and national organizations which are today and have been for at least two years been involved in programs of social and economic benefit (self-help) for Black people; the fund would receive increasing amounts annually for 20 years.

Absolute "forgiveness" of all college "loans" to Blacks.

The immediate release of all Black Liberation Army, "Indians", and other jailed freedom fighters, including whites jailed for helping the Black Liberation Army.

With the approval of the Black community, the release of Black prisoners who are drug-free, have not committed heinous crimes, and who have been in prison two years or more.

Exemption from all federal (income) taxes for 20 years.

The ten projected Pan-Afrikan College campuses are each to have a first-year endowment of a billion dollars. This endowment would also include students who work diligently, including those released from prisons.

A provision of $25,000 to each man, woman, and child, descendants of persons once held as slaves, who choose to return to Afrika or Jamaica.

It is PG-RNA's wish, as well as that of the New Afrikan People's Organization, to acquire Alabama, Georgia, Louisiana, Mississippi and South Carolina, as an independent Black state (similar to Canada), for those interested in sovereignty.

WE DEMAND REPARATIONS (FOR AFRICAN PEOPLE)

...Hundreds of millions, tens of generations of African people who have toiled, suffered, perished, and survived, the plantations, chain gangs, penitentiaries and apartheid ghettos on both sides of the Atlantic Ocean. This is for the millions who lost their lives in the big sea as "human cargo" in route to the Americas and Europe, during the world's worst war, the

international "HELLACAUST", or slave trade.

The purpose of "REPARATIONS" is simple. My goal is to help popularize the growing movement of people of African descent in North America (and Africans all over the Diaspora and on the continent of Africa) to redress past enslavement, and continuing colonialism, super-exploitation and oppression. A portion of the proceeds from the sales of this song are being contributed to N'COBRA (National Coalition of Blacks for Reparations in America), our coalition fighting for Reparations.

There is really no amount of money, nor enough gold or diamonds in the earth, to properly repay African people for the tremendous loss of life, and SELF, that we have experienced. The costs are incalculable! The time has come for African people to make it their top priority, the achievement of some economic righting of the wrongs perpetuated by the governments and corporations who sanctioned and got wealthy from the fruits of trading and breeding African people, and super-exploiting our labor. We DEMAND REPARATIONS, NOW! IT'S TIME TO NEGOTIATE!

In my opinion, our demands for Reparations could fall in the following categories (in no particular order). I encourage discussions in the following:

Cash

In North America, we should demand a cash payment (minimally, in the tens of thousands of dollars) for each man, woman, and child of African descent. This cash payment should be made directly to the individual, or guardians in the case of minors, to use at their discretion (for the purchase of property, business creation, investments, travel, relocation away from the U.S., the pursuing of dreams, etc.). Additional monetary payments should be made to our designated organizations.

On the continent of Africa, South and Central America, and the Caribbean, demands might include liquidating the so-called "debt" to U.S. and European governments and corporations, along with cash payments.

Land

In U.S. / North America, we must demand the redistribution of millions of acres of plantation land to African people, particularly in the "South", that is soaked with the sweat, blood and bones of our ancestors. The payment of "FORTY ACRES AND A MULE" to the enslaved Africans, was proposed by Congress in 1865, after the "Civil War". However, the bill was vetoed by then President Andrew Johnson. Even in cases where our people have legally owned the land, we have been cheated and terrorized out of it. In the "North", and major urban areas, we should demand a turning over of mostly inner-city properties, many now vacant, for redevelopment by organizations of predominately African people.

The land issue must be addressed on the continent of Africa, and throughout the Diaspora, as well. No true change and improvements in our living standards can come until a revolution in the ownership of the land is accomplished!

Education

In North America, enslaved Africans were robbed of our languages, culture, and traditions of living. Our people were not only victims of the mighty lash but subjected to the most horrific and racist brainwashing ever documented. This miseducation continues to this day, educationally and culturally.

Our Reparations demand must be for a true internationalist curriculum, which provides proper account of the significant role-played by Africa and its sons and daughters in the development of humanity.

In addition to changes in curriculum, our call must be for full funding by the governments and corporations of primary and secondary public education. Historically, African-American institutions, and the development of qualified new ones, deserve financial redress. Full scholarships for the descendants of slaves to the trade school, college, or university of choice, must be a major demand. Free preparatory instruction – to prepare students for higher education – should be made available.

Health

It is not surprising that in U.S. / America, people of African descent are suffering, disproportionately, from physical, mental, and spiritual ailments. Our quality of living and life span is generally worse and shorter than nearly all other sectors of the population. This stems from a legacy of having the worse nutrition, housing, medical care, and poverty imposed on our families. As a reaction to mass poverty, brutality and terror, Africans have developed disproportionate addictions to harmful foods, tobacco, alcohol and narcotics. Our Reparations movement should demand health-care, OF CHOICE and ON DEMAND, at any medical facility in the "U.S." (or, elsewhere). Full support for our health care institutions is a must.

Freedom

While African people in the U.S. / North America make up only 12% of the population, we comprise the majority of the incarcerated population. This is not surprising, since we have been "incarcerated" for nearly 500 years (on slave ships, plantations, prison farms, ghettos, and jails). In fact, the "federal" and "state" governments and corporations continue their drive for super-profits through the incarceration of mostly young African people. What else could explain the fact that billions and billions of dollars are allocated, each year, for prisons, and the new "plantations" known as "boot camps"? Poor communities, of all nationalities, are so economically desperate that they are selling their futures to secure the minimal "development" and jobs that come with more penal construction.

The overwhelming majority of inmates are jailed due to economic poverty and political injustice in the so-called "criminal justice" system. Our Reparations should include the release of the majority of men and women of African descent, and the establishment of "new life" programs run by designated community institutions. Those currently incarcerated deserve Reparations as well. If our foreparents had been paid their forty acres and a mule, many of our people wouldn't have been forced into a life of "crime" in order to survive.

Self-Determination

Along with the above economic demands, African people must be extended the right to self-determination, the opportunity to determine our own future. For too long, others have "spoken" for us, decided what was "best" for our people, communities, families, and futures. Conventions and plebiscites, similar to our mass movements during and after the "Civil War" and reconstruction, should occur.

African people, as an oppressed national people in North America, must be given the full right to decide whether to remain a part of the current political, economic and educational systems, or to break away and form separate ones.

House of Representatives Bill 40

Congressman John Conyers of Michigan has introduced an important bill in the U.S. Congress calling for a study of the affects of slavery and how the issue can be addressed. Personally, I have a problem with the bill. I feel that each day our people wait for more "studies", more of us die. We should be formulating our specific demands right now. Conyer's bill definitely deserves a hearing in the House of Representatives, and in the Senate. Currently, the bill sits in the House "Judiciary Committee". We must begin a major campaign to insure that hearings are held. Letters, calls, and meetings with our Congresspeople should be a priority. No support for Reparations should equal removal from office!

We should demand that our elected officials at all levels, and those running for office, actively support Reparations for African-Americans. In the final analysis, No Reparations should translate into disruption of the governmental and corporate production processes! There can be no talk of addressing "crime", education, health-care, "welfare reform" and "democracy", until amends are made for one of the greatest crimes of all times – the enslavement and continued super-exploitation of African people!

Actions You Can Take to Support Reparations for African People!

1. Discuss Reparations daily with your family, friends, and co-workers. Talk up the issue at he dinner table, on streets, jails, B-ball courts, taverns, campuses, everywhere there is more than one person. Rap about how you want us to get "paid", how best to use Reparations! Popularize the recent Reparations victory in Rosewood, Florida.

2. Become a member of N'COBRA. Organize a local N'COBRA chapter in your area. Hold fun(d)raising events to support N'COBRA.

3. Get your union, community group, church, fraternity and social club to support Reparations for African people, and endorse N'COBRA.

4. Register to vote and make calls on elected officials and candidates demanding they actively support Reparations for African people.

5. Organize and participate in actions for Reparations in your local area, and in Washington, DC and New York (the United Nations, etc.).

6. Fight for the land! Get involved in battles to recapture land in historically African-American communities.

7. File reparations "claims" against your city, county, and state governments, especially in the "South". Join in class-action suits.

8. Support the struggles for Reparations of African people in the Caribbean, South and Central America, Europe, and Africa.

There is no question that strong emotions are evoked by the possibilities of a Reparations program. Jahahara Harry Armstrong's recommendations have some highly valid suggestions for the successful implementation of fair restitution. However, his is not the only avenue under consideration.

THE LOST/FOUND NATION OF ISLAM

The Lost/Found Nation of Islam, a faction of the Nation of Islam founded in 1977 after the death of leader Elijah Muhammad, contends that the remedy for African-Americans must include land for an independent Black nation and that the United Nations, not the United States Congress, should be the target for Black appeals. In July 1994, the group submitted a petition to the United Nations requesting a forum "so that African-American human rights grievances pertaining to reparations and self-determination can be expressed, systematically and officially recorded, evaluated and remedied," according to Silas Muhammad, the organization's leader.

They insist that land outside the United States is the best reparation option.

The National Commission for Reparations supports the notion that the cure for

America's ills lie in the payment of reparations to the descendants of enslaved Africans. In 1995, under the direction of Silas Muhammad, a petition was filed with the United Nations Sub-Commission on Human Rights titled: Reparations Petition for U.N. Assistance under Resolution 1503 (XLVIII) on Behalf of African-Americans in the United States of America.

THE MOORISH SCIENCE TEMPLE OF AMERICA

In 1913, The Moorish Science Temple was founded by Noble Drew Ali, prophet of Allah. He proclaimed that "Negroes" were actually Moors (originally Blak-a-Moors), descendants of Moroccans of the 16th and 17th centuries (the ancient Moabites), and had inhabited the northwestern and southwestern shores of Africa, before being exported to Spain, and then brought to the U.S.

Sheik John Hawk-Bey delivered to the President a copy of his Consent for Reparations Petition, based on the initial Emancipation Proclamation that was issued on September 22, 1862, by President Abraham Lincoln, and passed the United States Congress on December 15, 1862. In it he demands as a first action that the...

> *...President of the United States ...release and pay out to each indigenous person of African descent their Just portion in Compensation for the Slave labor of our forefathers and mothers. The establishment of communities on our land here in the United States of America with the understanding that this is only the beginning phase for the ultimate restoration of our Nation States. The recognition is to be national and international in its scope detailing the necessity of this effort for our actual Freedom and the steps involved in the fulfillment of restoring nationhood which includes a true acknowledgment of the history and genealogy of Persons of African descent who were held in servitude both before and during slavery, and an acknowledgement of the efforts that our enslavement and the failure to enforce the laws designed to restore our wholeness had up to the present generation. It will also be necessary to establish an Executive Office for the purpose of facilitating information, technical and vital services between other branches and offices of the Executive Branch including the military, and indigenous Persons of African descent who are availing themselves of this Freedom. And last but not least is our demand for a public national and international apology for this dastardly crime. The Maintenance is to*

include financial support to all Persons of African descent who are making an effort for their actual Freedom (pursuant to Paragraph 2 of the Emancipation Proclamation), which will include the purchase of homes, and financial support for schools, vital services, and protection. This maintenance must give relief from federal, state, and local taxes and the return of all federal, state, and local taxes that have been collected.

Our Ancestry, Our Inheritance

In their slew of efforts to destroy Black history and culture, captors were notorious for separating families, (which increased their profits as well) to destroy them from the root. The science of tracing ancestry is called genealogy. Genealogical research is fundamental to healing wounds created during and subsequent to captivity and enslavement. History, as it has been taught, is not only a distorted rendition of past events, but has globally perpetuated the dominance and power of an exploitative minority ruling class over the majority of people of color around the world. However, the research and study of our ancestors can re-link the bonds that have been shattered and give a more accurate understanding of who we really are - our true history.

When attempting to trace the ancestry of Africans in the Americas and Caribbean (as well as other countries outside of Africa), take special consideration due to our unique circumstances. Due to the breakdown of our family structure and the categorization of our people, the puzzle of genealogy for people of African descent is far more difficult to piece together than any other group. Furthermore, African Americans were not included in the Federal Census until 1820, so families who have been able to preserve family records and heirlooms extending before the 1820s are most fortunate. It is important to note that even after Blacks were included in census records, women's surnames were often eliminated. The gradual loss of matrilineal branches is a tragic consequence of this practice. The distinction between "Black" and "mulatto" was often determined by complexion, so many individuals, born to two "Black" parents were labeled "mulatto", as well. Although many children were born from a Black woman impregnated by her white "master", the white relative is generally not recorded with the Black family. The birth records of children who were adopted, and people who change their names in some way for religious reasons or otherwise, are also important issues to be aware of when researching genealogy. The birth parents of those children are often difficult to ascertain, but are noteworthy for documenting future generations.

You can employ an experienced researcher or genealogist who, for varying fees, can trace your ancestry more extensively than you might be able to. If you hire someone, you should review all of your past accumulated records and data so they won't duplicate your efforts. Genealogical societies can provide you with a list of certified researchers willing to help with your research in any country.

In 1986, when the Tarbutton (a/k/a Carter) case was dismissed, I (Horace) began my own investigation of what had actually occurred. Once I reviewed the records, I realized how pivotal a role the heirs played. Genealogy, I learned, creates a window to understanding our ancestry and history. Legally, you must be able to document your ancestry to receive your inheritance in questionable situations, or when there is no will or trust. One recorded case illustrates the importance of investigating your own genealogy. In 1923, a Black town in Rosewood, Florida, was destroyed by a white lynch mob. Nearly 73 years after the destruction, a settlement was reached for the descendants of those Black families. In order to receive their reparations, they first had to prove their ancestry.

Genealogy offers tremendous insight for medical and health purposes, and provides an in-depth analysis of physical and personal character traits. Genetics and environment mold all of us and understanding those influences can be invaluable. It is the most hands-on approach to knowing oneself and our familial origins. Children deserve a more accurate documentation of their ancestry/history for future reference and research, as opposed to stringing together oral translations of the past that are unsubstantiated.

For this reason, committees should be established within families to continuously research our ancestry. In Utah, the Mormon Church has compiled the genealogy of virtually everyone in the United States. Other groups such as Quakers, Jews, and the Amish, amongst others, have done so as well. It is unconscionable to depend on memory or word of mouth when we should record our ancestry as well. We owe it to our children and theirs to have a reliable record of our family histories so maybe they can trace our lineage back to a village in the Songhai region of Africa if we don't.

Developing A Family History Program

The process of tracing your family history begins by questioning the elders of your family and constructing a miniature family tree. Although the word "interviewing" sounds formal, that is what you will be doing. Interview them or ask another relative or family friend to talk with or about them. Before you visit your relatives, write a brief note telling them about the kinds of information you want from them. Then give them a few weeks to look for scrapbooks or mementos, which most likely will jog their memories about the past.

If a personal visit is not possible, then you will need to compile an informal questionnaire. Draft it in "fill in the blank" style so your relatives will not feel overwhelmed by answering your questions by mail. Tell them about your project and try to stir up their enthusiasm. Remember to include a stamped, self-addressed envelope for the reply, if possible.

Documentation

A family history should be more than a collection of names, dates and places. It should be a collection of documents. Here's where to look:

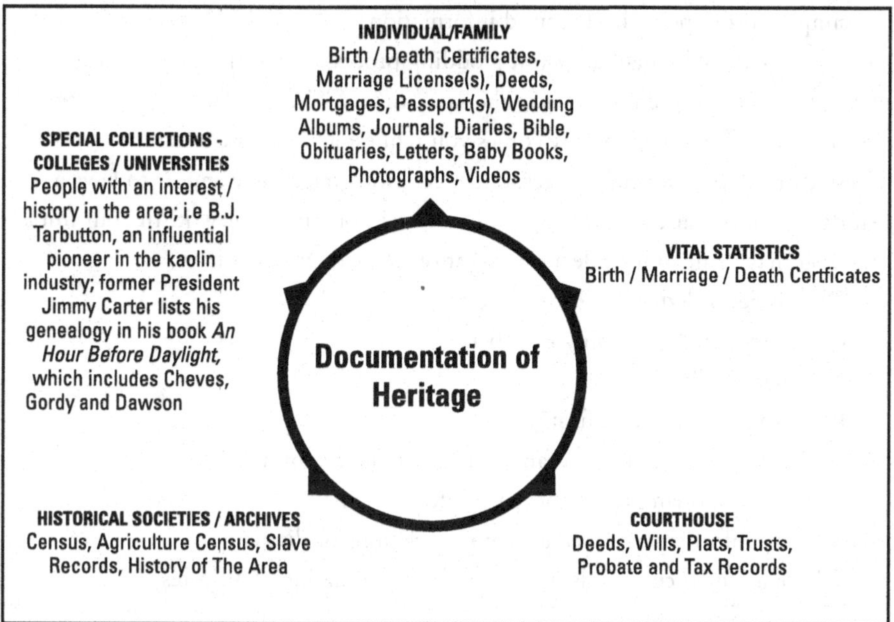

Family records, old letters, scrapbooks, diaries, photo albums, newspaper clippings, and legal documents are like fingerprints, left behind by your relatives to help you solve the mystery of your past. In other words, exhaust family sources first. Our foreparents are an important part of our heritage.

Become familiar with public libraries, genealogical/historical societies and their periodicals, private libraries with special genealogical collections, state libraries or archives, the internet, and cemeteries where family members are buried. Also, the nations' capitols hold a wealth of census records. They have military records, veterans' pensions, and veterans' bounty land grants as well as ships' passenger lists and naturalization records.

Out Of Town Sources

When you need information from out of town sources, telephoning, faxing, and mailing are still your most economical means of data retrieval. Libraries and historical societies often have people to answer letters with genealogical questions.

- Always enclose a stamped, self-addressed envelope for the reply.
- Offer to pay for any photocopies your reply may require. Many people save time by enclosing $1 or $2 in their initial request.
- Restrict your request to one or two items of specific information. Provide simple, to-the-point background information.

Genealogy done by mail is a slow, plodding process, but you can speed it up by sending letters to different sources at the same time. Write to relatives for additional information. Offer to pay for any copies you request and enclose a stamped, self-addressed envelope for return correspondence. However, if they appear to have a great deal of information, you may want to visit in order to review it. In your initial letter, you may want to include a check-list of items they might have:

- Old diaries or letters
- Old photographs of family members
- Marriage certificates
- Birth and/or death certificates
- Wills, trusts, or deeds with family members names on them
- Old Bibles showing family heritage information
- Military information - medals, commendations or discharges
- School attendance records, report cards or graduation certificates

In all cases, your initial letter to relatives should explain what line of the family you're exploring. Offer to share your family heritage with them when you're finished.

If sufficient information about your family has survived through the years, your chances of filling in family branches are better. Then your venture depends on how well the records were preserved. If you are not sure where your relatives lived, you can attempt to locate copies of your ancestors' birth, marriage and death certificates.

As you research deeds and wills in your courthouse, legal terminology will probably raise some questions. There may be unfamiliar words and phrases. Copy the phrases in question and then look them up in your courthouse's law library reference books.

The further back in time your search carries you, the more genealogical idiosyncrasies you are likely to encounter. Deciphering handwriting is often a challenge.

You will understand how names and dates could have changed by accident when clerks were unable to read the handwriting of someone requesting an official document.

Correspondence Record Keeping Chart

To organize all of the information you will accumulate, create a Correspondence Record Keeping Chart. This format makes it easier to tell at a glance whom you have written, when, what you asked them to do, how much money you sent for them to use for copies, when you received a reply, what the reply said, and where you placed the information on your charts.

DATE SENT	MONEY SENT	FOLLOW-UP LETTER	ANSWER DATE	LETTER WRITTEN TO	SUBJECT(S)	RESULTS	CHART & LOCATION

Correspondence Record Keeping Chart

Tips

Here are a few check-points to follow when corresponding with someone about genealogical information. Typed letters are always best, but if that isn't possible, take time to write everything legibly.

Make a copy of every letter you write. To maintain a complete file, you need to know everything you've asked for, so you don't repeat your request to the same person. If you do need to write a follow-up letter, use the first letter as a reference. By comparing the reply with the original request, you'll know which of your questions were answered and which ones you'll have to have answered somewhere else.

Keep your letter simple. When you write to a relative, it isn't necessary to relate the entire family history to make your point. A few opening sentences to explain who you are, and what you're doing, is sufficient. Then, get to the point of your question. After you've traded information back and forth several times, it might be thoughtful to call the person to explain what you're doing and some of the things that may help you.

Don't hide your questions. Be as direct as possible.

Whenever you ask for information that requires photocopying, always include money to pay for the copies. If someone sends you copies you didn't ask for (because you didn't realize they might be available), send them the money after you receive them. Copies can cost from $0.10 to $0.25 each, so be certain to include enough to cover the cost at the higher figure.

Include a self-addressed stamped envelope (SASE). It will usually encourage your correspondent to give you an answer. The only time return postage isn't necessary is when writing to a state or federal agency.

Finally, say "thank you". A few words showing you recognize their efforts will go a long way toward helping you get similar good treatment from people again.

Family folklore and genealogy are not the same thing. Folklore considers the story as important as the information it conveys. Genealogy is concerned mainly with factual information. However, genealogical research allows you to look into your family heritage. Here are some suggestions:

Ask questions that require a narrative answer. Interviews that only require "yes" and "no" answers are boring.

Recognize that there is some information you just won't get. Maybe your relatives don't feel comfortable giving you personal or sensitive information about their lives. If the information is absolutely essential, then perhaps another relative can intercede on your behalf and get the information for you.

Realize that what you're doing puts you in a somewhat awkward position. You are no longer a niece or nephew, grandson or granddaughter, but an interrogator. This role may make both of you uncomfortable. A low-key approach in familiar, comfortable surroundings will probably help overcome this situation.

Be interested in the conversation. Even though you're asking the questions, don't hesitate to take an active part in the conversation. Don't dominate the discussion. Be a good listener.

Know what questions you want to ask, but don't be afraid to let your informant elaborate at length. Many times "going off on a tangent" brings up interesting situations you might never have thought about.

If you're recording the material, leave the recorder running unless you're asked to turn it off. Turning the recorder off indicates you're judging what the relative is saying and have decided some of the conversation isn't worth recording.

Don't hesitate to use props. Documents, letters, photos, scrapbooks, anything at all that will stimulate memories and generate conversation is well worth the effort.

Respect the people you're about to interview. Schedule your session at times they'll find convenient. Remember, if you're talking to older people, they often tire easily. It's better to have several short sessions than one marathon meeting. Don't ignore family members who have expressed an interest in your project. Just because you didn't ask them for an interview doesn't mean they have nothing to contribute. Hear them out. You may be pleasantly surprised at what they have to offer.

Try to keep the people you've interviewed up to date on your project. While you don't have to report weekly, an occasional note about some of the interesting things you've found will make them realize how important their contribution really was. Many times, your informant will think of additional things and call you back for more conversation.

One last point about your recording tapes: label each one with the names of the people interviewed, the date and place of the interview. Keep each tape as part of your permanent record rather than use the same tape for the next interview. Use 90 minute tapes to minimize the number of potential tape changes during the interview. In the future, it might give your grandchildren the opportunity to hear their great, great-grandmother's or grandfather's voice.

The Interview

The following is a guide of questions to ask:

What do you know about your family surname, its origin, its meaning? Did it undergo any changes? Do you remember any stories about how the changes took place?

Are there any traditional first names, middle names or nicknames in the family?

What stories have been handed down about your parents, grandparents, and other relatives? How have these people described their lives to you? What have you learned from them about their childhood, adolescence, schooling, marriage, work, religion, political activity, recreation? Did they enjoy discussing the past? Did their memories seem to be concentrated in certain time periods and ignore others? Are there certain things about your heritage you'd like to know, but couldn't find out? Did various relatives tell you the same story in different ways? How did their versions differ?

Is there a notorious or infamous character in the family's past? What stories have you heard about him/her?

How did your parents, grandparents and other relatives happen to meet and marry? Are there family stories about lost love, jilted brides, unusual courtships, arranged marriages, elopements and runaway lovers?

Have any particular historical events effected your family? (Enslavement, The Revolutionary War, The Civil War, Reconstruction, Jim Crow, The Harlem Renaissance, World War I & II, Vietnam, Civil Rights Movement, etc.)

Are there any stories about relatives who made or lost great fortunes? Can the stories be substantiated?

What holidays (national, religious or family) have always been important in the family? Does the family celebrate holidays in an unusual way? Who started the custom? Why?

Does the family ever hold reunions? How often? When? Where? Who is invited? Who comes? Does someone keep a record of these reunions? Who? Are photographs taken at each reunion? By whom?

Do you know of any other people who became part of your household? When? Why? What were they called, i.e. aunt, uncle, cousin?

Is there a family cemetery or burial plot? Who is buried there? Who made the decision to use that area?

Does the family have any special heirlooms? How were they acquired and by whom? What sort of things are they? Are there any stories connected with them? Who has these things now?

Do you have any photo albums, scrapbooks, slides or home movies? Who created them? Whose pictures are shown? Who keeps them up to date? Are they available for you to look at?

Remember, any one of those questions could take the better part of an afternoon. So don't be impatient and expect to go back again. If your interview manners follow the recommendations you've just read, your return visit will be welcome.

How To Write For Official Records

Record-keeping is more sophisticated today because computers store volumes of information about every one of us. But begin your search on the assumption that there is an official certificate filed IN THE PLACE WHERE THE EVENT HAPPENED, for every birth, death and marriage that transpired. When writing to Vital Statistics offices, here's what you should be sure to include:

– Full name of the person whose certificate you want.
– Sex and race of that person.
His or her parents' names, including mother's maiden name.
– Exact date of birth, death or marriage (month, day and year)
– Exact place of birth, death or marriage (include the hospital if any).

You can request the full copy (the certificate in its entirety) or the short form (less information, but also less expensive). You may have to write two letters: one to find out the cost and the second one to place your order. If you include enough information so the document can be easily obtained, the fee should be moderate. The charge is for looking up the certificate. If a person is still living, it's best to have him/her obtain the documents. Some Vital Statistics offices won't supply this information to others.

The Family History Library of the Church of Jesus Christ of Latter-Day Saints possess' the largest single source of genealogical information in the world. The Mormons' interest in genealogical research stems from their belief that family relationships are meant to be eternal. The Mormons believe that families will remain together throughout eternity, along with their ancestors and descendants. Members of the church trace their ancestry to prepare for a "sealing" ceremony, which binds their families together forever. Before the families can be "sealed" together, they must trace all of their ancestors.

They have compiled and catalogued information on over 10 million families. Some 60 million names can be found in the International Genealogical Index. They have copied such documents as parish registers, marriage bonds, cemetery records, deeds, military records, land grants and probate records.

The library in Salt Lake City, Utah holds over one million rolls of microfilm and 200,000 printed volumes. Over 30,000 new rolls and 3,000 printed volumes are added each year. Records are microfilmed every day in some 38 countries around the world.

This information is available to Mormons and non-Mormons alike. It can be obtained by contacting your nearest Mormon Library. For instance, the Church has copied and indexed parish registers in some countries. A computer listing of this index for the surname you are researching is available for a small fee. Although the Library will answer one or two specific questions, they do not have sufficient staff to provide you with a list of accredited researchers. When requesting this list, be sure to specify the country or countries in which you are searching, as they have specialists for particular areas. You will then be able to select your researcher and negotiate any financial arrangements.

The Mormons have done extensive microfilming of records around the world. They will provide you with a small booklet for each country outlining the information they are able to provide. Although the Mormon records are vast and comprehensive, they are a starting point and not the final word. Use them as a guide to further your research, and always be prepared to examine other sources.

<u>Main Library</u>

The Family History Library of the Church of Jesus Christ of Latter Day Saints
35 N. West Temple Street
Salt Lake City, Utah 84150 U.S.A
Phone: (801) 240-2331

African Ancestry, Inc.

African Ancestry, Inc. (www. africanancestry.com) has become the exclusive licensee of a prominent genetic researcher's extensive database of genetic lineages from Africa. The company, wholly owned by African American investors, is selling DNA - based genealogy tests to members of the public who wish to determine if they have African ancestors. African Ancestry's novel African Lineage Database™ is the largest of its kind in the world. African Ancestry's database includes DNA sequence information that Dr. Kittles collected from natives of the West and Central African regions from which individuals were procured for the Trans-Atlantic slave trade. African Ancestry also has access to DNA sequence information that other sources have collected throughout the continent.

Rick Kittles, PhD, received his PhD. in Biological Sciences from George Washington University. Dr. Kittles went to Howard University in 1998 and helped to establish a national cooperative network to study the genetics of hereditary prostate cancer in the African American community. Dr. Kittles has set-up a state-of-the-art laboratory to conduct molecular genetic studies. As co-director of Molecular Genetics at the National Human Genome Center at Howard University, he is also in charge of large-scale, high throughput genotyping and DNA sequencing. Dr. Kittles' research exploits gene genealogy in studies of population history and disease associations. He has had a strong research focus on using DNA to trace ancestry of African Americans and has published on prostate cancer genetics of African Americans and genetic variation in the African Diaspora. "The bridge to the past collapsed with the advent of the slave trade, and we're reconstructing it by using DNA. Tracing ancestry through DNA can lead us to some insight about our potential ancestors and potential places of ancestry. For untold numbers of people, knowing that is a lot better than knowing nothing".

This wealth of information, for the first time, is being marshaled in order to help African Americans genetically determine their African ancestry. Others who believe or suspect that they may have African ancestry can as well purchase a test that will compare their DNA sequence information with DNA sequence information in the firm's database. Unlike other tests on the market, in addition to telling an individual if she does in fact share genetic lineages with African peoples, African Ancestry's testing process can also pinpoint from which region in Africa her lineage originates.

Eighty percent of African Americans that Africana.com recently surveyed say they believe it would be important to use DNA to determine their ancestry through DNA testing. Genealogy experts suggest that as the African American middle class continues to grow, so will the demand for genealogy testing.

African Ancestry's database contains DNA sequence information from almost 10,000 individuals representing 82 West and Central African populations. In addition, the firm uses DNA sequence data gathered from other populations throughout the continent. No DNA sequence information can be traced back to a specific person in Africa. Blind sampling methods were used to obtain DNA sequence data from individual people. The firm offers two DNA-based genealogy tests and each test costs $349 US

If African Ancestry does not find an African match for ancestry, the firm will, with the customer's consent, search a European database for a match. The firm does not have lineage data on other human populations.

African Ancestry's results are quite accurate. For about seven out of ten people tested the firm will find identical matches in its database. For the remaining people, the firm will find closely related lineages with a greater than 90 percent confidence level.

Mitochondrial DNA Analysis:

Mitochondrial DNA (mtDNA) are chromosomes that are inherited exclusively from the mother. This DNA provides a solid record of your maternal descent. Your mtDNA comes exclusively from your mother's, mother's, mother...for hundreds of generations. The MatriClan™ Service analyzes the genetic sequence of your mitochondrial DNA. African Ancestry's scientists compare your genetic sequence against an exclusive database containing thousands of mitochondrial DNA samples from females throughout Africa. The matching mitochondrial DNA that is found determines the ancestral region of your maternal ancestors.

Y-Chromosome Analysis:

The Y-Chromosome provides information on paternal lineage. It is found only in males and is passed UNCHANGED from father to son over hundreds of generations. As a result, each male's Y-chromosome is the same as his father's, his father's father, and so on up the line. The PatriClan™ service analyzes the genetic sequence of the Y-chromosome. African Ancestry's scientists compare your genetic sequence against an exclusive database containing thousands of Y-Chromosome samples from males throughout Africa. The matching Y-Chromosome that is found determines the ancestral region of your paternal ancestors.

Both the MatriClan™ and PatriClan™ Test Kits are based on cells swabbed from the inside of your cheek. It is simple and easy to use. When you order the service, you receive a kit containing the following items:

– Two cotton swabs in plastic packaging
– Simple, easy-to-follow instructions
– Information form
– Terms and conditions
– Postage-paid return envelope

Results:

Once their scientists determine whether you share ancestry with a particular African region, the results of your MatriClan ™ / PatriClan ™ Test (s) will be sent to you. You will receive your results within six weeks. In addition to your results, you will receive:

– Your DNA sequence
– Certificate of Ancestry
– Color map of Africa highlighting your specific ancestral region

Confidentiality

Samples are handled with confidentiality. Their procedures require them to destroy your DNA samples when the results are determined.

African Ancestry
5505 Connecticut Avenue, NW
Suite 297
Washington, DC 20015
info@africanancestry.com
Phone: [202] 439 - 0641
Fax: [202] 318 - 0742

The Soundex System

The National Archives has microfilm copies of card indexes that can be useful in obtaining United States Federal Census records for the 1880 (partial), 1900, 1910 and 1920 censuses. When using census records, it is recommended that you begin your research in the most recent available indexed census. At present, only Federal Censuses through 1920 are open to the public. To protect the privacy of living American citizens whose names appear in the schedule, population schedules are closed for 72 years after the census is recorded.

In its efforts to index the U.S. censuses in the late 1930s, the federal government devised the Soundex system. The names from the census records were extracted, coded and placed onto cards. After coding, the cards were then sorted according to certain Soundex rules. The result was a listing of people from the censuses whose names, although spelled differently, were grouped together because they "sounded" alike.

Finding the Soundex code for a given surname is one of the most valuable tools in genealogical research. It facilitates using government documents that are arranged by the Soundex Index. Other federal records that have been indexed using this system include ship passenger lists and military records. Many state and local records are soundexed as well.

The Soundex coding system is useful because it allows you to find a person in the census even though his/her name may have been recorded under various spellings. The advantage to this type of index is that phonetic spellings are grouped with what may be considered the standard spelling for the name. This helps to compensate for an unusual spelling of the surname. Surnames that sound the same but are spelled differently, like Smith and Smyth, have the same code and are filed together in the index.

To locate a particular surname in the Soundex Index, you must first find its code. Finding the Soundex code for a person's name is easy to do. Every Soundex code consists of a letter and a 3-digit number. The letter is always the first letter of the surname. Then numbers are assigned to the remaining letters of the surname.

The Soundex Coding Guide	
THE NUMBER:	KEY LETTERS OR EQUIVALENTS:
1	B,P,F,V
2	C,S,K,G,J,Q,X,Z
3	D,T
4	L
5	M,N
6	R

The letters A,E,I,O,U,Y,W and H are not coded. The first letter of a surname is not coded. Every Soundex number must be a 3-digit number.

Additional Rules

Names with Prefixes

If your surname has a prefix - like Van, Von, De, Di, or Le - you should code it both with and without the prefix because it might be listed under either code. (Mc and Mac are not considered prefixes.)

Names with Double Letters

If your surname has any double letters, they should be treated as one letter. Thus, in the surname Lloyd, the second L should be slashed out; in the surname Gutierrez, the second R should be slashed out.

Names with Letters Side by Side that Have the Same Number on the Soundex Coding Guide

Your surname may have different letters that are side by side and have the same number on the Soundex Coding Guide; for example, PF in Pfister (1 is the number for both P and F); CKS in Jackson (2 is the number for C,K, and S). These letters should be treated as one letter. Thus, in the name Pfister, F should be slashed out; in the name Jackson, K and S should be slashed out.

Coding Your Ancestral Surname

Step 1

On line 1, write the surname you are coding, placing one letter in each box.

Step 2

On line 2, write the first letter of the surname in the first box.

Step 3

On line 1, disregarding the first letter, slash through the remaining letters A,E,I,O,U,W,Y and H.

Step 4

On line 2, write the numbers found on the Soundex Coding guide for the first three remaining unslashed letters. Add zeros to any empty boxes. Disregard any additional letters.

Using The Soundex Card Index

Once your ancestor's name is correctly coded, you are ready to use the microfilmed Soundex card index. The index is organized by state, thereunder by Soundex code, and thereunder alphabetically by the first name or initial of the individual for whom you are searching. After you locate the first name, look for the surname and then the county. When you find the person you're looking for on the microfilm roll, you'll discover that the index card lists quite a bit of information about the individual (although not as much information as contained in the actual census schedules).

It is important to note that the 1880 and 1910 Soundex indexes are not as complete as the 1900 and 1920 ones. For the 1880 census, Soundex entries include only those households containing a child age 10 or below. The Soundex cards on the microfilm roll show the name, age, and birthplace of each member of such households. There is a separate cross-reference card for each child age 10 or below whose surname differs from the head of the household's.

To begin research in the 1900, 1910 or 1920 censuses, you must know at least your ancestor's full name and state or territory of residence. It is also helpful to know the full name of the head of the household in which your ancestor lived. For the 1900 census, there is a complete Soundex Index to all household heads, with cross-reference cards for all persons with different surnames. For the 1910 census, there are Soundex indexes on microfilm for: Alabama, Georgia, Louisiana, Mississippi, South Carolina, Tennessee and Texas.

"Miracode" is an indexing method similar to the Soundex system. It has been used to develop indexes for Arkansas, California, Florida, Illinois, Kansas, Kentucky,

Michigan, Missouri, North Carolina, Ohio, Oklahoma, Pennsylvania, Virginia and West Virginia. There are no indexes for the remaining states and territories.

After you've located a person's name in the Soundex Index, copy the enumeration number and line number from the displayed Soundex card, in order to use the census schedules.

The microfilm for census schedules is usually organized by year, state, and county. Many libraries can order any states' from the American Genealogical Lending Library (ALGLL).

When viewing census schedules, first look for the state and county. Then, find the enumeration district number (that appeared in the Soundex Index for the particular person), followed by the sheet number, and finally the line number. Special forms are available for transcribing census information. You can generally get them for a small fee at Latter-Day Saints (LDS) branch libraries, historical societies, or places with genealogical research rooms. The forms are different for each census year, and you will want to make several copies of each.

If you're still uncertain on how to work out the Soundex code for a surname of interest, the codes to over 500,000 surnames have been published in a book called The Soundex Reference Guide, which is available in most large libraries and also from the AGLL.

For more information on how to locate a family in the census schedules (after finding the Soundex code), contact the American Genealogical Lending Library (AGLL), P.O. Box 244, Bountiful, UT 84011.

Family Associations, Surname Registers & Reunion Committees

To further assist you in your genealogical research, family associations often exist for descendents of a particular surname. These associations have a considerable amount of information to offer about a specific surname and/or its variants.

The information they provide can be valuable in helping you find other people researching your family name. It can also assist in making contact with family members, sharing information about family history and family reunions, and discovering whether or not people of the same surname connect on the family tree.

In addition to family associations, there are other special research services discussed herein, which may prove helpful to the genealogist.

If a family association does not exist for your surname or you want to find information on another family name, contact a surname register.

Surname registers give access to the names and addresses of researchers and the surnames they are researching, plus a way to discover or inform others about your research. Some of these organizations may not be primarily genealogical in nature, focusing more on gathering information about current generations.

Figuring Relationships

To be related, two individuals must have a common ancestor at some point in their ancestry. The kinship, or degree of relationship, is dependent on the closeness of blood, not time, to that common ancestor.

Full brothers and sisters have the same common ancestors (their parents), and there is a close degree of relationship between them. A cousin is not as closely related because different ancestors are involved which are not common to each other. To find the relationship, you have to start with the common ancestor.

Direct Ancestors

These are people from whom you descend: father, mother, grandfather, grandmother, great-grandfather, etc. The pedigree chart shows your direct (blood) line. As your pedigree extends beyond your great-grandparents, an additional "great" is added to each generation, indicated by a number. Your 2nd great-grandfather means your great-great-grandfather.

Collateral Lines

Collateral relatives have everything but "father" or "mother" in their titles: aunts, uncles, nephews, nieces, and cousins of every sort. These are the brothers and sisters (and their children) of direct line ancestors

Cousins

The children of brothers and sisters are first cousins to each other. The children of first cousins are second cousins to each other. The children of second cousins are third cousins to each other, etc. When cousins are not of the same generation (not on the same horizontal line), such as the following example, of Michelle Cotton and Denise Nicole Cheeves, the relationship is determined by the number of generations the cousins are removed from each other.

Example:

Common Ancestor:		
	Jeff Carter Jr.	
Ruby Carter Nelson	Sister	Lillian Carter Cheeves
Michelle Cotton	First Cousin	Horace Cheeves
Venice Cotton	Second Cousin	Denise Nicole Cheeves

Michelle Cotton and Horace Cheeves are first cousins (1c). Denise Nicole Cheeves, the daughter of Horace Cheeves, is not on the same line (same generation), as Michelle Cotton, so they cannot be just cousins. They are first cousins one generation removed (1c1r), because Denise Nicole is one line down from Michelle. Denise Nicole's son would be a first cousin two generations removed from Michelle Cotton (1c2r), because he was two lines down. Venice Cotton and Denise Nicole Cheeves are second cousins (2c), because they are on the same line (same generation).

On a family group sheet on a collateral/allied line (aunts, uncles, or cousins), you will normally be related by blood only to the husband or wife. You designate "in-law" by the abbreviation, "il". If you want to write your relationship on a family group sheet showing your mother's brother as the husband, you would be the niece or nephew to the husband, and the niece-il or nephew-il to the wife. Your relationship to your first cousin and her husband would be 1c-il to the husband, and a 1c to the wife. Any kind of first cousin, even a 1c57r (first cousin, 57 times removed), is closer than any second cousin (2c). If a person is both your blood relative and an in-law, take the blood relationship. Any blood relationship is closer than any in-law relationship.

Family Questionnaire

List the names and present ages of your grandparents, parents, and all of your brothers and sisters, in the order of their birth, (include any who died & at what age). Add three words describing each person the way you saw that person:

– as a child (approximately 4 to 10 years of age)

– as a teen (approximately 13 to 18 years of age)

– as a young adult (approximately 20 to 30 years of age)

– over 30

Of all your family members, including parents and siblings, which one was or is most like you? In what ways (i.e. look, talk, act, etc)?

– as a child

– as a teen

– as a young adult

– over 30

Which one was or is most different from you? In what ways?

– as a child

– as a teen

– as a young adult

– over 30

How did you go about getting your way?

– as a child

– as a teen

– as a young adult

– over 30

What kinds of compliments did you receive from your parents, school, family & friends?

– as a child

– as a teen

– as a young adult

– over 30

What kinds of criticism did you receive from you parents, school, family & friends?

– as a child

– as a teen

– as a young adult

– over 30

What emphasis did your mother place on family, education, religion/spirituality, and civic responsibilities?

What emphasis did your father place on family, education, religion/spirituality, and civic responsibilities?

What was your favorite childhood story, book, or fairy tale? What was your favorite part of the story? With whom did you identify?

If you could wave a magic wand and change anything or anyone about your life, what would you change?
– as a child
– as a teen
– as a young adult
– over 30

What problems did you have in your childhood that you still have now?

Picture the house you lived in when you were a child, and imagine yourself playing in a secluded spot by yourself. Try to remember a specific place and actually "see" yourself right there now (in your room, outside of your house, the backyard, etc.).

What is your earliest recollection? It needs to be a specific incident, though it needn't be particularly important. Not a general recollection like, "We used to go to grandmom's, and I was sitting on the back porch when I saw my cousins playing…" The recollection should not be a family story that you grew up hearing about, but rather one that you just remembered before writing. Think back and identify the specific picture in your memory that you remember best. Imagine that the recollection is a movie and you are going to freeze the action at the most vivid "freeze frame" of that short movie. Then imagine the emotion that you felt at that particular "freeze frame moment", and write that down.

How would you like to be remembered?

		1	2	3	4	5	6	7	8	9
	CA	SON	G SON	GG SON	2GG SON	3GG SON	4GG SON	5GG SON	6GG SON	7GG SON
1	SON	BRO	NEP	G NEP	GG NEP	2GG NEP	3GG NEP	4GG NEP	5GG NEP	6GG NEP
2	G SON	NEP	1c	1c1r	1c2r	1c3r	1c4r	1c5r	1c6r	1c7r
3	GG SON	G NEP	1c1r	2c	2c1r	2c2r	2c3r	2c4r	2c5r	2c6r
4	2GG SON	GG NEP	1c2r	2c1r	3c	3c1r	3c2r	3c3r	3c4r	3c5r
5	3GG SON	2GG NEP	1c3r	2c2r	3c1r	4c	4c1r	4c2r	4c3r	4c4r
6	4GG SON	3GG NEP	1c4r	2c3r	3c2r	4c1r	5c	5c1r	5c2r	5c3r
7	5GG SON	4GG NEP	1c5r	2c4r	3c3r	4c2r	5c1r	6c	6c1r	6c2r
8	6GG SON	5GG NEP	1c6r	2c5r	3c4r	4c3r	5c2r	6c1r	7c	7c1r
9	7GG SON	6GG NEP	1c7r	2c6r	3c5r	4c4r	5c3r	6c2r	7c1r	8c

Relationship Chart

Key To Chart:

1. Locate the position of yourself in the column at the left from the Common Ancestor (CA), marked 1-9.
2. Locate the position of the person you are tracing the relationship to in the column across the top, designnating his descent from the Common Ancestor (CA), marked 1-9.
3. The Correct Relationship will be found where the parallel and horizontal lines cross.

Examples:

1. The relationship of No. 1 on the left and No. 1 on the top is brother or sister.
2. The relationship of No. 2 on the left and No. 4 on the top is 1c2r, or first cousin, two generations removed.

Use the terms, son or daughter, brother or sister, grandson or granddaughter, nephew or niece, etc. as it might apply.

Common Abbreviations

CA – common ancestor
C or COU – cousin; 2c1r – second cousin, one generation removed
In-law – il
BRO – brother
SIS – sister
DAU – daughter
SON – son
NEP – nephew
NIECE – niece
G Son – grandson
GG SON – great-grandson
2 GG SON – great-great-grandson, or second great-grandson
G NEP – grand nephew
GG NEP – great-grand nephew
2 GG NEP – second great-grand nephew

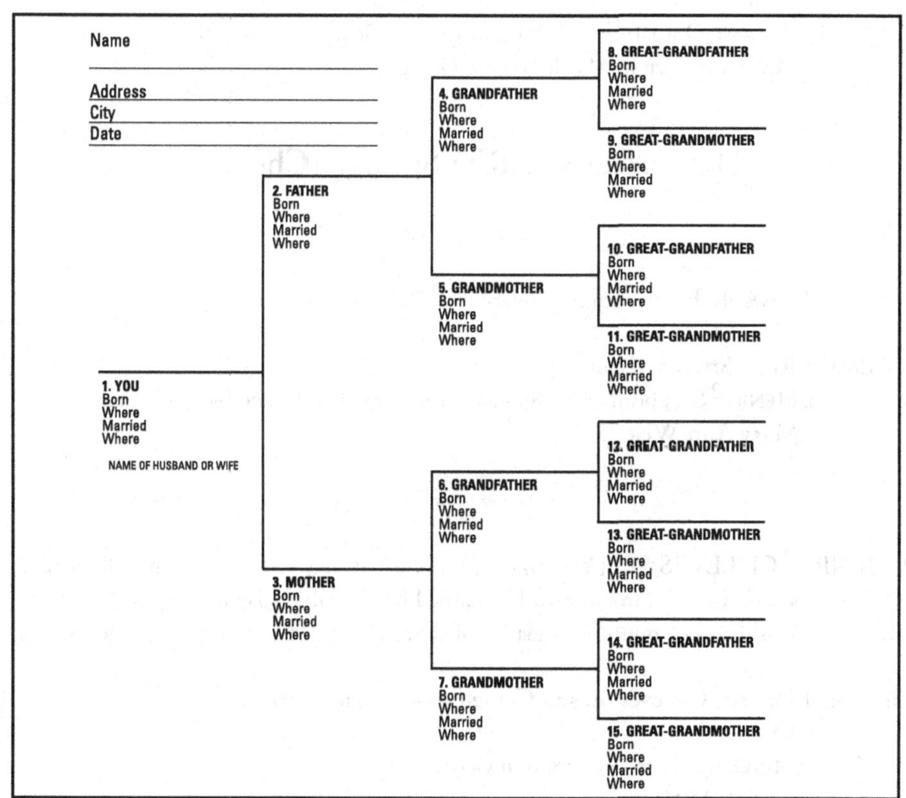

Pedigree Chart

Descendants of Burrell Carter

Generation One

1. **BURRELL[1] CARTER** was born in May 1833 in Georgia. He married **Mary Ann Lane** in Georgia.

Children of **Burrell[1] Carter** and **Mary Ann Lane** were as follows:

\+ 2. i. **MILLY[2]**, born circa 1861 in Georgia.
\+ 3. ii. **JEFF SR.**, born circa 1862 in Georgia; married **Ella Hooks;** married **Easter Gordy;** married **Delia Howard.**
\+ 4. iii. **GRACE 'GRACIE'**, born circa 1864 in Georgia.
\+ 5. iv. **JOHN**, born circa 1866 in Georgia.
\+ 6. v. **BURRELL 'BURL' JR.**, born circa 1868 in Georgia.
7. vi. **SALLIE** was born circa 1871 in Georgia.
\+ 8. vii. **VIRGIL**, born circa 1873 in Georgia.
\+ 9. viii. **SUSIE**, born February 1874 in Georgia; married **John Cheeves;** married **Jordan Lord.**
10. ix. **(INFANT DAUGHER)** was born in 1880 in Georgia.
11. x. **MARY** was born in March 1883 in Georgia.

Descendants of Rita Strange (Cheeves)

Generation One

1. **RITA[1] STRANGE** was born in Sandersville, Washington County, Georgia.

Children of **Rita[1] Strange** include:

\+ 2. i. **HENRY[2] SR.**, born May 1834 in Georgia; married **Cenie (———-)**; married **Mary Ann Wise.**

Generation Two

2. **HENRY[2] CHEEVES SR.** (*Rita[1] Strange*) was born in May 1834 in Georgia. He married **Cenie (———-)** in Georgia. He married **Mary Ann Wise** on 14 July 1880 in Washington County, Georgia He died on 25 July 1908 in Georgia at age 74.

Children of **Henry[2] Cheeves Sr.** and **Cenie (———-)** were as follows:

\+ 3. i. **JOE[3]**
4. ii. **ABNER** was born circa 1858 in Georgia.
5. iii. **GUSSIE ANN.**

Children of **Henry**[2] **Cheeves Sr.** and **Mary Ann Wise** were as follows:

- 6. i. **HENRIETTA**[3] was born circa 1864 in Georgia.
- \+ 7. ii. **JOHN**, born August 1867 in Georgia; married **Susie Carter.**
- 8. iii. **MILLEDGE** was born circa 1869 in Georgia.
- \+ 9. iv. **DOVIE**, born circa 1872 in Georgia; married **Randall Rogers.**
- \+ 10. v. **DAVID 'COOT'**, born July 1873 in Washington County, Georgia; married **Hattie Johnson.**
- 11. vi. **WILLIAM** was born circa 1877 in Georgia.
- 12. vii. **DAVIE** was born circa 1879 in Georgia.
- \+ 13. viii. **LOU**, married **Sip Davis.**
- 14. ix. **DANIEL** was born circa 1870 in Georgia.
- \+ 15. x. **HENRY JR.**, born 13 May 1884 in Sandersville, Washington County, Georgia; married **Clara Bell Trawick.**
- \+ 16. xi. **LENNIE**, married **William Hodges.**
- \+ 17. xii. **CARRIE**, born 22 December 1885 in Sandersville, Georgia; married **Samuel 'Sam' Gordy.**

Descendants of Porter Boyer

Generation One

1. **PORTER**[1] **BOYER** was born in Georgia. He married **Georgeanne** (—?—) in Georgia.

Children of **Porter**[1] **Boyer** and **Georgeanne** (—?—) were as follows:

- \+ 2. i. **MARSHALL**[2], born in Georgia; married **Ida Solomon.**
- \+ 3. ii. **CHARLES 'CHARLIE'**, born in Georgia; married **Mamie Adams.**
- 4. iii. **MAUD** was born in Georgia. She married **Abe Wise** in Georgia. She married **Leonard Walker** in Georgia. She married **Burton Fuller** in Georgia.
- \+ 5. iv. **JOHNNIE**, born in Georgia; married **Mollie** (—?—).
- \+ 6. v. **NANCY**, born in Georgia; married **Ed Williams.**
- \+ 7. vi. **FANNIE**, born in Georgia; married **Julius Swint.**
- \+ 8. vii. **MARY**, born in Georgia; married **Tom Swint.**
- 9. viii. **SARAH** was born in Georgia. She married **Henry Allen.**
- \+ 10. ix. **BENNIE**, born in Georgia; married **Parrie Lee Adolphus.**
- \+ 11. x. **MATTHEW**, born in Georgia; married **Mamie** (—?—).
- \+ 12. xi. **SAM 'SAMMIE'**, born 15 October 1892 in Milledgeville, Georgia; married **Lillian Hood.**

Descendants of James Hooks

Generation One

1. **JAMES[1] HOOKS** was born circa 1833 in Georgia. He married **Ella Kelsey.** He married **Mary (——-)**. He died circa 1891.

Children of **James[1] Hooks** and **Ella Kelsey** were as follows:

+ 2. i. **ROBERT[2] SR.**, born 6 June 1869; married **Clara Lane.**
+ 3. ii. **ADAM 'ADD'**, born circa 1875 in Washington County, Georgia; married **Kizzie Trawick.**
+ 4. iii. **RACHEL**, born March 1876 in Washington County, Georgia; married **William 'Will' Turner.**
  5. iv. **REUBEN** was born circa 1878 in Georgia.

Children of **James[1] Hooks** and **Mary (——-)** were as follows:

  6. i. **JORDAN[2]** was born circa 1859 in Georgia.
+ 7. ii. **MACK**, born December 1861 in Washington County, Georgia; married **Judy Mason.**
  8. iii. **LEE** was born circa 1863 in Georgia.
+ 9. iv. **ANNA**, born circa 1866 in Washington County, Georgia; married **Doss Dixon.**
+ 10. v. **MARY**, born 1866 in Washington County, Georgia; married **Western Wiggins.**
+ 11. vi. **ELLA**, born September 1870 in Washington County, Georgia; married **Jeff Carter Sr.**

Descendants of Bybe Butts

Generation One

1. BYBE[1] BUTTS.

Children of **Bybe[1] Butts** and **Catherine (——-)** were as follows:

+ 2. i. **FREDDIE[2]**, married **Carrie (——-).**
+ 3. ii. **WILLIAM 'LUMP'**, married **Jessie Renfrow.**
+ 4. iii. **LULA**
+ 5. iv. **EPHRAIM**, married **Mamye (——-).**
+ 6. v. **THOMAS 'TOMMIE'**
  7. vi. **MATTIE.**
+ 8. vii. **MILAS (SR.)**, born 4 July 1883; married **Roeanor Dawson.**
+ 9. viii. **BEVERLY 'LEE'**

Descendants of Mr. Trawick

Generation One

1. MR.[1] TRAWICK.

Children of **Mr.**[1] **Trawick** include:

+ 2. i. JACK 'JOHN'[2], born circa 1822 in Washington County, Georgia.
+ 3. ii. BENJAMIN, born circa 1835 in Washington County, Georgia; married **Julia** (———).
+ 4. iii. SAMUEL, born 1840 in Washington County, Georgia; married **Fannie** (———).

Descendants of Jim Gordy

Generation One

1. **JIM**[1] **GORDY**; Jim Gordy was a white plantation owner. Esther Johnson was an enslaved Black woman on the plantation.

Children of **Jim**[1] **Gordy** and **Esther Johnson** were:

+ 2. i. BERRY[2] SR., married **Lucy Hellum.**

Generation Two

2. **BERRY**[2] **GORDY SR.** (*Jim*[1]); Freed from slavery when he was a child. He was raised on a farm outside Oconee now known as Gordy Church area. He married **Lucy Hellum** in Washington County, Georgia. They had twenty-three children; all but nine died before adulthood.

Children of **Berry**[2] **Gordy Sr.** and **Lucy Hellum** were as follows:

3. i. MAMIE[3] was born in Sandersville, Washington County, Georgia.
+ 4. ii. JOHN, born in Sandersville, Georgia; married **Mamie Hooks.**
5. iii. LULA was born in Sandersville, Washington County, Georgia. She married **Morgan Butts** in Sandersville, Georgia.
+ 6. iv. CHARLIE, born in Washington County, Georgia; married **Pearl Bouyer.**
+ 7. v. BERRY 'POP' JR., married **Bertha Fuller.**
+ 8. vi. JOSEPH 'JOE', married **Lee Alice Reese.**
+ 9. vii. SAMUEL 'SAM', born 1878 in Washington County, Georgia; married **Carrie Cheeves.**
+ 10. viii. EASTER, born circa 1883 in Georgia; married **Jeff Carter Sr.**
+ 11. ix. LUCY 'NIG', born 10 April 1896 in Sandersville, Washington County, Georgia; married **Albert Butts;** married **Mark Lane Wood.**

Descendants of Sampson Dawson

Generation One

1. **SAMPSON[1] DAWSON** married **Mamie Robinson.**

Children of **Sampson[1] Dawson** and **Mamie Robinson** were as follows:

+ 2. i. **HOMER[2]**, born in Sandersville, Washington County, Georgia; married **Lora Ella 'Laura' Carter.**
+ 3. ii. **HERMAN,** born in Sandersville, Washington County, Georgia; married **Effie Walker.**
  4. iii. **LILLIAN** was born in Sandersville, Washington County, Georgia.
  5. iv. **CASSIUS** was born in Sandersville, Washington County, Georgia.
  6. v. **WILLIE LOUIS** was born in Sandersville, Washington County, Georgia.
  7. vi. **BESSIE** was born in Sandersville, Washington County, Georgia.
  8. vii. **ALPHEUS** was born in Sandersville, Washington County, Georgia.

Descendants of William 'Tump' Peeler

Generation One

1. **WILLIAM 'TUMP'[1] PEELER** was born in North Carolina. He married **Susie Temple.** He died in 1912 in Washington County, Georgia.

Children of **William 'Tump'[1] Peeler** and **Susie Temple** were as follows:

+ 2. i. **MAUDE[2]**, born in Washington County, Georgia.
+ 3. ii. **BERNIECE**, born in Washington County, Georgia.
+ 4. iii. **CLAUDIA**, born in Washington County, Georgia; married **Walter Wiggins.**
  5. iv. **BOOKER** was born in Washington County, Georgia.
+ 6. v. **DONNIE**, born in Washington County, Georgia.
  7. vi. **JOHN** was born in Washington County, Georgia.
  8. vii. **FREDDIE** was born in Washington County, Georgia.
+ 9. viii. **CLEVELAND**, born 25 December 1889 in Sandersville, Washington County, Georgia; married **Leola Rogers.**

References

Introduction: Maafa - The African Holocaust

From Slavery to Freedom
John Hope Franklin and Alfred A. Moss, Jr.

The Journey of the Songhai People
Calvin R. Robinson, Redman Battle and Edward W. Robinson, Jr.

Before the Mayflower
Lerone Bennett, Jr.

Education For A New Reality In The African World
John Henrik Clarke

Remembering Slavery - African Americans Talk About Their Personal Experiences Of Slavery And Emancipation
Edited by Ira Berlin, Marc Favreau, and Steven F. Miller with a foreword by Robin D.G. Kelley

The Royal Africa Company
K.G. Davies

The Blackheath Connection - Questions on Slavery
Dan Byrnes

Freedom and Crisis: An American History, Vol. 1, New York, 1981, pg. 33
Allen Weinstein and Frank Otto Gatell

Photographs of Elmina Castle and Goree Island Courtesy of The d'zert Club

Traders, Planters and Slaves: Market Behaviour in Early English America, Cambridge: Cambridge University Press
David W. Galenson 1986

maafa.org/jhclarke.html

angelfire.com/ny2/maafacom/maafa.html

swagga.com/slavdeck.htm

Ghanadata.com

africaonline.com

ferris.edu/news/jimcrow/what.htm

americanradioworks.org/features/remembering/transcript.html

toptags.com/aama/docs/jcrow.htm

Chapter I: Legacy

Sworn affidavits and depositions; tax receipts and deeds on file at county courthouses; personal documents; personal interviews with witness' and relatives; lawyers

Jim Crow Guide
Stetson Kennedy

ferris.edu/news/jimcrow/what.htm

Chapter II: The Kaolin Cartel

Cotton to Kaolin: A History of Washington County, Georgia 1784- 1989
Washington County Historical Society

Red Clay, Pink Cadillacs and White Gold
Charles Seabrook with Marcy Louza

The Eleventh Circuit Judicial Inquiry
The Special Committee of the Judicial Council

Sworn affidavits and depositions; tax receipts and deeds on file at county courthouses; personal documents; personal interviews with witness' and relatives; lawyers

Photograph of the Sandersville Railroad, courtesy of Atlanta Journal-Constitution

Photograph of woman biting 'chalk'/kaolin, and photgraph of men at kaolin pit, courtesy of Lynn Johnson

Chapter III: NAKLo.

Atlanta Journal-Constitution

pbs.org/wnet/jimcrow/stories_events.html

Chapter IV: One-Eyed Jacks

Court transcripts; affidavits; interviews

Chapter V: Saruge

A Case for Reparations
Boris I. Bittker

Remembering Slavery - African Americans Talk About Their Personal Experiences Of Slavery And Emancipation
Edited by Ira Berlin, Marc Favreau, and Steven F. Miller with a foreword by Robin D.G. Kelley

The Chicago Weekend
The Black Arcade Liberation Library, 1970 Recompiled and reedited by Kenneth T. Spann

Psychiatry's Betrayal
The Citizens Commission on Human Rights

Library of Congress Prints and Photographs Division, Washington D.C.

Emerge Magazine, February 1997

Mahogany Press

Reparations Petition
Silis Muhammad and U.B. & U.S. Communications Systems, Inc.

Complaint of the Provisional Government of the Republic of New Afrika (North America)

Essence Magazine, April 1993

N'COBRA

Strong-Arm Productions

americanradioworks.org/features/remembering/transcript.html

matahnation.com

powernomics.com

Chapter VI: Our Ancestry, Our Inheritance

Genealogical seminar at Pacific Lutheran University

info@africanancestry.com

Corporation of the President of The Church of Jesus Christ of Latter-Day Saints. Copyright 1985, 1990

Printed in the United States
by Baker & Taylor Publisher Services